Late Antiquity: Eastern Perspectives

edited by

Teresa Bernheimer and Adam Silverstein

Gibb Memorial Trust
2012

Published by

The E. J. W. Gibb Memorial Trust

ISBN 978-0-906094-53-2

A CIP record for this book is available from the British Library

Further details of the E. J. Gibb Memorial Trust and its publications
are available at the Trust's website

www.gibbtrust.org

Printed in Great Britain by
Short Run Press
Exeter

Contents

Acknowledgements

The editors wish to thank Damien Bove for help with the maps, H. Namir Spencer for help with the index, the Khalili Family Trust for use of the cover illustration from the Nasser D. Khalili Collection of Islamic Art, and Val Lamb at Oxbow for typesetting the book (amongst many other things).

List of Contributors

TERESA BERNHEIMER
SOAS

FRANÇOIS DE BLOIS
SOAS

MICHAEL R. JACKSON BONNER
University of Oxford

PATRICIA CRONE
Institute for Advance Study, Princeton

JAMES HOWARD-JOHNSTON
University of Oxford

GEOFFREY KHAN
University of Cambridge

ADAM SILVERSTEIN
King's College London

D. G. TOR
University of Notre Dame

LUKE TREADWELL
University of Oxford

PHILIP WOOD
University of Cambridge

1

Introduction

Adam Silverstein and Teresa Bernheimer

Where and when does 'Late Antiquity' end? From among these questions it is hardly surprising that the latter has attracted more scholarly attention than the former. After all, 'Late Antiquity' is a phrase whose two components are time-related; defining the period covered by the phrase is thus crucial. In the four decades since Peter Brown's *The World of Late Antiquity* first appeared and the field of late antique studies began to gather real momentum, scholars have debated the place of early Islam within the late antique world, thereby determining *when* 'Late Antiquity' ends. Whereas earlier generations, such as Pirenne's, might have argued for excluding 'Islam' from this world – on the grounds that its rise led to decisive discontinuities with the preceding period – most scholars in recent decades have made the opposite case,[1] stressing the many important points of continuity – in everything from art and architecture,[2] to language, popular and high culture, and religion – from Late Antiquity to the first century or so of Muslim rule. The workshops entitled "Late Antiquity and early Islam" (and the related volumes published by Darwin Press entitled *Studies in Late Antiquity and early Islam*) clearly embraced this point, while also implying that the phrase 'Late Antiquity' itself does *not* on its own include early Islam. Early Islam's increasing integration within the world of Late Antiquity is captured in the more recent work *Late Antiquity: A Guide to the Post-Classical World*, whose title does not 'add' early Islam but whose contents do – and not only does 'Islam' get its own chapter (by Hugh Kennedy),[3] but one of the volume's three editors, Oleg Grabar, was himself an Islamicist.[4]

[1] Note, however, Judith Herrin's statement that "His [Henri Pirenne's] thesis that the advent of Islam in the Mediterranean sealed the end of Late Antiquity remains valid" (J. Herrin, *The Formation of Christendom*, Princeton 1987, 134).

[2] See, for instance, the important work by G. Fowden, *Qusayar Amra: Art and the Umayyad Elite in Late Antique Syria*, Berkeley 2004.

[3] The important point can be made (*pace* C. Robinson, "Reconstructing early Islam: truth and consequences" in H. Berg (ed.) *Method and Theory in the Study of Islamic Origins*, Leiden 2003, 101–134) that isolating 'Islam' in its own chapter rather than integrating it fully within the volume's other chapters actually implies Islam's exclusion from full membership within the 'world' of Late Antiquity.

[4] Most recently, see R. Hoyland, "Early Islam as a Late Antique Religion" in S. Johnson (ed.) *The*

To an extent, the continuity between the pre- and early-Islamic periods was appreciated by scholars even before the publication of Brown's *World of Late Antiquity*: Gaston Wiet's short article "L'Empire néo-byzantin des omeyyades et l'empire néo-sassanide des Abbasides"[5] appeared in the early 1950s. Moreover, the fact that the subtitle of Brown's book is *AD 150–750* indicates that already in the early 1970s it was acknowledged that it is something other than the rise of Islam that caps the period. Precisely when within the period of 'early Islam' Late Antiquity ends is probably impossible to determine, and the answers are likely to vary based on the criteria applied.[6] More on this below.

Although, as stated, 'Late Antiquity' is essentially a term of periodization, this period must also be contained geographically – otherwise scholars of Late Antiquity might be beholden to awkward discussions about T'ang China and Gupta India, to say nothing of contemporary Mesoamerica. *Where*, then, does Late Antiquity end?

To answer this (or, for that matter, any question of geography), it is important to establish one's intellectual coordinates. 'Late Antiquity' is an intellectual construct devised by what might be called – for lack of a better term – 'westernists' to study 'westerners'; that is to say, those who, when looking down onto the Eurasian world from above, are physically and intellectually centered on Europe and the Mediterranean. 'Late Antiquity', therefore, *begins* in the lands of southern Europe and the eastern Mediterranean that produced 'Classical Antiquity' and where it was consciously transformed in the period discussed here. Already in Classical Antiquity, though, the *oikoumene* included lands well to the east of the Mediterranean, taking in the Achaemenid Empire, the eastern borders of which extended to modern Afghanistan and Pakistan. It is, in fact, to 'western' sources such as the works of Herodotus and Xenophon that we owe much of our knowledge of Achaemenid history, and though the relationship between the two sides was often dominated by rivalry if not outright war – the Greco-Persian wars lasted half a century – Greek authors were not incorrigibly hostile to their eastern neighbors, with Xenophon's choice of Cyrus the Great as his model of an 'Ideal Ruler' being an obvious example of this. And in the post-Achaemenid period, Alexander the Great's adoption of the Persian title 'King of Kings' (as well as an array of Persian court-practices) further indicates the esteem in which 'the east' was held.[7]

The relative decline of 'Persian' power in the post-Achaemenid period (the occasional

Oxford Handbook of Late Antiquity (Oxford, forthcoming). We wish to thank the author for making a draft of his article available to us. Many recent studies that treat this topic are indebted on this issue to G. Fowden, *From Empire to Commonwealth: Consequences of Monotheism in Late Antiquity*, Princeton 1993, esp. ch. 6, "Islam: World Empire, then commonwealth".

5 In *Cahiers d'Histoire Mondiale* 1 (1953), 63–71.

6 It should be noted, however, that acceptance of early Islam (by whatever definition) within 'Late Antiquity' is more common amongst those working on the 'eastern' half of Late Antiquity than amongst 'westernists'. Thus, G. Bohak (*Ancient Jewish Magic: A History*, Cambridge 2008, 143) defines Late Antiquity as "roughly from the third to seventh century CE", whereas M. G. Morony's 'Magic and Society in Late Sasanian Iraq' in S. Noegel, J. Walker, and B. Wheeler (eds), *Prayer, Magic and the Stars in the Ancient and Late Antique World* (Philadelphia 2003), dealing with the same topic, assumes continuity into early Islamic times.

7 On Alexander's acceptance by 'easterners' themselves, see R. Stoneman, *Alexander the Great: A Life in Legend*, New Haven 2008.

Parthian success *vis à vis* the Seleucids notwithstanding), however, allowed the Romans and Later Romans to develop a largely justifiable sense of superiority over their easterly neighbors. It was thus, as James Howard-Johnston puts it in his contribution to this volume, "hard for Romans to reconcile themselves with the existence of an equipollent eastern neighbour, once loose Parthian rule was replaced by a more managerial Sasanian regime." And though relations between the Byzantines and the Sasanians were often very fractious, neither side could afford to underestimate the other as their fates were interdependent. The *world* of Late Antiquity, as Peter Brown so aptly termed it, was thus inhabited by equal partners and scholars of late antique studies have, for the most part, acknowledged the Sasanians' as cohabitants in this 'world'.

The fact remains, however, that such acknowledgement of the Sasanians as equal partners with the Byzantines rarely translates into equal coverage for the eastern part of the late antique world in studies of the period. Thus, while the volume *Late Antiquity: A Guide to the Post-Classical World* included an Islamicist amongst its editors, the absence of a Persianist is telling. Coverage of the Sasanians is fully integrated into the book's main chapters (unlike, as we have seen, 'Islam', which inhabits its own chapter) but never is the Sasanian Empire treated in anything like as much detail as the Byzantine side is. The second paragraph of the editors' Introduction to the work is worth quoting in full,[8] both for what it does and does not say:

> In 800, also, from Central Asia to the plateau of Castile, an Islamic caliphate, created at headlong speed by the Arab conquests of the 7th century, had gained stability by settling back into the habits of the ancient empire it had replaced. The tax system of the Islamic empire continued with little break the practices of the Roman and Sassanian states. Its coins were *denarii, dinars*. The system of post-horses and of governmental information on which its extended rule depended was called after its Roman predecessor *veredus, al-barid*. Its most significant enemy was still known, in Arabic, as the empire of *Rum* – the empire of Rome in the east, centered on Constantinople.

Continuity into the Islamic period is demonstrated here using four examples: 1) the system of taxation; 2) the unit of coinage; 3) the system and name of the imperial post; and 4) the identity of the two rival powers. The first example acknowledges the Sasanians alongside the Byzantines in a very general way. The fourth example seems to imply that the caliphs *replaced* the Sasanians as the new rivals of *Rum*. It is the second and third examples that reflect the volume's propensity for the 'west': for while we hear of Byzantine *denarii* we hear nothing of the silver *drahms* favored by the Sasanians[9] (and, as *drachmas*, known to the Byzantines too), which were adopted as *dirhams* under the caliphs. And although the caliphal term *barīd* may well be related to *veredus* (or, equally plausibly, to *veredarius*, 'courier'), virtually every other postal-term used by the caliphs was of Sasanian provenance and the Sasanians are at least as likely to have shaped the *Barīd* as they Byzantines were.[10]

---

[8] Bowersock, Brown, and Grabar, *Late Antiquity*, vii.

[9] On which, see T. Daryaee, *Sasanian Persia: The Rise and Fall of an Empire*, London 2009, 144.

[10] On all this, see A. Silverstein, *Postal Systems in the Pre-Modern Islamic World*, Cambridge 2007, ch. 1, and esp. 28–29.

This inequality of coverage is a feature of the field of late antique studies as a whole, and may be explained in a number of ways. First, as the concept of 'Late Antiquity' was devised by 'westernists' it is understandable that the Later Roman/Byzantine lands would benefit – at least to begin with – from more scholarly attention than eastern lands do. Second, a field with such a Romano-centric pedigree is likely to be dominated by scholars whose philological expertise largely restricts them to sources produced in lands to the west of the Euphrates. Naturally, though the world of Late Antiquity may be centered on Byzantium for these scholars, Byzantium's relations with its neighbors, and especially its eastern rival, is a topic that requires the attention of those working in the field. Studies on the relations – both peaceful and, more commonly, belligerent – between Byzantium and the Sasanians have thus appeared, and these are almost exclusively the works of westernists looking eastwards rather than vice versa.[11] In this way, the Sasanians do appear in the consciousness – and publications – of 'westernists', but only insofar as they relate to the Late Roman/Byzantine world. There has thus been no question but that where and when 'Late Antiquity' ends are questions for 'westernists' to answer.

In early 2008, shortly after the establishment of the Oxford Centre for Late Antiquity (OCLA), we decided to organize a seminar series to put the eastern half of Late Antiquity on the map on its own terms. The series was entitled "Late Antiquity: Eastern Perspectives" and contributors were asked nothing more specific than to present a paper on an aspect of their research, bearing in mind the seminar's aim "to situate Iran within the broader world of Late Antiquity." The present volume is the product of that series, albeit an indirect one: not all the chapters included here were presented in the series, and not all the papers presented in the series are included here.

A series of eight seminars can only go a short way towards redressing the imbalance described here. What is more, in holding the seminars under the auspices of OCLA we were at once championing Iran's perspective on Late Antiquity yet also, paradoxically, presupposing that the essentially European concept of Late Antiquity is an intellectual construct to which ancient Iranians and those who study them comfortably belong. The Iranologist Raheem Shayegan, for instance, has argued *against* including the Sasanian Empire within 'Late Antiquity',[12] on the grounds that the transformations that occurred in Byzantine lands, which characterize 'Late Antiquity', did not take place in the Sasanian Empire. To his arguments the following three points may be added.

First, 'Antiquity' from a Persian perspective ends with the rise of Islam, not with events

---

[11] See, for instance, Beate Dignas, Engelbert Winter, *Rome and Persia in Late Antiquity: Neighbours and Rivals*, Cambridge 2007. And see A. Farahani's review in *Bryn Mawr Classical Review* 2009.03.51 and S. R. Hauser's review of the German original of the work, in *Bryn Mawr Classical Review* 2002.05.06, both of which point out the book's "Eurocentric" approach to the Sasanians. And see A. D. Lee, *Information and Frontiers: Roman Foreign Relations in Late Antiquity*, Cambridge 1993, on the Roman Empire's diplomatic (and other) relations with its neighbours to the east and north.

[12] In M. Morony, "Should Sasanian Iran be Included in Late Antiquity", *e-Sasanika* 6 (2008), 2. Morony's article argues forcefully *against* Shayegan, while other Sasanologists, e.g. Touraj Daryaee (author of *Sasanian Iran (224–651 CE): Portrait of a Late Antique Empire*, Costa Mesa 2008; and "The Persian Gulf Trade in Late Antiquity", *Journal of World History* 14 (2003), 1–16), take the Sasanians' inclusion in Late Antiquity for granted.

of whatever nature that took place in the second or third centuries CE. The entire period of Iranian history, from mythologized origins until the coming of Islam is covered by the phrase *Ērān-i bāstān*, 'ancient Iran', and the parameters of this period are reinforced by the scope of the Iranian national epic, the *Shāhnāme*, which ends abruptly with the Muslim conquest of Iran. From an Iranian perspective, then, it is early Islam that most accurately represents a transformative period of *late* Antiquity; and it is therefore unsurprising that the Persian translation of Morony's article on the Sasanians' place in Late Antiquity begins with a detailed footnote in which the Persian neologism coined to represent 'Late Antiquity' is explained to readers for whom the concept is otherwise devoid of significance.[13]

Second, while the "westernists'" inclusion of Sasanian and early Islamic 'Iran'[14] within Late Antiquity is surely a gesture of inclusivity and an acknowledgement of a certain measure of parity between the two empires, this openness can be justified by the Classical worldview but not the ancient Iranian one.[15] The Greek division of the [populated] regions of the world into 'climes' (*klimata*; sing. *klima* – literally 'inclination') posited a series of horizontal bands, east–west slices of the world, determined in relation to a clime's proximity to the sun. The first few and last few climes were deemed to be too hot or too cold to produce the highest forms of civilization; the fourth, middle clime was the most conducive to productivity and it was, crucially, inhabited by both the Greeks and Iranians. Theoretical parity between the two sides was therefore achievable from a 'western', Greek perspective and Procopius could write, for instance, of Khusraw I's superiority as a just ruler over Justinian without falling foul of the prevailing [theoretical] worldview.[16] The ancient Iranian worldview(s), however, held that the world is divided into seven *kishvars*, the six least-favored ones forming a circle around the middle region of *Ērānshahr*.[17] The idea of parity (let alone equality) between 'Iran' and others (the technical term for 'others' being *an-Ērān*) is incompatible with this worldview, and while the Byzantines could welcome the Sasanians into their world, from the perspective of ancient Iranian geography, the Sasanians could not – strictly speaking – accept the invitation.

Third, on a related note, the theoretical superiority of *Ērānshahr* was reflected practically in statements of both the region's elites and its general populace. Not only did Pahlavi texts (perhaps predictably) proclaim Khusraw II "Lord of the seven *kishvars*" (*haft kishvar*

[13] In *e-Sasanika* 6 (2008), 9 n. 15. The translator settled on the phrase *pesā bāstān* for 'Late Antiquity', but not without reservations.

[14] The term is used loosely here, to reflect those regions under Persian rule.

[15] A good summary of the 'western' attitude towards others in Late Antiquity may be found in G. Clarke, *Late Antiquity: A Very Short Introduction*, Oxford 2011, ch. 6 ("Barbarians"). We wish to thank the author for making a pre-publication draft of her book available to us.

[16] Take for example Procopius's complaint about Justinian's curtailing of the Byzantine *Cursus Publicus* (*Anecdota*, XXX: 8–9) at a time when Khusraw I "increased the salaries of his spies and profited by this forethought. For nothing that was happening among the Romans escaped him" (ibid., XXX: 18). Naturally, such potentially provocative statements about Justinian were relegated to his *Anecdota* but there is no hint of Jāḥiẓian irony in this comparison.

[17] On ancient Iranian geographical conceptions and the exclusivity of the *kishvar*-system's worldview, see T. Daryaee, "The Idea of *Ērānšahr*: Jewish, Christian, and Manichaean Views in Late Antiquity" in C. G. Cereti, *Iranian Identity in the Course of History*, Rome 2010, 91–108, esp. 97–106.

xwadāy)[18] but, as Philip Wood shows in his contribution to this volume, Syriac sources written by Sasanian Christians referred to Yazdegird as "ruler of the entire world, east and west." Though such hyperbole could be dismissed as mere propaganda, it should be noted that Iranian geographical texts (and related materials)[19] – which are realistic enough to accept the existence of *an-Ērān* – demonstrate the contempt with which the territorial claims of Iran's rivals were viewed. Shāpūr I's inscription at Ka'be-ye Zardosht, from the beginning of the Sasanian period, includes within "*Ērānshahr*" such regions as Arabia, Albania, Oman, and India;[20] while the *Shahrestānhā-ye Erānshahr*, from the end of the period, also includes Africa (*friga*).[21] Already Darius I, in the Behistun inscription, describes the boundaries of his empire in terms that are likely to have bewildered or even offended some of his neighbors; and the Achaemenid-era *Book of Esther* famously begins by describing Xerxes I's realm grandiosely as comprising 127 provinces, spanning from India (*hoddu*) to Ethiopia (*kush*).[22]

Moreover, it is clear that even the region's ordinary inhabitants held views somewhat incompatible with the notion of parity between the two empires in Late Antiquity: not only did Sasanian Christians, from no later than the fifth century CE,[23] pride themselves on their separate identity as Iranians but Jewish communities in Babylonian appear even to have adopted a version of the Iranian concept of *Arya* by arguing that Babylonian (hence, Sasanian) Jews were of superior lineage to that of their Palestinian (hence, Roman) coreligionists. As the Talmudic rabbis put it: "All countries are dough [i.e., of mixed 'ingredients'] compared to the Land of Israel. And the Land of Israel is dough compared to Babylonia."[24] The Babylonian rabbis thus delineated the geographical boundaries of the Land of Israel – crucial for the application of certain details of Jewish law – not positively,

[18] In D. Monchi-Zadeh, "*Xusrov i Kavatan ut Retak*: Pahlavi Text, Transcription, and Translation" in *Monumentum Georg Morgenstierne II*, Acta Iranica 22, Leiden 1982, 63.

[19] It is difficult to speak of a genre of Sasanian 'Geography'. On this, see D. Shapira, "Was there Geographial Science in Sasanian Iran?", *Acta Orientalia Academiae Scientiarum Hung.* 54ii–iii (2001), 319–338.

[20] The inclusion of Oman is important in confirming that 'Arabia' in this inscription means something other than this region.

[21] *Šahrestānīhā ī Erānšahr* (ed./trans. T. Daryaee, Costa Mesa 2002) 26, l. 33.

[22] *Esther* 1:1. The precise dating of *Esther* is disputed, but Sh. Shaked has shown ("Two Judaeo-Iranian Contributions: 1. Iranian Functions in the Book of Esther", Irano-Judaica 1 (1982), 292–303) that the work contains accurate knowledge of Achaemenid life. Ancient Iran's relations with 'Kush' are reflected in the Medieval *Kushname*, a Persian epic on a half-Persian/half-Ethiopian hero sent by an ancient shāh to conquer Africa, who switches allegiances.

[23] On which see generally S. P. Brock, "Christians in the Sasanian Empire: the Case of Divided Loyalties" in *Studies in Church History* 18 (1982), 1–19, and particularly Daryaee, "Idea of *Ērānšahr*", 95.

[24] Babylonian Talmud, Tractate *Kiddushin*, 71a. Later debates over the ethnic credentials required of the Exilarch are tantalizingly similar to early Islamic conceptions of the 'Alid family on the one hand, and to pre-Islamic ideas of Aryan lineage on the other. In either case, it would seem that there is an identifiable 'superiority-complex' of sorts that emanates from Iranian lands, even amongst non-Zoroastrian communities. See also T. Bernheimer, "Postscript: A Davidic Parallel", in *A Social History of the 'Alid Family from the Eighth to the Eleventh Century*, unpublished D.Phil Thesis, Oxford 2006.

by sketching the borders of the Holy Land, but negatively, by describing the boundaries of Babylonia "of pure lineage", with the excluded regions to the west representing the Land of Israel.[25]

The Iranian superiority-complex as reflected in geographical notions survived well into the Islamic period, as evidenced in the work of Ibn Khurradādhbih, widely considered the father of Arabo-Islamic geography. He writes: "We shall begin, then, by mentioning the Sawad region, since the Persian kings [of old] used to refer to it as *del-i Ērānshahr*, that is 'the heart of Iraq'."[26] Moreover, the fact that Sasanian-era Pahlavi geographical works continued to be copied into the Abbasid period indicates that the ancient Iranian ideas endured long after the rise of Islam, which introduced its own worldviews (some of which were inconsistent with traditional Iranian concepts).[27]

Much as the Sasanians might have rejected the invitation to join the world of Late Antiquity, there are two reasons to include them in it. First, with the benefit of a millennium and a half of hindsight, it is clear that the Byzantine and Sasanian empires were actors on a shared stage and often forged their own characters and practices on the basis of their relations with each other. And although, as seen, from the fifth century Christians on either side of the Euphrates regarded themselves as distinct from their coreligionists across the border, and Jews in Babylonia adopted Iranian ideas of ethnic superiority over Jews in Roman Palestine, the historical record shows that both Jews and Christians crossed the Byzantine-Sasanian border effortlessly, both physically in their travels,[28] and intellectually, in scholarly exchanges and disputes with coreligionists on either side of the divide.[29] Thus, patriotism and other posturing aside, the populations on *both* sides of the divide clearly inhabited a single, inter-dependent 'world', and – importantly – they often appeared to be aware of this reality.

---

[25] See A. Oppenheimer (with B. Isaac, and M. Lecker), *Babylonia Judaica in the Talmudic Period*, Wiesbaden 1983, index s.v. "Babylonia of pure lineage." It should be pointed out that, similarly to the ancient Iranians, the Jews of Late Antiquity are unlikely to have subscribed to this periodization as rabbinic Jews subscribe(d) to a competing division of the period's history into tannaitic, amoraitic, saboraitic (or, 'stammaitic', following Weiss-Halivni), and Gaonic periods. Moreover, the ramifications of such divisions were crucial to the formation of *halakhah* and rabbinic culture more generally.

[26] Ibn Khurradādhbih, *Kitāb al-Masālik wa-l-Mamālik*, ed. M. J. de Geoje, Leiden 1889, 5.

[27] On the endurance of Iranian geographical ideas in Arabo-Islamic geographies, and on the emergence of a competing 'Islamic' worldview, see A. Silverstein, "The Medieval Islamic Worldview: Arabic Geography in its Historical Context" in K. Raaflaub and R. Talbert (eds), *Geography, Ethnography, and Perceptions of the World from Antiquity to the Renaissance*, Oxford, 2009.

[28] On which, see A. Silverstein "Jews and News: the interaction of private and official communication-networks in Jewish History" in S. E. Alcock, J. Bodel, and R. Talbert (eds), *Highways, Byways, and Road Systems in the pre-Modern World* (forthcoming). On the non-Roman Jewish communities of Late Antiquity, see the important remarks in F. Millar, "The Many Worlds of the Late Antique Diaspora: Supplements to the 'Cambridge History of Judaism' vol. IV", *JJS* 59 (2008), 120–138.

[29] It is interesting to note that the rise of Islam and the creation of an Islamic – and thereafter, an Islamicate – empire from Iberia to India served to divide Christian communities between east and west, yet served to unite Jewish ones (though not, as often assumed, through the gaonic academies in Iraq).

This world is also discernable at elite levels. One example of this, worth mentioning here since the otherwise slippery notion of 'influence' is given in this case a philological backbone, is the functionary known in Byzantium as the *a secretis*, in Sasanian lands as the *rāzbān*, and in caliphal times (perhaps) as the *kātib al-sirr*. This 'secret bearer' performed functions common to all empires (courier duties and the like), but under different titles; what is striking here is the calque (whether Byzantine-Sasanian or Sasanian-Byzantine) that indicates conscious bureaucratic emulation on the part of the two rivals.[30]

Second, as 'Late Antiquity' is a modern, scholarly construct that offers modern scholars a particular perspective on (and, hence, approach to) a particular period and region of history, what ancient Iranians might have thought of this categorization – and their relevance to it – is besides the point: our evidence suggests that there *was* an identifiable 'world' to which the Byzantines, Sasanians, and early Muslims belonged. The questions thus remain: where and when does this world of 'Late Antiquity' end?

Earlier it was implied that the two questions are separable, with modern scholars tending to answer the latter question by accepting that the first century or so of Islamic civilization was more 'late antique' than it was medieval. Late Antiquity would thus end *c*. 750 or *c*. 800 CE, or with the Abbasid Revolution as the turning point, or perhaps the reign of Hārūn al-Rashīd (d. 809), which has the advantage of coinciding with the coronation of Charlemagne in 800, as the terminus. Others, adopting a cultural (specifically Hellenistic) – rather than political – yardstick for measuring Late Antiquity's endurance under Islam, have even suggested *c*. 1000 CE as the endpoint. In Wisnovsky's words:

> "Those scholars of Late Antiquity and of medieval Europe who ponder about when the late-antique era ended and the medieval began, can infer from my book that at least as far as the history of metaphysics is concerned, the decisive moment occurred around 1001, in the Samanid library in the city of Bukhara in the Central Asian province of Transoxania, far outside their traditional area of focus."[31]

For our purposes, Wisnovsky's statement is most important for linking a question of *periodization* with *geography*.

This volume includes chapters that, in their different, ways also link the 'when' of Late Antiquity's terminus with the 'where'. Although scholars have argued for the extension of Late Antiquity's reach to such places as Ethiopia and the Hijaz,[32] while others have recently demonstrated that 'Late Antiquity' has come to encompass and increasingly large

---

[30] Though the *a secretis* and *kātib al-sirr* are relatively well-known, the *rāzbān* has received little scholarly attention. Byzantine sources were certainly aware of this Persian functionary and it is likely that the calque itself (for *rāzbān* is Persian for 'bearer of secrets') did not escape them. See *Chronicon Paschale 284–628 AD* (trans. M. Whitby and M. Whitby), Liverpool 1989, 126, 185, and 187.

[31] R. Wisnovsky, *Avicenna's Metaphysics in Context*, London 2003, 266. Quoted in Hoyland, "Early Islam as a Late Antique Religion" (forthcoming).

[32] Ethiopia: S. Munro-Hay, *Aksum: An African Civilization of Late Antiquity*, Edinburgh 1991; and the Hijaz: J. E. Montgomery, "The Empty Hijaz" in: J. E. Montgomery (ed.), *Arabic Theology, Arabic Philosophy. From the Many to the One: Essays in Celebration of Richard M. Frank*, Leuven, 2006, 37–97, esp. 43, where Montgomery writes: "I aim to show how the *qaṣīda* can, in fact, be (or rather: ought to be) read so as to form part of the Late Antique phenomenon ..."

and unwieldy region,[33] this volume is concerned with a single – albeit vast – region of the late antique world. As such, the chapters of this volume (and any conclusion derived from them) cannot pertain to the whole of 'Late Antiquity' but may instead serve as a case-study for those wishing to re-evaluate or refine our understanding of the term by considering narratives and perspectives other than those emanating from Byzantium or, more generally, 'the West'.[34] Thus, as Wisnovsky implies above, *when* 'Late Antiquity' ends depends on *where* within the world of Late Antiquity we are looking, and – we might add – from what perspective. As the perspective of this volume is decidedly 'eastern', it is the continuity of (or disruption to) Sasanian – and more generally, ancient Persianate – culture that will determine Late Antiquity's limits.[35]

Before proceeding, it should be stressed that the 'eastern' region under discussion is often ill-defined. For while some forty years ago Peter Brown himself said that "it is time ... to look at the sixth century world through more eastern eyes"[36] it is clear that his focus was mostly limited to Mesopotamia.[37] This is a westernist's view of the eastern perspective – Mesopotamia, with its Jewish academies, Christian administrators, and Aramaic culture, is shallow water for Byzantinists who have focused on such Roman provinces as Syria, Palestine, and 'Arabia'. Westernists seeking to incorporate the 'eastern' perspective on Late Antiquity into their work often speak simply of 'the Sasanians', and are thus justified in focusing on the western regions of the Sasanian Empire, which were relatively Christianized, from which many of the sources used by these scholars emanate, and with which the Byzantines had most of their interaction for geographical reasons.

A frequently-adduced justification for largely ignoring the 'Persian' regions of the Sasanian Empire (or for ignoring the Sasanians altogether) is that the sources for these regions are inadequate – or even non-existent – for the reconstruction and analysis of Sasanian history. One of the aims of this volume is to disprove such notions: not only do all the chapters below demonstrate that the 'eastern' voices of Late Antiquity are there to be heard, but individual chapters contribute directly to our understanding of these sources. Francois de Blois, Patricia Crone, and Michael Bonner scrutinize a number of superficially similar Islamic-era passages about the Sasanians, yielding important results for Sasanian historiography. Phillip Wood also shows that nuanced readings of sources such as the *Chronicle of Seert* allow us to disentangle the Sasanian-era materials that were preserved in later sources. These chapters illustrate the ways in which sources in Pahlavi, Avestan, Arabic,

[33] Morony ("Should Sasanian Iran", 3) has charted the curious phenomenon of the broadening of definitions of 'Late Antiquity' over time, rather than the expected sharpening of the term.

[34] Armenia, for instance, could provide its own corrective to the Romano-centric view of Late Antiquity, as could numerous other regions.

[35] Herein lies a major difference between our approach and Wisnovsky's; for he is applying 'western' (in this case Hellenistic) criteria to the question of Late Antiquity's terminus, while finding an 'eastern' answer to the question. Conversely, our view is that if we accept that the Sasanians represent a legitimate 'voice' in Late Antiquity, then it is the survival of that voice that is being traced to determine its extent in time.

[36] Brown, *World of Late Antiquity*, 159.

[37] This point was noted in Morony, "Should Sasanian Iran", 1. That his book concludes with discussion of Abbasid Iraq is yet further evidence that Brown's 'east' is Mesopotamia.

Syriac, and New Persian have been reworked by those with political-religious agendas. Furthermore, Geoffrey Khan's contribution to this volume offers us an edition and annotated translation of some documentary sources from the eastern half of the region under consideration here. Thus, alongside the new interpretations and contextualisations of older, literary sources are new, documentary ones. What these contributions show is that while the source-material for the eastern parts of Late Antiquity may seem daunting in its linguistic variety and may require sophisticated analysis to be of use to historians, one could not claim that the materials are not there to be analysed. James Howard-Johnston's double length article in this volume demonstrates that a judicious use of our sources allows us to produced detailed reconstructions of Sasanian institutions, in this case the Sasanian army.

An important point to emerge from the chapters that touch upon sources from or concerning the Sasanians is the centrality of 'eastern' historiography to our quest for Late Antiquity's terminus. Scholars who have considered "Islam's" inclusion within 'Late Antiquity' have interpreted the question in terms of continuity vs. change: If the Umayyad and early Abbasid caliphs and their societies can be shown to have displayed the necessary characteristics (whatever these may be) of Late Antiquity then the latter's timeline could be extended forwards by a century or two. What the issue of Sasanian historiography raised in the aforementioned chapters shows is that 'extending the timeline' of Late Antiquity into the Islamic period is an overly-simplistic approach to the question at hand. The reconfiguration of the Near East's centres of political power in the aftermath of the Muslim conquest disrupted any such neat-continuity: what was a provincial centre in Damascus became an imperial capital (and local administrators found themselves running a machine that is likely to have been too big for them); and what had been an imperial centre in Ctesiphon was relegated to provincial status, only to re-emerge in the late eighth and early ninth century, for a sort of swan-song of Sasanian imperial culture. Accordingly, taking Sasanian historiography as a case-study, it is clear that then endurance of 'eastern' Late Antiquity into the Islamic period was *delayed* – lying dormant during most (if not all) of the Umayyad period, during which aspects of '*western*' Late Antiquity were being continued by the caliphs.

The same could be said of Sasanian administrative traditions. Geoffrey Khan's contribution to this volume is pivotal in this context. The documents he discusses come from early-Abbasid Bactria, a region that tests our definitions of Late Antiquity's geographical extent. For although the region was never that firmly under the Sasanians' control (and local languages endured, not only during the Sasanian period but long into the Islamic one),[38] the administration was 'Persianate' and some of the administrators mentioned in the documents have Iranian names and titles – even a century and a half after the rise of Islam. Aspects of late antique administration are clearly in evidence here. However, as Khan points out, the documentary record suggests that it is only in the early Abbasid period that caliphal control over this region was centralized, with only loose and

[38] On the Bactrian-language documents see N. Sims-Williams, *Recent discoveries in the Bactrian language and their historical significance,* Society for the Preservation of Afghanistan's Cultural Heritage (Afghanistan), 2004.

relatively informal ties to the centre having been the norm in the Umayyad period. In other words, the imperial administrative centralization that was one of the defining attributes of Late Antiquity was absent from this region for almost a century following fall of the Sasanians, only to be reintroduced in the second half of the eighth century. As with Sasanian historiography, the administrative practices of 'eastern' Late Antiquity did not continue uninterruptedly into the Islamic period. Determining the endpoint of Late Antiquity in 'the east' is thus more complicated than simply extending a timeline.

Another ramification of Khan's chapter is that neat – and, admittedly, intuitive – ideas about the continuation of Byzantine traditions in provinces to the west of the Euphrates and Sasanian traditions to its east, are also overly simplistic. Arabic administrative documents from Egypt indicate that in the third century AH *Persian* administrative traditions – whose Sasanian pedigree is often beyond question – were consciously introduced into "*western* regions" of the caliphate, such as Egypt. The relevance of the "'eastern' perspective" on Late Antiquity is thus not limited to 'the east',[39] and questions about where and when Late Antiquity end are more complex than they might appear.

In his paper on 'Urban Militias', Luke Treadwell also deals with a region that is 'eastern' even within the context of our 'eastern' perspective on Late Antiquity. Unlike Khan's paper, which – in focusing on administration – concerns issues of imperial bureaucracy and centralization, Treadwell's piece focuses on 'local' organisations that operated in spite of (or, at the very least, alongside) official institutions. The archaeological record in this case might be particularly useful in our quest for Late Antiquity's termini: though the local traditions in this region are unapologetically 'Iranian' and as such suggest a measure of continuity from pre-Islamic times, the construction of new *ribāṭ*s in the third century AH, serving new functions, demonstrate *dis*continuity on a number of levels. Not only did the Soghians in the immediately preceding period attempt nothing like the proliferation of *ribāṭ*s that characterises the third century AH, but the political context for this activity is the fragmentation of the Abbasids' empire and the emergence of [semi-]independent dynasties in the eastern regions of the caliphate. Put another way, the urban militias are probably more 'medieval' than they are 'late antique' – the Samanids' introduction of *iqṭāʿ*s being particularly telling in this regard.

While the landscape and governance of 'the east' may have been undergoing a transformation during the third century AH, the prestige of Sasanian traditions ensured that long after characteristics commonly associated with 'Late Antiquity' gave way to 'medieval' ones Iran's late antique past continued to exert its influence on medieval Islamic culture and civilisation. A number of contributions to this volume highlight the legacy of eastern late antique traditions on the following period, with Patricia Crone, Phillip Wood, and Deborah Tor treating the themes of religion, historiography, and rulership respectively. Tor's piece argues that the Iranian-ness of Islamic political theory was not in conflict with 'Islamic' rule but rather it became inherent to it, once the caliphal institution itself failed.

[39] Returning to the example of late Antique postal traditions being continued into the Islamic period, it should also be pointed out that in the early ninth century, particularly during the reigns of al-Ma'mūn and al-Muʿtaṣim, certain Sasanian-era postal techniques and terminology were introduced for the first time into the caliphal *barīd* (see Silverstein, *Postal Systems*, 26 and n. 114).

We should therefore be unsurprised to find that Niẓām al-Mulk, writing in the late eleventh century, drew on legends about Sasanian shāhs in attempting to provide guidance for Muslim rulers.

Ultimately, of course, it would be impossible to pinpoint either a physical or temporal borderline for 'Late Antiquity' that would satisfy all scholars, with the many competing definitions and interpretations of the term that have been offered. What is hoped is that this volume will raise significant questions about some of the assumptions that continue to pervade the field of late antique studies, particularly for those whose intellectual coordinates are 'western'.

2

A New Look at Mazdak[1]

François de Blois

MAZDAK'S COSMOLOGY ACCORDING TO MUSLIM SOURCES

The incidents surrounding Mazdak are surely the most heatedly debated episode in Sasanian history.[2] Our understanding of these happenings is shaped primarily by the Arabic historians, beginning with Ṭabarī (some 400 years after the events), who had their information mainly from now lost Arabic translations of historical or quasi-historical writings of the late Sasanian period. Their story can be summarised very briefly: Mazdak the son of Bāmdād was a religious leader who came forward during the reign of Kavād, that is to say, after 488. His teachings, like those of most prophets, were not new; we are told namely that he revived the teachings of a certain Zarādusht-i Khurragān, who, according to one Syriac source, was a contemporary of Manes. Mazdak was (allegedly) a communist; he taught that property and women should be held in common. Rather surprisingly, he enjoyed the protection of the emperor, who adopted his views, at least as far as the sharing of women is concerned. But after the death of Kavād in 531, his son Khusraw I had Mazdak and his followers put to death. The principal contents of this report are broadly corroborated by contemporary Byzantine sources. Both Procopius and Agathias, though without mentioning Mazdak by name, confirm that Kavād, already during his first reign (488–496), introduced some shocking innovations with regard to women and marriage, and a slightly later Byzantine author, John Malalas, speaks of the suppression of certain people, whom he calls Manichaeans, during the early part of the reign of Khusraw.

[1] The transliteration of Avestan and Pahlavi words differs slightly from the system used elsewhere in the volume.

[2] The principal secondary literature is: Th. Nöldeke, *Geschichte der Perser und Araber zur Zeit der Sasaniden, aus der arabischen Chronik des Tabari*, Leiden 1879 (455–67: Über Mazdak und die Mazdakiten); A. Christensen, *Le règne du roi Kawād I et le communisme mazdakite*, Copenhagen 1925; O. Klima, *Mazdak*, Prague 1957; idem, *Beiträge zur Geschichte des Mazdakismus*, Prague 1977; E. Yarshater, 'Mazdakism', *The Cambridge history of Iran*, iii (2), Cambridge 1983, 991–1024; P. Crone, 'Kavad's heresy and Mazdak's revolt', *Iran* 29, 1991, 21–42 (with a comprehensive synthesis of the historical data). My own interpretation of Mazdakism is almost diametrically opposed to the previously held views, but I have chosen to refrain from polemic. I add only that the first of the two parts of this paper was read (in a form not very different from the present one) already at the Quatrième conférence européenne d'études iraniennes, in Paris, in September 1999.

Muslim authors, specifically those writing on religious sects, claim moreover that certain religious movements in Islamic Persia revived the teachings of Mazdak. This accusation is levelled in particular against the followers of Muqannaʿ, of Bābak, and the various sects who expected the return in glory of Abū Muslim, the founder of the Abbasid state. Even patently Islamic sects like the Ismailis are sometimes accused of being covert Mazdakites, and the heresiographers not rarely equate Mazdakites, Manichaeans (*zanādiqa*), and Muslim heretics (*malāḥida*) all with one another. It seems to me, however, that the historical and doctrinal identity of the so-called Neo-Mazdakites of the eighth century and later, with the followers of Mazdak, in the fifth and sixth centuries, needs to be demonstrated rather than taken for granted.

The fact is that, although all the sources affirm that Mazdak was a religious teacher, none of the historians says anything substantial about the religious content of his teachings. Until now, all attempts to reconstruct Mazdak's doctrines have relied essentially on one source, the section on the Mazdakites in the big heresiographical and doxographical compendium of Shahrastānī (d. 548/1154), which contains a detailed account of Mazdakite cosmology, ostensibly quoting an important authority of the mid ninth century, Abū ʿĪsā al-Warrāq. Shahrastānī's book has been available to scholars for a long time, through Cureton's edition of 1842–46,[3] followed by Haarbrücker's German translation of 1850–51,[4] and the passage has been exploited fully by everyone who has written on Mazdak. But in the last decades our knowledge of Arabic heresiographical literature has made quite significant advances, notably through the discovery of a number of works by early Muʿtazilite authors preserved in the libraries of the Yemen. The great theological encyclopaedia of ʿAbd al-Jabbār al-Asadʾābādī (d. 415/1025), published in Egypt in the 1960s,[5] contains an account of Mazdak which has close textual similarities with that quoted by Shahrastānī. Like Shahrastānī, ʿAbd al-Jabbār cites the authority of Abū ʿĪsā al-Warrāq, but at the beginning of the chapter devoted to the refutation of dualism ʿAbd al-Jabbār makes it clear that his account of the dualist sects is in fact taken mainly from the Shiite author Ḥasan b. Mūsā al-Nawbakhtī. His explicit quotations from Nawbakhtī contain in turn citations from Abū ʿĪsā. It is thus evident that ʿAbd al-Jabbār did not quote Abū ʿĪsā at first hand, but via Nawbakhtī, and the same is true of Shahrastānī. A further important new source is a theological work by a later Muʿtazilite author, Ibn al-Malāḥimī, a native of Choresmia, and a contemporary of Shahrastānī. A unique incomplete manuscript of this work was discovered by Wilferd Madelung, who published it together with Martin McDermott in 1991.[6] In the last section of the extant portion of this work Ibn al-Malāḥimī devotes himself to the refutation of the so-called *dahriyya* (vaguely: atheists), then of the

---

[3] Shahrastānī, *Book of religious and philosophical sects*, ed. W. Cureton, London 1842–1846, now superseded by the critical edition by Muḥammad Fatḥallāh Badrān, Cairo 1947–1955.

[4] Shahrastānī, *Religionspartheien und Philosophen-Schulen*, ed. T. Haarbrücker, Halle 1850–51. This has now been superseded by the richly annotated French translation by D. Gimaret, G. Monnot, and J. Jolivet: *Livre des religions et des sectes*, Paris 1986 *et seqq.* (the second volume does not seem to be dated), where the section on Mazdak is translated by Monnot.

[5] ʿAbd al-Jabbār al-Asadʾābādī, *al-Mughnī fī ʾabwābi t-tawḥīdi wa l-ʿadl*, 16 vols., ed. M. M al-Khuḍayrī, Cairo 1960–65.

[6] Ibn al-Malāḥimī, *al-Muʿtamadu fī ʾuṣūli d-dīn*, ed. M. McDermott and W. Madelung, London 1991.

Manichaeans, Mazdakites, Marcionites, Bardesanites and Zoroastrians, among others, quoting in his account of their doctrines large extracts explicitly from Abū ʿĪsā al-Warrāq. These quotations are considerably more extensive than those given by other authors and clearly derive from Abū ʿĪsā at first hand. The most important section is the one devoted to Manichaeism. It was long ago suggested that Abū ʿĪsā was one of the sources used by Ibn al-Nadīm in the famous detailed description of Manichaeism in his *Fihrist*. The new source confirms this, but it also enables us for the first time to distinguish clearly those sections in the *Fihrist* that derive from Abū ʿĪsā from those which Ibn al-Nadīm had from another, in fact superior, genuine Manichaean source, and thus to separate the Manichaean from the pseudo-Manichaean material in the Fihrist. I have written about this elsewhere;[7] here we are concerned with Mazdak.

The new sources show that Shahrastānī's account of Mazdakism falls into three sections, which are not differentiated by the author. I shall discuss each of these separately. The first section reads as follows:

> [Abū ʿĪsā] al-Warrāq reported that the doctrine of the Mazdakiyya is like the doctrine of many of the Manichaeans as concerns the two essences and the two principles except that Mazdak used to say that Light acts by intention and choice and Darkness acts at random and by accident. And Light is knowing and perceptive, but the Dark is ignorant and blind. And that the mixture (of the two principles) was by accident and at random, not by intention and choice. And likewise salvation will be only by accident and not by choice. And Mazdak used to forbid people from engaging in disagreement and hatred and fighting one another, and since most of these (forbidden activities) happen only because of women and goods, he declared women free (for all) and lifted restrictions on goods and made (all) people a partnership with regard to them in the same way that 'they are partners with regard to water and fire and forage'.[8] And it is said of him[9] that he ordered (his followers) to kill themselves (or: to kill people?)[10] in order to liberate

[7] See my paper 'New light on the sources of the Manichaean chapter in the *Fihrist*', in *Quinto congresso internazionale di studi sul manicheismo*, ed. A. van Tongerloo and L. Cirillo, Turnhout 2005, 37-45; further: *Dictionary of Manichaean texts II: Texts from Iraq and Iran*, ed. F. de Blois and N. Sims-Williams, Turnhout 2006 (21–88: my 'Glossary of technical terms and uncommon expressions in Arabic – and in Muslim New Persian – texts relating to Manichaeism'). My book *Two Arabic accounts of Manichaean cosmology, by Abū ʿĪsā al-Warrāq and al-Ḥasan ibn Mūsā an-Nawbaxtī. Synoptic edition of the extant fragments, translation and annotation* is basically finished, but publication has been delayed by (for me) insoluble technical difficulties.

[8] As Monnot points out, this phrase is a Muslim *ḥadīth*. This is one of a number of instances where Shahrastānī dresses up the quotations from his sources with Islamic phraseology.

[9] *wa ḥukiya* (or: *ḥakā*)*ʿanhu* can mean: 'it is said of him (i.e. Mazdak)', or: 'it is said on his (Abū ʿĪsā al-Warrāq's) authority', or: 'He (Abū ʿĪsā al-Warrāq) said of him (Mazdak)'.

[10] *ʾamara bi qatli l-ʾanfus* is ambiguous. *qatlu n-nafs*, lit. 'killing the self/soul', is an ordinary enough idiom for 'killing oneself, suicide'(with unspecified subject, alongside *qatala nafsahū*, 'he killed himself') and so *qatlu l-ʾanfus* could mean 'killing themselves' (again without a specified subject, alongside *qatalū ʾanfusahum*, 'they killed themselves'). On the other hand, the plurals *ʾanfus* and *nufūs* are also used to mean 'persons, people', so *qatlu l-ʾanfus* could merely mean 'the killing of people' (the article before the second word making the *ʾiḍāfa* construction determinate), though I should think that 'selves' is more common for *ʾanfus* and 'people' for *nufūs*. Both interpretations seem possible also in the passage where Shahrastānī (Cureton, 92; Badrān, 216; Gimaret *et al.*, i, 384),

them(selves?)[11] from evil and from the mixture of Darkness.[12]

The same information, in very much the same wording, though partly in a different order, can be found in the earlier author ʿAbd al-Jabbār, again ostensibly quoting Abū ʿĪsā, though, as mentioned, in fact quoting him at second hand, through Nawbakhtī. The passage reads:

> Report on the doctrine of the Mazdaqiyya. [Abū ʿĪsā] al-Warrāq reported that their doctrine is like the doctrine of many of the Manichaeans as concerns the two essences, but they claim that Light acts according to intention and Darkness acts at random. And the Magians report about Mazdaq that he used to lift restrictions on goods and women and to claim that he did this in order to make people abandon enmity and fighting, because these things happen because of goods and women. And he is the one who summoned the king Qubādh to his sect, and Qubādh followed him, but Kisrā Anūsharwān opposed him, and he is the one who killed him and his followers. And Mazdaq used to believe that Light is knowing and perceptive and Darkness is ignorant and blind and that the mixture (of the two principles) was at random, not by intention. And his companions claimed that he was a prophet and that he lifted restrictions on marriage and on killing those who oppose him. And he only ordered (his followers) to kill themselves (or: to kill people?) in order to liberate them(selves?) from the mixture of Darkness.[13]

Here now is the corresponding passage in Ibn al-Malāḥimī:

> Abū ʿĪsā (al-Warrāq) said: Before the time of Mānī <some people> used to uphold the doctrine of the two (principles), and it is said that Mānī took from them much of his doctrine. They used to claim that Light and Darkness were both living from all eternity, except that Light is perceptive and knowing, and Darkness is ignorant and blind, and that it was constantly moving in an arrogant sort of way, and while[14] it was in this state,

speaking about the Kharijite sect of Najadāt, cites Kaʿbī as stating that these believe 'that dissimulation (*at-taqiyya*) is permissible in word and in deed, without exception, *wa ʾin kāna fī qatli n-nufūs*' (variant: *n-nafs*), that is, either: 'even if this involves the killing of people', or: 'even if this involves them killing themselves', that is: executing the fellow members of their own sect. As we shall see presently, ʿAbd al-Jabbār makes exactly the same statement about the Mazdakites as Shahrastānī, but Ibn al-Malāḥimī writes that Mazdak believed *bi l-qatli li takhalluṣi l-ʾarwāḥi mina l-ʾabdāni tuḍarru bihā.* I suspect that in the first half of this sentence it is Shahrastānī and ʿAbd al-Jabbār who have preserved Abū ʿĪsā's wording intact and that Ibn al-Malāḥimī has replaced the ambiguous expression *qatlu l-ʾanfus* (which he must have understood to mean 'killing people') by *al-qatl*; the former seems to me in any case the *lectio difficilior.* I add that the Sufic concept of *qatlu n-nafs* in the sense of killing off the base (individual) soul as a prerequisite for the development of higher spiritual values is hardly relevant in the present context.

[11] The pronominal object of *li yukhalliṣahā* refers to *al-ʾanfus* in whichever of the two meanings one ascribes to it.

[12] Shahrastānī, *Kitābu l-milali wa n-niḥal*, ed. Cureton, 192–3; ed. Badrān, 631–7; trans. Monnot, I, 663–6.

[13] ʿAbd al-Jabbār, *al-Mughnī fī ʾabwābi t-tawḥīdi wa l-ʿadl*, v, ed. al-Khuḍayrī, 16.

[14] Edition: *fa yubnā* (misprint?); read: *fa baynā.*

> behold, one of its (personified) impulses[15] knocked against one of the *borders[16] of Light, and it swallowed a bit of it in ignorance, not by intention, and it went into its belly (etc., etc. ...). They said: And when the Supreme Light saw this he went up to the two of them (i.e. Darkness and the devoured bits of Light) and constructed this world from the two of them so that he might endeavour to extract the light which (Darkness) had swallowed, for he was not able to do so without this scheme. Abū ʿĪsā said: These people and the *Manichaeans agree in many of their doctrines and futile arguments. He said: It has also been reported to me that the Mazdaqiyya today, or at least the majority of them, adhere to this doctrine, and it has also been reported to me that they incline towards the doctrine of the Manichaeans, except that they claim that Mazdaq – and he is the one from whom they take their name – was a prophet and that the messengers come one after another, whenever one departs another comes forward, and they claim that Mazdaq gave permission to them that men have intercourse with each other's wives and gave them license to kill those who oppose them, and it is reported that Mazdaq believed in killing in order to liberate the spirits (*ʾarwāḥ*, that is: pneumata) from the bodies in which they are suffering.[17]

I have highlighted the passages which show close literal agreement with the two previously quoted authors. But despite the literal agreement there is a substantial difference in content between Ibn al-Malāḥimī's quotation from Abū ʿĪsā and the words that the other authorities ascribe to the same author. Here, in Ibn al-Malāḥimī, we have an account of certain dualists 'before the time of Mānī' from whom 'Mānī took much of his doctrine'. They are not further identified, but the statement that they taught that the mixture of light and darkness was not provoked intentionally (as the Manichaeans believed), but was the result of an accidental collision of the elements has an unmistakable affinity with the doctrine which Syriac Christian authors ascribe to Bardesanes, who, of course, did live 'before the time of Mānī'. As quoted here, Abū ʿĪsā claims no knowledge of the cosmological doctrines of Mazdak. He does quote, in a decidedly distancing way ('it has been reported to me ...') two conflicting accounts of 'the Mazdaqiyya today', that is to say, the so-called Neo-Mazdakites of the ninth century: one report has it that they share the doctrine of the afore-mentioned anonymous dualists, the other says that they 'incline towards the doctrine of the Manichaeans'. Only at this point does Abū ʿĪsā proceed to give a few data about Mazdak and how he allowed men 'to have intercourse with each other's wives' etc.

The common source used by ʿAbd al-Jabbār and Shahrastānī, that is to say, Nawbakhtī, not only shortened Abū ʿĪsā's account, but also misrepresented it. While Abū ʿĪsā quotes in a noncommittal way two conflicting reports of 'the Mazdaqiyya today', Nawbakhtī has retained only one of them, quotes it as the doctrine of Mazdak himself, and ascribes to Mazdak the cosmology which Abū ʿĪsā gave as that of the anonymous dualists with whom the 'Mazdaqiyya today' are alleged to agree.

---

15 Vocalise: *hammāmātihā*. For *al-hammāmah*, 'intention, the Thoughtful One, enthymesis', see our *Dictionary of Manichaean texts* II, 83–86, and the references and literature cited there, supplemented now by W. Sundermann, 'God and his adversary in Manichaeism: the case of the "Enthymesis of Death" and the "Enthymesis of Life"', *Religious texts in Iranian languages*, ed. F. Vahman and C. V. Pedersen, Copenhagen 2007, 137–149.

16 Text: *ʿalā ḥāssatin min ḥawāsi n-nūr*. Read (with Shahrastānī, 196): *ʿalā ḥāshiyatin min ḥawāshī n-nūr.*

17 Ibn al-Malāḥimī, *al-Muʿtamadu fī ʾuṣūli d-dīn*, ed. McDermott and Madelung, 583–584.

A few pages after his account of the Mazdakites, Shahrastānī[18] also gives a brief description of an unspecified 'group of dualists', with a shorter version of the account which Abū ʿĪsā gave of these people 'before the time of Mānī', but in this passage Shahrastānī has nothing to say about Mazdak. It would seem that he used two different sources both deriving from the same passage in Abū ʿĪsā: first Nawbakhtī for the doctrines of Mazdak, and then another source for the teachings of these unspecified dualists.[19]

It emerges from this that Abū ʿĪsā does not really say anything about Mazdak's cosmology. The supposed quotation from Abū ʿĪsā in Shahrastānī and ʿAbd al-Jabbār is an extrapolation from a larger context.

The second part of Shahrastānī's description of Mazdakism follows the above quoted first section without any break. It reads:

> And his belief concerning the principles and the elements is that they are three: water and fire and earth, and when they mixed with one another there originated from them the regulator (*mudabbir*) of good and the regulator of evil, and what is pure in them is the regulator of good and what is murky in them is the regulator of evil.

It has always struck me that this clearly contradicts what we have been told in the first part of Shahrastānī's account. First we hear that Mazdak taught 'two principles', like the Manichaeans, but now we are told that he believed in 'three principles', water, fire and earth, out of which good and evil emerge. The word for 'principle' is the same in both passages (*aṣl*). Both can hardly be correct. The reason for the error becomes clear from our new source. Ibn al-Malāḥimī reports (apparently from Abū ʿĪsā) the same doctrine as in this passage, but he ascribes it not to the Mazdakites, but to an entirely different sect, the Kantaeans, an obscure para-Christian group who apparently lived in southern Mesopotamia. He writes:

> As for the Kanthāniyya, and they are (also called) the Ṣiyāmiyya, some people attached them to the Christians and it is claimed that they had a sanctuary which was called *Kanthā from which they took their name, and some people claimed that they say the principles of the world are three: water and earth and fire, and that they mixed with one another and there arose from them the regulators for good and evil.[20]

In his initial report on the discovery of Ibn al-Malāḥimī's book, Madelung correctly drew attention to the similarity between the doctrine that Ibn al-Malāḥimī ascribes to the Kantaeans and the one which Shahrastānī ascribes to the Mazdakites.[21] But he was wrong to suggest that this might indicate that Mazdak had been influenced in some way by the Kantaeans.[22] What we have here is not merely the same doctrine, but similar wording in two Arabic texts and it seems impossible to doubt that there is a literary connection between the two. Shahrastānī has evidently wrongly attributed Abū ʿĪsā's account of the

---

[18] Shahrastānī, *Book of religious and philosophical sects*, ed. Cureton, 196.

[19] The second source is perhaps Muḥammad b. Shabīb, whom Shahrastānī cites a few lines earlier as a witness concerning the Bardesanites.

[20] Ibn al-Malāḥimī, *al-Muʿtamadu fī 'uṣūli d-dīn*, 589.

[21] W. Madelung, 'Abū ʿĪsā al-Warrāq über die Bardesaniten, Marcioniten und Kantäer', in *Studien zur Geschichte und Kultur des vorderen Orients* (Festschrift B. Spuler), Leiden 1981, 210–224.

[22] ibid., 224.

Kantaeans to the Mazdakites. The most innocent explanation for this misattribution would seem to be that a page was missing in Shahrastānī's copy of Nawbakhtī and that consequently the text about the Kantaeans followed immediately after the one on the Mazdakites.

A few pages later Shahrastānī also has a few words to say about the Kantaeans:

> A group of the dialecticians report that the **Kanϑāniyya* claimed that the principles are three: fire and earth and water ... [23]

Here again we must assume that Shahrastānī has unwittingly quoted from two different books both dependent on Abū ʿĪsā, first, apparently, a defective copy of Nawbakhtī, where the description of the Kantaeans had got attached to that of the Mazdakites, and then some other source where the same doctrine is attributed (correctly this time) to the Kantaeans.

The third and longest section of Shahrastānī's account is not found in any independent source.[24] It contains a large number of Persian words, not glossed by Shahrastānī, and it seems most likely that he had it from a book in Persian, more precisely: in New Persian.[25] It reads as follows:

> And it has been reported on his authority[26] that the one whom he worships is sitting on his chair in the upper world in the way that the *khusraw* is sitting in the lower world, and in front of him there are four powers: the power of discretion and understanding and recollection and joy, just as before the *khusraw* there are four individuals: *mōbadhān mōbadh*, and the grand *hirbadh*, and the *ispahbadh*, and the *rāmishgar*, and these four regulate the affairs of the people of the world by means of seven of their ministers: *sālār* and *pēshkār* and (...) and (...) and *kārdān* and *dastūr* and *kōdhak* and these seven rotate in twelve spiritual beings:[27] *khwābanda* [=Taurus], *dihanda-sitānanda* [=Gemini], *buranda* [=Scorpio], *khuranda* [=Cancer], *daranda* [=Leo], *chīnanda* [=Virgo], *kahanda* [=Libra], *zananda* [=Sagittarius], *kananda* [=Capricorn], *āb-dih* [=Aquarius], *suranda* [=Pisces], *pāyanda* [=Aries]. And every man in whom were gathered these four powers and the seven and the twelve became godlike (*rabbānī*) in the lower world and the obligation (to perform religious duties?) was lifted from him. He said: In the upper

---

[23] Shahrastānī, 196.

[24] The account of Mazdak in the Indo-Persian *Dabistān i madhāhib* derives from Shahrastānī (evidently from one of the two extant New Persian translations of his book) dressed up with material of the author's own invention, and imbedded in a mendacious fable of how the author had heard it all from real-life Mazdakites in the seventeenth century, who had in their hands a book by Mazdak himself. I remind readers that the same disreputable author claims also to have met face to face with followers of Musaylima, the Arabian contemporary and rival of Muḥammad.

[25] The use of the word *khusraw* not as the proper name of a specific king, but as a general word for 'Persian king', is specific to New Persian. It is thus misguided to see this as an extract from a Mazdakite book in Middle Persian.

[26] *wa rawā* (or: *ruwiya*) *ʿanhu* is again ambiguous: 'it has been reported on his (Abū ʿĪsā al-Warrāq's? or Mazdak's?) authority', or: 'he (Abū ʿĪsā) reported on his (Mazdak's) authority'.

[27] The 'seven ministers' and the 'twelve spiritual beings' are of course the planets and the signs of the zodiac respectively, whereby Monnot (see his translation, 664–5) has shown that the Persian names for the latter (in part corrupt in the manuscripts) refer to the traditional iconography of the 12 signs.

> world the *khusraw* regulates only through the letters the sum of which is the Supreme Name, and whoever has any conception of these letters, to him opens the great mystery, but whoever is deprived of it remains in the blind state of ignorance and forgetfulness and stupidity and grief, the opposites of the four spiritual powers. They are (divided into) sects: the Kōdhakiyya, and Abū-Muslimiyya, and the Māhāniyya, and the Ispēdhjāmagiyya. The Kōdhakiyya are in the environs of Ahwāz and Fārs and Shahrazūr, and the others are in the environs of Sughd Samarqand and Shāsh and Īlāq.

There is no reason to think that this has anything to do with Abū ʿĪsā. Abū ʿĪsā was interested in Iranian religions essentially only as examples of various versions of dualism, but this passage has nothing dualistic about it, nor does it actually have any link with Iranian religious traditions. The idea that the cosmos is ruled by astrological phenomena and that the divinity rules 'through the letters the sum of which is the Supreme Name' reminds us, if of anything, of Ismailism. The last sentence of the passage makes it clear that it has to do with the so-called Neo-Mazdakites of Islamic Persia. The Kōdhakiyya, Abū-Muslimiyya and 'White-robed ones' (Persian *sapēdh-jāmagān*, Arabic *mubayyaḍah*) are mentioned elsewhere in connection with 'Neo-Mazdakism'. On the other hand, the Māhāniyya are considered by Ibn al-Malāḥimī (apparently from Abū ʿĪsā), ʿAbd al-Jabbār (from Nawbakhtī, from Abū ʿĪsā) and Ibn al-Nadīm (perhaps also from Abū ʿĪsā) as being connected with Marcionism and are here apparently wrongly grouped together with the others.

To summarise so far: Shahrastānī's account of Mazdakism has three components. The first is taken from Nawbakhtī's garbled version of Abū ʿĪsā's description of Mazdak, in which (through Nawbakhtī's fault) a noncommittal remark about the dualistic beliefs of the 'Neo-Mazdakites' of the ninth century has been transformed into an account of Mazdak's cosmology. The second has nothing to do with any kind of Mazdakism. The third derives from a report in New Persian (evidently from the eleventh or twelfth century) on the beliefs of the 'Neo-Mazdakites'. For the cosmology of Mazdak and his contemporary followers we are left actually with nothing.

MAZDAK'S ETHICS: ASCETICISM OR LIBERTARIANISM?

As regards the ethical teachings of Mazdak, we have not only the above-cited Muslim sources but also a brief, but important, passage in a Zoroastrian religious text, namely in the *zand* (that is: translation cum commentary) of the canonical Avestan scripture *Vendidad* 4,49.[28] The passage is part of what is clearly an attack on asceticism. We are told, namely, that the man who marries is better than the one who is celibate, the man who has children is better than the one who has none, the man who has riches is better than the poor man, the man who eats meat is better than the one who does not, and among the achievements of this red-blooded child-breeding, property-holding, meat-eating man is the fact that:

> *ashəmaoγəm anašauuanəm aŋuharəstātəm pəšanaiti*

[28] See *Vendidâd: Avesta text with Pahlavi translation and commentary*, ed. Dastoor Hoshang Jamasp, I. Bombay 1907. The Middle Persian (Pahlavi) text of *Vendidad* 4,49 has recently been transcribed and translated in A. Cantera, *Studien zur Pahlavi-Übersetzung des Avesta*, Wiesbaden 2004, 201–2.

What these four words of Avesta actually mean does not really concern us here; it will suffice to say that *aŋuharəstāt-*[29] is very problematic. The zandist analysed it, doubtless wrongly, as the privative prefix *a-*, then a derivative of the root *x^var-*, 'to eat', and then (apparently) some form of the word *sāstar-*, '(wicked) commander',[30] and rendered it with the one-off formation *a-xwarišn-īh-sāstār*,[31] 'the commander of non-eating'. The whole of the 'translation' thus reads:[32]

> *ahlomōγ ī an-ahlaw ī a-xwarišn-īh-sāstār pahikāred,*
>
> "He contends with the unrighteous heretic, the commander of non-eating",

followed by the gloss:

> *čiyōn Mazdak ī Bāmdādān, kē-š xwēš sagr xward u-š kasān pad suy ud marg dād u-š pahikār abāg Astwihād.*
>
> "like Mazdak, son of Bāmdād, who ate himself full and consigned others to hunger and death, and his struggle is (thus) with Astwihād" (the demon of death).

The practice of fasting is, of course, well known in Judaism, Christianity and in para-Christian religions like Manichaeism, as it is later in Islam, but it is foreign to Zoroastrianism. So one might consider this passage as indicating merely that the Mazdakites engaged in the (for Zoroastrians) abhorrent practice of fasting. But the fact that the gloss goes on to say that Mazdak 'consigned' his followers 'to hunger and death', and indeed seems to equate Mazdak with the demon of death, implies that it is a question not simply of fasting but of voluntary starvation. One could then possibly link this with the statement in two of our Muslim sources to the effect that Mazdak imposed *qatlu l-ʾanfus* (that is: either suicide or homicide)[33] as the path to salvation of the soul. The imputation that Mazdak was a hypocrite, who 'ate himself full' while condemning others 'to hunger and death', is, of course, a polemical *topos*. But it is, I think, legitimate to separate the informational content of this passage from its polemical content, especially since the underlying Avestan text (as understood by the zandist) speaks only of 'non-eating' and not of hypocrisy.

---

[29] Thus in Geldner's edition of the Avesta. Chr. Bartholomae, *Altiranisches Wörterbuch*, Strassburg 1904, col. 1767, reads *haŋuharə-stāt-* and proposes 'der im Verborgenen sich befindet, sein Wesen treibt', comparing Sanskrit *sasvár*, 'secret'. J. Kellens, *Les noms-racine de l'Avesta*, Wiesbaden 1974, 266–8, gives his cautious approval to Bartholomae's etymology, but also draws attention to the problems that it involves.

[30] The zandist presumably had passages in mind like *Yasna* 65,8, *Vendidad* 21,1, *Yasht* 3,7 and 3,10, where the words *ashəmaoγō, anašauua* and *sāsta* occur in close succession.

[31] Some manuscripts have *ʾḥwlšn y sʾstʾl*, others omit the *y*. On the basis of the former variant I propose *a-xwarišn-īh-sāstār*: *a-xwārišn* is a bahuvrīhi ('whose eating is not'), *-īh* makes it abstract ('the act of not eating'), in a genitival tatpuruṣa with *sāstār* 'commander'. Cantera, loc. cit., following Dastoor Hoshang, reads *a-xwarišn* and regards *sāstār* as a gloss, translating: "der gegen den unfrommen Ketzer, der fastet, [den Irrgläubigen] kämpft". I suggest that my reading gives a better sense. The difference is in any case slight.

[32] As always with Zoroastrian Middle Persian it is necessary to construct the reading from the variants offered by the assorted manuscripts, as I have done here, but without any actual emendations. Cantera's reading is not significantly different.

[33] See footnote 10.

The problem with all of the sources about Mazdak is that they contain what seems to be grossly contradictory information. On the one hand we are told that Mazdak taught asceticism, fasting, and even voluntary starvation 'in order to liberate souls from the bodies in which they are suffering', but at the same time that he allowed men 'to have intercourse with each other's wives', so he was apparently an ascetic and a libertine at one and the same time. And then we are told that he 'lifted restrictions on goods', but at the same time that he enjoyed the patronage of the emperor Kavād, a person whom one would not expect to be particularly keen on abolishing private property. All modern authors have been aware of this discrepancy and their general tendency has been to play down the reports that connect Mazdak with asceticism and instead to depict the Mazdakites either as communist revolutionaries or as hedonistic advocates of free love.[34] I think it might be worth looking at it, just for the sake of argument, the other way around.

To begin with, it has to be said that the sources are decidedly vague with regard to Mazdak's alleged 'communism'. But if the Mazdakites were ascetics, it is reasonable to think that they lived in monastic communities where they practiced poverty, chastity and humility, and had no private possessions but rather shared their belongings with the other members of the community, as is the case in monastic orders in other religions. Outside of the monasteries there would have been a larger circle of catechumens (as they were called in early Christianity), or auditors (as the Manichaeans called them), who married and had children and tilled the fields, but who perhaps also pooled their belongings (as did some of the Christian sects that emerged after the Reformation), and indeed the whole concept of private land-holding is famously fluid in the Iranian countryside, where the land is even today periodically redistributed among the farmers. In any event: communal ownership, whether in a monastic community or in a closed village economy, is no threat to the privileges of the landlords, or of the state, who will collect their tributes and taxes regardless of how the fields are divided between the labourers. Communism in the ancient and mediaeval world is not a revolutionary movement; if anything it is a conservative or indeed atavistic force.

If the Mazdakites believed that the world is evil, that souls are entrapped in bodies, that it is necessary to "liberate souls from the bodies in which they suffer", it would follow that procreation, however it is achieved, is fundamentally sinful, because it prolongs the existence of an evil world and perpetuates the entrapment of the souls. From this perspective marriage is no better than concubinage, but, by the same reckoning, concubinage is no worse than marriage. And indeed, for those catechumens who might eventually find the inner strength to renounce the world and devote themselves to a life of blessed chastity, concubinage is less of an impediment than marriage, as it is easier to shake off. These could well have taken Augustine's famous words as their motto.[35]

I cite as a parallel to this the reports about the mediaeval dualists whom their enemies

[34] I am sure it would make an interesting study if someone would investigate the history of Mazdakite studies from the view-point of modern social history. The earliest European authors treat the Mazdakites as dangerous subversives. Then, Eastern European and leftist Iranian scholars glorify Mazdak as a communist revolutionary, while anti-communist writers depict him as a fun-loving libertarian.

[35] *Conf.* 8.7.17: *da mihi castitatem et continentiam, sed noli modo.*

call "Manichaeans" or "Cathars", but who actually styled themselves simply as "Christians".[36] They taught that the world was created by an evil god, that souls are held captive in the world and that procreation is evil because it aids the Creator. The elect, the *perfecti*, lived blessed lives of chastity and poverty, but they were protected by a body of *credentes*, who lived ordinary mundane lives, but who had the opportunity to renounce the world on their deathbeds and be elevated into the rank of *perfecti* and thus achieve salvation, which they too are claimed to have hastened by voluntary starvation. The *credentes* would normally have been married, but their Catholic opponents accused them of practicing some mediaeval, talismanic form of contraception, so as not make themselves guilty of perpetuating the work of the Creator, and also claim that they engaged in "unnatural" – that is to say: non-reproductive – forms of sexual intercourse. All this may or may not be true, but it is surely comprehensible in the context of an anti-cosmic dualism.

According to this model the Mazdakites too would have been anti-cosmic ascetics, who shared their belongings, and who allowed, presumably, their catechumens to marry, but at the same time encouraged them to satisfy the weaknesses of their flesh in other, less permanent, unions, so as to make it easier for them to abandon them when they were ready to do so. This then would have been what their opponents called "lifting restrictions on goods and women".

To what extent Kavād actually supported Mazdak is a question debated in modern scholarship.[37] Without reopening this debate I would nonetheless maintain that such a scenario is entirely plausible. Of course, Kavād was not an ascetic. If he found Mazdakism useful, then it would have been as an instrument for undermining the power of the Zoroastrian clergy, in the same way that his ancestor Shāpūr had used Manes to strengthen his own position against the priesthood, the same way also that, 700 years later, the Count of Toulouse allied himself with the Christian dualists in his struggle against the Catholic clergy and their supporter, the King of France. Asceticism does have the capacity to dispense an aura of sanctity on otherwise totally worldly rulers should they take upon themselves the patronage of the holy men, and this all the more easily if it does not demand too much of them in terms of moral rectitude.

The model that I propose is that Mazdakism is part of a long tradition of anti-cosmic, encratic, dualist Christian and para-Christian asceticism, stretching from Marcion and Manes to the Christian dualists of mediaeval Europe. It is a tradition that is as foreign to

[36] In the context of mediaeval religious polemic 'Manichaean' means 'dualist' and 'Cathar' means 'encratic'. In my paper 'Dualism in Iranian and Christian traditions', *JRAS* 2000, 1–19, I have argued that the so-called Cathars in mediaeval Europe were not Neo-Manichaeans but Neo-Marcionites. The best study of the daily life of the Christian dualists in Southern France is of course the famous book by E. Le Roy Ladurie, *Montaillou, village occitan*, Paris 1975, based mainly on a prudent sifting of the records of the inquisition.

[37] I refer in particular to the interesting paper by Crone cited in note 2. Crone's argument (briefly) is that Kavād was a follower not of Mazdak, but of his predecessor Zarādusht, and that the emperor accepted the pooling of women, not of goods. This was during his first reign. Mazdak emerged only during the second reign of Kavād, or that of Khusraw, preached the collectivisation of women and of goods, was supported by the masses, but not by royalty. There are advantages in this chronology, but, if Zarādusht and Mazdak really belonged to the same tradition, then Kavād's assumed support of the former does seem to pose the same questions as his alleged support of the latter.

and inimical to the pro-cosmic ethical dualism of Zoroastrianism as it is to the pro-cosmic monotheism of catholic Christianity, of Judaism, and of Islam. It is a tradition that despises the flesh, but at the same time takes into account the weakness of the flesh. It involves an anti-sexualism that has so low a regard for procreation that it sees no difference between matrimony and fornication, but in so doing it blurs, intriguingly, the border between stringent moralism and moral indifference.

3

Buddhism as Ancient Iranian Paganism

Patricia Crone

In his book on India Bīrūnī says that in ancient times the whole region from Khurasan through Fars, Iraq and Mosul to the border of Syria followed the religion of the Shamaniyya and continued to do so until Zoroaster appeared.[1] At first sight this makes no sense. The religion of the Shamaniyya (Sanskrit *śramaṇa*, Pali *samaṇa*, ascetics, monks) is Buddhism; the normal form of the word in Arabic is Sumaniyya, a vocalisation I shall freely use even though it must have arisen by mistake.[2] But how could Bīrūnī claim that the whole of the Iranian culture area had once been Buddhist? The answer is that well before his time Sumanism had come to be used as a general term for an ancient form of paganism of which Buddhism was seen as a survivor. In this light, some of Bīrūnī's information on the Sumaniyya is very interesting.

The idea of Buddhism as ancient paganism is presented in its clearest form in Ḥamza al-Iṣfahānī (wrote 359/961) and Khwārizmī (wrote between 367/977 and 372/982). We may start with Ḥamza. According to him, all the nations of the world had once followed a single religion, which had prevailed until the coming of the revealed laws (*ẓuhūr al-sharāʾiʿ*). This single religion had been known by two names: in the eastern regions its adherents were called Sumaniyyūn (Buddhists) and in the western regions Kaldāniyyūn (Chaldaeans). Both still survived, the Sumanīs in India and China, the Chaldaeans in Harran and Edessa. In Khurasan the Sumanīs were now known as Shamanān, while the survivors of the Chaldaeans had taken to calling themselves Sabians since the time of Maʾmūn.[3]

Later Ḥamza provides some further details. Idolatry was instituted (*ḥuddithat*) in the

This article has been greatly improved by the comments of Michael Cook and Kevin van Bladel on an earlier draft.

[1] Bīrūnī, *Kitāb fī taḥqīq mā li'l-Hind*, ed. E. Sachau, London 1887, 10f; ed. Hyderabad 1958 (the edition I have used), 15f; tr. E. C. Sachau, *Alberuni's India*, London 1910, i, 21 (henceforth cited in the form *Hind*, 10f/15 = i, 21).

[2] For all this, see G. Monnot, 'Sumaniyya', *EI*².

[3] Ḥamza al-Iṣbahānī, *Tawārīkh sinī mulūk al-arḍ wa'l-anbiyāʾ*, ed. J. M. P. Gottwaldt, Leipzig 1844, 5; ed. (with *Taʾrīkh* for *Tawārīkh*) Beirut 1961, 11 (henceforth cited in that order, separated by a slash); cf. D. Gimaret, 'Bouddha et les Bouddhistes dans la tradition musulmane', *Journal Asiatique* 257, 1969, 288f.

reign of king Ṭahmūrath, he says. It arose because some people had lost their dear ones and made representations of them to console themselves, and eventually they came to worship them as intermediaries between man and God. It was also in the reign of Ṭahmūrath that fasting was instituted, originally because food was difficult to come by, but eventually it came to be seen as a form of religiosity and worship of God, and they practised it in an extreme form. The inventors of fasting (*al-mubtadiʿ lahu*) were poor people from among the followers of a man called Būdhāsaf. The followers of this religion were called Chaldaeans, and in the time of Islam they called themselves Sabians, though in reality the Sabians are a group of Christians living between the swamps and the desert who differ from the main body of Christians and who are counted among their heretics (*mubtadiʿīhim*). Ṭahmūrath, whose exploits included the building of Isfahan and Babel, held that every group which liked its own religion should be left alone, a principle followed in India to this day.[4]

Here there is no mention the Sumaniyya, only of the Chaldaeans, i.e. the pagans of Harran (and, in his first account, Edessa), who had adopted the name of Sabians to secure *dhimmī* status for themselves in the reign of Maʾmūn according to a famous story.[5] But the institutor of fasting among them is Būdhāsaf (Boddhisattva), placed in the reign of Ṭahmūrath, a king of the legendary Pīshdādid dynasty associated with eastern Iran who is here the ruler of Babel, too.[6] Both idolatry and fasting are said to have appeared in his reign for reasons that originally had nothing to do with religion. Būdhāsaf is the leader of a group whose poverty and fasting go well enough with Buddhism, but one would not have recognized him as a Buddhist figure if it had not been for his name.

Khwārizmī's account is similar and clearly shares a source with Ḥamza's first account, but he has some additional information. Once upon a time mankind (*al-nās*) were Sumaniyyūn and Kaldāniyyūn, he says. The former were idolaters and survive in India and China; the latter survive in Harran and Iraq (rather than Edessa) and are now called Sabians and Harranians, having adopted the name of Sabians in the time of Maʾmūn, though the real Sabians are a Christian sect. The Sumaniyya were followers of Suman and idolaters who believed in the eternity of the world (*qidam al-dahr*), the transmigration of souls, and the doctrine that the earth is always falling downwards. Their prophet was Būdhāsaf, who came forth in India, though others say that he was Hermes. Būdhāsaf appeared in the time of king Ṭahmūrath, who brought the Persian script.[7]

Here Būdhāsaf is more recognizable: he appears in India, his followers are the Sumaniyya, and both he and the Sumaniyya are idolaters who believe in the transmigration of souls, the eternity of the world, and a somewhat enigmatic doctrine regarding the downward

[4] Ḥamza, *Tawārīkh*, 29–32/31f (both editions have Yūdāsaf for Būdhāsaf); cf. Gimaret, 'Bouddha', 280f.

[5] Ibn al-Nadīm, *Kitāb al-Fihrist*, ed. R. Tajaddud, Tehran 1971, 385; tr. B. Dodge, *The Fihrist of al-Nadīm*, New York 1970, ii, 751f.

[6] Cf. A. Christensen, 'Les types du premier home et du premier roi, *Archives d'Études Orientales* 14, 1917–34, part i, 183ff; E. Yarshater, 'Iranian National History', in *Cambridge History of Iran*, 3 (1), ed. E. Yarshater, Cambridge 1983, 371.

[7] Khwārizmī, *Mafātīḥ al-ʿulūm*, ed. G. van Vloten, Leiden 1895, 36; cf. C. E. Bosworth, 'Al-Khwārizmī on various faiths and sects, chiefly Iranian', *Papers in Honor of Professor Ehsan Yarshater*, Leiden 1990, 12, 14f.

movement of the earth; as before, they survive in India and China. For all that, Būdhāsaf is still associated with the Iranian king Ṭahmūrath, and it is not just to the Sumaniyya that he is a prophet, but also to the Chaldaeans/Sabians, in competition with Hermes, the prophet with whom the Sabians are normally associated.[8] There is no mention of fasting.

A similar account of the origins of paganism was known already to Ibn al-Kalbī (d. 204/819). According to him, the religion practised under Ṭahmūrath was idolatry, and fasting first appeared in his time, originally because some poor people had trouble procuring food but eventually as a way of drawing close to God, in which capacity it continued until it was instituted by the revealed laws.[9] Unlike Ḥamza, Ibn al-Kalbī does not identify the poor people as followers of Būdhāsaf, but Būdhāsaf's presence should probably be taken for granted, for it is otherwise hard to see why the invention of fasting should be placed under Ṭahmūrath. Besides, other traditions which may also go back to Ibn al-Kalbī identify Būdhāsaf as the inventor of Sabianism.[10] Abū ʿĪsā al-Warrāq (d. 247/861 or later) and Ṭabarī duly tell us that Zoroaster's patron, Bīshtāsf (Vishtaspa) was a Sabian, i.e. a pagan, when Zoroaster brought Zoroastrianism to him.[11]

Masʿūdī (d. 345/956) also knew the history of paganism. Unlike Ḥamza and Khwārizmī, he does not tell us that mankind had once followed the same pagan religion, but rather gives his information in connection with specific peoples. In the first of three relevant accounts he says that the Iranians were pagans (*ʿalā raʾy al-ḥunafāʾ*) when Zoroaster brought his book[12] and explains their paganism as Sabianism, brought by Būdhāsaf to Ṭahmūrath.[13] Būdhāsaf's message was that perfection, nobility, complete soundness and the sources of life lay in the elevated roof above, i.e. the sky, and that the planets which came out and went in were the managers (of this world) and the cause of everything in the world, including the creation of composites out of simple elements, the perfection of forms (*tatmīm al-ṣuwar*), the lengths of lives, and more besides. He attracted people of weak minds with this view and was the first to preach the Sabian doctrine of the Harranians and Kīmārīs, the latter being followers of a type of Sabianism which was separate from that of the Harranians and found among people in the swamps around Wasit and Basra; Masʿūdī also refers to them as the pagans and Chaldaeans (*al-ḥunafāʾ waʾl-kaldāniyyīn*) who were the Babylonians still extant in the swamps.[14]

The paganism that Būdhāsaf brought to Ṭahmūrath is here Sabianism in the sense of

---

[8] Cf. K. van Bladel, *The Arabic Hermes*, Oxford 2009, ch. 3.

[9] Ibn al-Athīr, *al-Kāmil fī ʾl-taʾrīkh*, ed. C. J. Tornberg, Dār Ṣādir reprint, Beirut 1965–7, i, 61.

[10] Ṭabarī, *Taʾrīkh al-rusul waʾl-mulūk*, ed. M. J. de Goeje and others, Leiden 1879–1901, i, 176, 184; Ibn al-Athīr, *Kāmil*, i, 61.

[11] Cited in the forthcoming part of Ibn al-Malāḥimī's *Kitāb al-Muʿtamad fī uṣūl al-dīn*, ed. W. Madelung, 640; my thanks to Prof. Madelung and Sabine Schmidtke for letting me see the typescript); Ṭabarī, i, 683.

[12] Masʿūdī, *Kitāb al-tanbīh waʾl-ishrāf*, ed. M. J. de Goeje, Leiden 1894, 90f.

[13] Masʿūdī, *Tanbīh*, 90f; *Murūj al-dhahab* (cited as MM) ed. C. Barbier de Meynard and A. J. B. Pavet de Courteille, Paris 1861–77 (cited by volume and page); ed. C. Pellat, Beirut 1966-79 (cited by volume and paragraph), ii, 111f/i, §535; cf. iv, 49/ii, §1375, where Būdhāsaf is credited with a statement about kingship which was recorded in Persian on the gate of Nawbahār.

[14] Masʿūdī, *Murūj*, ii, 112/i, §535; cf. iv, 68/ii, §1397; idem, *Tanbīh*, 161.8.

Harranian religion, without any Buddhist features whatever. As the bearer of Sabian/Chaldaean religion Būdhāsaf was to undergo further developments: an astrologer by the name of al-Qasrī, cited by Maqdisī (wrote 355/966), held him to be a Babylonian of immense antiquity who possessed the science of the astral revolutions and who had calculated the age of the world as 360,000 years; he lived before Hermes, who lived long before Adam.[15] Since the present paper is about Buddhism, however, these developments can be left aside.[16]

In his second account Masʿūdī tells us that many Indians, Chinese and others hold that God and the angels have bodies. For this reason they made images of them and worshipped them until their wise men informed them that the planets and stars were live and endowed with intelligence (*nāṭiqa*), that the angels moved back and forth between them and God, and that everything in the world was due to them, so they worshipped them instead; but during the day and some nights they could not see them, so they made idols again. After various events which Masʿūdī says he omits, they abandoned the worship of the heavenly bodies until Būdhāsaf appeared in India. He was an Indian who went to Sind, Sistan, Zābulistān and Kirmān, claiming to be a prophet and a messenger of God, and an intermediary between God and his creation. He came to the land of the Persians in the time of Ṭahmūrath, or, according to some, in that of Jam(shīd) (Ṭahmūrath's brother and successor), and he was the first to make public the doctrines of Sabianism (here Masʿūdī refers the reader back to his earlier account). Būdhāsaf taught them asceticism and preoccupation with the things of the higher worlds in which people's souls originated and to which they would return, and he renewed (*jaddada*) the worship of idols.[17]

Here Sabianism is not primordial paganism, but rather a reformed version of it: idolatry represents the first step, and here as in Ḥamza it develops naturally, though it is also reinstituted by Būdhāsaf. The latter's Sabianism, consisting of astral worship and asceticism, is the second step, and astral worship also develops naturally, though again it is reinstituted by Būdhāsaf. How asceticism (fasting) had appeared we are not told, but in Ibn al-Kalbī and Ḥamza that too develops naturally, and Masʿūdī is clearly working with closely related material. He does not use the word Sumaniyya, but his Būdhāsaf is an Indian figure of whom we are implicitly told that his religion had once prevailed in eastern Iran.

In his third account Masʿūdī says that all of China used to adhere to the religion of their forebears (*man salafa*), that is the religion of the Sumaniyya (or Samaniyya, as Pellat vocalises it). He identifies Sumanism as idolatry comparable to that of Quraysh, implicitly referring back to his second account. One manuscript has the Chinese import their Sumanism from India, but in Pellat's edition the Sumaniyya are simply idolaters like the Indians. We do not see Būdhāsaf reform their gross idolatry here. Instead we are told that Dualist and Dahrī doctrines have appeared in China: the reference is presumably to Manichaeism and

[15] Maqdisī, *Kitāb al-badʾ waʾl-taʾrīkh*, ed. Cl. Huart, Paris 1899-1919, ii, 97; cf. ii, 146ff on his book on *qirānāt*.

[16] Cf. van Bladel, *Arabic Hermes*, 115–118.

[17] Masʿūdī, *Murūj*, iv, 42ff/ii, §1370f; cf. Baghdādī, *Uṣūl al-dīn*, Istanbul 1928, 321. The section down to the appearance of Būdhāsaf is from al-Nawbakhtī, citing Abū Maʿshar (cf. ʿAbd al-Jabbār, *al-Mughnī*, v, ed. M. M. al-Khuḍayrī, Cairo 1958, 155).

(real) Buddhism.[18]

The information about Būdhāsaf which does not reflect Iraqi paganism in the sources reviewed so far is this: Būdhāsaf was an Indian active in diverse parts of eastern Iran, a prophet, and a contemporary of king Ṭahmūrath; he founded or reformed ancient paganism, meaning idolatry, and his followers were poor people for whom he instituted fasting or who did so themselves; they were known as Sumanīs and were still found in India and China, and they believed that the world was eternal, that the souls transmigrated, and that the earth was always falling downwards.

Some of these details were also known to the heresiographers, who added a few of their own. To them, the Sumaniyya were a species of Dahrīs. Māturīdī (d. 333/944) explained that they (or the Dahrīs in general) held everything to be generated by mixtures and movements devoid of providence and wisdom, and that they only accepted knowledge based on the senses, so that they would not accept information about countries that one had not seen, for example.[19] They were *muʿaṭṭila*, as Maqdisī said, placing them in India and giving a well-informed account of their belief in reincarnation with reference to that country;[20] but he also identifies them as dualists with implicit reference to Khurasan,[21] and cites the Samanid geographer Jayhānī as saying that some Sumanīs regarded the Buddha (*al-budd*) as a prophet while others cast him as the creator in visible form.[22] According to Baghdādī (d. 429/1037), they had existed before the rise of Islam and reappeared after it; they believed in the eternity of the world, knowledge based on the five senses alone, and the equipollence of proofs (*takāfuʾ al-adilla*), as well as in reincarnation on the basis of merit (which he took to be incompatible with their epistemological principles).[23] Their view that the earth is always falling was familiar to Mātūrīdī, but Baghdādī reports it as Dahrī rather than specifically Sumanī.[24] The heresiographers say nothing about the Sumaniyya's relationship with Būdhāsaf, though Baghdādī knew him as a pseudo-prophet.[25]

With the exception of Maqdisī's account relating to India, all the information on Buddhism reviewed so far had reached the Muslims via eastern Iran. It must have been in eastern Iran that Būdhāsaf was linked with Ṭahmūrath. It was certainly there that the terms *shamanān* and Būdhāsaf were formed[26] and that the book which came to be known in Arabic as *Kitāb al-Bilawhar wa-Būdhāsaf* originated.[27] It was also there that Jahm b. Ṣafwān

---

[18] Masʿūdī, *Murūj*, i, 298f/i, §325; cf. Gimaret, 'Bouddha', 290 (where the Chinese get their Buddhism from India), 294-6 (on Buddhists as Dahrīs).

[19] Mātūrīdī, *Kitāb al-tawḥīd*, ed. F. Kholeif, Beirut 1970, 152; similarly Ibn al-Malāḥimī, *Kitāb al-Muʿtamad fī uṣūl al-dīn*, ed. M. McDermott and W. Madelung, London 1991, 29.ult., 44f.

[20] Maqdisī, *Badʾ*, i, 144, 197ff; iv, 9; cf. Gimaret, 'Bouddha', 298f.

[21] Maqdisī, *Badʾ*, iv, 24; similarly Ibn al-Murtaḍā in Gimaret, 'Bouddha', 294.

[22] Maqdisī, *Badʾ*, iv, 19.

[23] Baghdādī, *al-Farq bayna 'l-firaq*, ed. M. Badr, Cairo 1910, 253f; idem, *Uṣūl al-dīn*, 320.

[24] Baghdādī, *Uṣūl*, 319f.

[25] Baghdādī, *Farq*, 333.

[26] Cf. W. Sundermann, 'Die Bedeutung des Parthischen für die Verbreitung buddhistischer Wörter indischer Herkunft', *Altorientalische Forschungen* 9, 1982, 100ff; N. Sims-Williams, 'Indian Elements in Parthian and Sogdian', in K. Röhrborn and W. Veenker (eds.), *Sprachen des Buddhismus in Zentralasien*, Wiesbaden 1983, 133, 137.

[27] Cf. D. M. Lang, 'Bilawhar wa-Yūdāsaf', *EI*^{2}; Gimaret, 'Bouddha', 282ff.

(d. 128/746) disputed with Sumaniyya,[28] probably at Tirmidh, on the border between Sogdia and Bactria (Ṭukhāristān), where he was based and where there certainly was a Buddhist population.[29] It must have been via debates such as Jahm's that the Sumanīs came to be known as empiricists and skeptics, and that their doctrine regarding the downwards movement of the earth reached Iraq, where it was known already to Nazzām (d. 220–230/835–45): the latter had frequented Sumanīs and other believers in the equipollence of proofs in Baghdādī's opinion.[30] A story set in Basra in the 740s–60s presumes Sumanism to have been sufficiently well known at the time for a Basran to be attracted to it.[31] Ibn al-Nadīm (d. 380/990) had actually read about Būdhāsaf in a Khurasani book and knew him to be the prophet of the Sumaniyya, a religion followed by most Transoxanians before Islam and in ancient times (*qabla ʾl-islām wa-fīʾl-qadīm*); but all he says about it is that Būdhāsaf forbade his followers to say no, which sounds like an innuendo.[32] He also reports that some held *al-budd* to be an image of Būdhāsaf *al-ḥakīm*, and both he and others have further information about the devotees of *al-budd*.[33] But *al-budd* is not often linked, let alone identified, with Būdhāsaf before Bīrūnī.[34]

FROM IRANIAN BUDDHISM TO BŪDHĀSAF THE SABIAN

How did Būdhāsaf come to be the institutor of ancient paganism? Given the scarcity of the material, the answer has to be conjectural, but we may start by noting that Buddhism and Iranian paganism had blended in eastern Iran to the point that they will have looked much the same to a Zoroastrian. Thus the Sogdians, who were often Buddhists outside Sogdia (where their Buddhist writings have been found), do not seem often to have been Buddhists at home, but even so, they were quite ready to incorporate the Buddha in their eclectic pantheon. A house built around 700 at Panjikant, where both Iranian and other deities (above all the Babylonian goddess Nana) were worshipped, had a reception room with huge images of the owner's main deities as well as smaller figures of other gods and goddesses, including a modest Buddha equipped with the halo and tongues of flames characteristic of the local deities: the owner seems to have been a non-Buddhist who had

---

28 J. van Ess, *Theologie und Gesellschaft im 2. und 3. Jahrhundert Hidschra*, Berlin and New York 1991–1997, ii, 503f.

29 P. Leriche and S. Pidaev, 'Termez in Antiquity', in J. Cribb and G. Hermann (eds.), *After Alexander: Central Asia before Islam*, Oxford 2007, 189f; Hsüan-tsang (d. 664) in S. Beal, *Buddhist Records of the Western World*, i, London 1906, 39.

30 Māturīdī, *Tawḥīd*, 152, cf. 155; Baghdādī, *Farq*, 113; Gimaret, 'Bouddha', 293, 295f.

31 Abū ʾl-Faraj al-Iṣbahānī, *Kitāb al-aghānī*, Cairo 1927–74, iii, 146f (in a story bringing together *mutakallims* of all persuasions represented in Basra at the time).

32 Ibn al-Nadīm, *Fihrist*, 408; tr. Dodge, ii, 824; cf. P. Crone, *The Nativist Prophets of Early Islamic Iran: Rural Revolt and Local Zoroastrianism*, Cambridge 2012, cf. 17 ('wife-sharing').

33 Ibn al-Nadīm, *Fihrist*, 411.5; tr. Dodge, ii, 831; Gimaret, 'Bouddha', 274ff.

34 Cf. Gimaret, 'Bouddha', 274ff. Ibn al-Nadīm lists Persian books on al-Budd, Būdhāsaf, and Būdhāsaf and Bilawhar (*Fihrist*, 364.–2; tr. Dodge, ii, 714), suggesting that they entered the Persian tradition as separate figures.

added the Buddha to his religious repertoire, clearly thinking of him as a deity.[35] A terracotta Buddha figure dating from the fifth/early sixth century or later has also been found at Panjikant, made by a local artist who may have seen images of the Maitreya Buddha, but who did not follow any Buddhist prototype. The mould was made for serial production, so there were many Sogdians who liked to call upon the Buddha even though they were not what one could call Buddhists.[36] Buddhist objects owned by non-Buddhists have also been found in Samarqand, Kish and Nasaf.[37] The Buddhists in their turn absorbed (or, as converts, retained) Iranian concepts such as dualism,[38] spoke of *Buddha Mazda*, depicted the Buddha with the above-mentioned tongues of flames, which are assumed to reflect Iranian tradition,[39] and sometimes cast him as the creator in visible form, suggesting *ḥulūlī* views of the type also espoused by Muqannaʿ.[40] Above all, both the Buddhists and the Sogdians revered the *dēvs* as divine beings instead of branding them as demons after the fashion of the Zoroastrians. At Panjikant the inhabitants used Zoroastrian fire ritual and burial modes, but whereas the Zoroastrian creed included profession of hatred for the *dēvs*,[41] the last king of Panjikant was called Dēvaštīč, "*dēv*-like", or in other words "divine";[42] the scribe of a letter probably addressed to him was called *dywgwn*, rendered "the devilish" by the translators, though it is hard to see why the *dyw* in his name should be more devilish than that in *dywʾštyc*;[43] and a Sogdian Dēvdād, son of Dēvdasht (alias Abū ʿl-Sāj b. Yūsuf), turns up in Afshīn's troops along with his nephew Dēvdād b. Muḥammad.[44] Modern scholars debate whether the *dēvs* revered by Dēvaštīč and his likes were survivors of ancient Iranian religion or Indian imports bought by Buddhism.[45] To the Zoroastrians, it will have been a non-question: the two religions were one and the same.

It was presumably the Buddhists of eastern Iran who had linked Būdhāsaf with the Pīshdādid dynasty in order to endow their religion with native credentials, but from a Zoroastrian point of view, they thereby identified him as the founder of the *dēv*-worshipping paganism that Zoroaster was to oppose. At some point the Pīshdādid and Kayānid kings travelled to Iraq, where they replaced the Achaemenids as rulers of ancient Iran and Babel in the historical memory of the Iranians. Here Būdhāsaf entered a discussion of the origins

---

35 B. I. Marshak and V. I. Raspopova, 'Wall Paintings from a House with a Granary, Penjikent, 1st Quarter of the Eighth Century AD', *Silk Road Archaeology* i, 1990, 123–176, esp. 151ff.

36 B. I. Marshak and V. I. Raspopova, 'Buddha Icon from Panjikent', *Silk Road Archaeology* 5, 1997–98, 300.

37 K. Abdullaev, *The Buddhist Iconography of Northern Bactria-Tokharistan*, forthcoming.

38 Cf. above, note 21.

39 B. Stavisky, 'Buddha-Mazda from Kara-tape in Old Termez (Uzbekistan): a Preliminary Communication', *Journal of the International Association of Buddhist Studies* 3, 1980, 89–94; D. A. Scott, 'The Iranian Face of Buddhism', *East and West* 40, 1990, 54.

40 Cf. above, note 22.

41 Yasna 12.1; also prefaced to some Yashts, e.g. nos 5, 19.

42 W. B. Henning, 'A Sogdian God', *Bulletin of the School of Oriental and African Studies* 28, 1965, 253; cf. F. Grenet and E. de la Vaissière, 'The Last Days of Panjikent', *Silk Road Art and Archaeology* 8, 2002, 155–196.

43 Grenet and de la Vaissière, 'Last Days of Panjikent', 172, 175

44 C. E. Bosworth, 'Sādjids', *EI*².

45 C. Herrenschmidt and J. Kellens, 'daiva', *Encyclopaedia Iranica*.

of idolatry which had begun well before the rise of the Sasanians, let alone the coming of Islam. The best known founder of idolatry in Babel was Nimrod, a wicked king. Contrary to what one might have expected, Būdhāsaf was not simply identified with him, however, perhaps because he was not a king himself or perhaps because Nimrod was already associated or identified with Bēwarāsb, an evil king of the Pīshdādid dynasty who ruled after Ṭahmurath and Jam(shīd) and who was also known as Azdahāg.[46] Būdhāsaf was however confused with Bēwarāsb. In the *Dēnkart* the wicked (Az)dahāg, i.e. Bēwarāsb, is a pre-Zoroastrian king of Babel who bewitched mankind into following the idolatry which Zoroaster opposed.[47] In the traditions perhaps going back to Ibn al-Kalbī, the institutor of Sabianism is actually called Bēwarāsb;[48] but he appears in the reign of Ṭahmūrath and is not a king himself, so he retains the key characteristics of Būdhāsaf.[49] (Bēwarāsb also figures as a *ḥakīm*, i.e. Būdhāsaf, in the fourth/tenth-century *Rasāʾil ikhwān al-ṣafāʾ*).[50] As the institutor of Chaldaean/Sabian idolatry, however, Būdhāsaf is undoubtedly continuing an old Iraqi debate about the origins of idolatry in which the protagonist used to be Nimrod and/or Bēwarāsb, even when he retains his Buddhist name.

BĪRŪNĪ

We may now turn to Bīrūnī. A great deal of what he says comes from the sources already examined. In his section on pseudo-prophets (*al-mutanabbiʾūn*) in his *Āthār*, written in 390f/999f, he mentions that Būdhāsaf appeared in India one year into the reign of Ṭahmūrath, brought the Persian script, and preached the religion of the Sabians (*millat al-ṣābiʾa*); many followed him; the Pīshdādid kings and some of the Kayyānids, who were settled at Balkh, venerated the sun, moon, planets and the elements until the coming of Zoroaster, and there were still survivors of such Sabians in Harran, where they are known as the Ḥarrāniyya.[51] All this is what we have read in Ḥamza, al-Khwārizmī, and Masʿūdī, except that here it is Būdhāsaf, not Ṭahmūrath, who brings the Persian script. A little earlier in his *Āthār*, Bīrūnī tells us that before the coming of the revealed laws (*ẓuhūr al-sharāʾiʿ*) and the appearance of Būdhāsaf, people (*al-nās*) were Shamaniyyūn in the east. They were idolaters and survive today in India, China and among the Toghuz Oghuz; the

---

[46] Ṭabarī, *Taʾrīkh*, i, 174, 201ff; P. O. Skjaervø, 'Zarathustra in the Avesta and in Manicheism. Irano-Manichaica IV', in *La Persia e l'Asia centrale. Da Alessandro al X secolo* (Accademia Nazionale dei Lincei, Atti dei Convegni 127), Rome 1996, 608f; cf. also Movsēs Xorenacʿi cited there and at 609n.

[47] *Dēnkart*, VII.4, 72 (tr. W. E. West, *Pahlavi Texts*, Oxford 1897, 66f); cf. Skjaervø, 'Zarathustra', 611.

[48] See above, note 10.

[49] Differently F. Rosenthal (tr.), *The History of al-Ṭabarī*, i, Albany 1989, 345n, against Christensen, 'Types', i, 206, but without discussion.

[50] *Rasāʾil ikhwān al-ṣafāʾ*, Beirut 1957, ii, 204.11, 205.12 (here written Bīrāst, but compare the Urdu translation as rendered in J. Wall, *The Ikhwan-us-suffa*, Lucknow 1880, 8, 9).

[51] Bīrūnī, al-*Āthār al-bāqiya ʿan al-qurūn al-khāliya*, ed. and tr. C. E. Sachau, Leipzig 1923 and London 1879, 204.18. (I do not give separate reference to the translation since it preserves the pagination of the Arabic text in the margin.)

Khurasanis call them Shamanān.[52] "It is even said that before the despatch of the messengers all mankind (*al-nās*) formed a single nation of idolaters", he adds in his *Hind*.[53] With the exception of the Toghuz Oghuz, this is what we are told in al-Khwārizmī.

Bīrūnī continues in his *Āthār* that the idol temples (*bahārāt aṣnāmihim*), monasteries (*farkhārāt*)[54] and other remains (*āthār*) of the Sumaniyya are extant in the borderland between Khurasan and India, where he had presumably seen them himself. The Sumaniyya believed in the eternity of the world (*qidam al-dahr*), reincarnation of the soul, and that the celestial sphere (*al-falak*) is endlessly falling in the void (*khalā'*) and that this is why its motion is circular: they claimed that when a round object is moved (*uzīla*), it will rotate as it descends.[55] This is an amplified version of what we read in Khwārizmī, suggesting that he and Khwārizmī were excerpting from the same source. He adds that some of them believe that the world has been created in time and that it will last a million years, divided into four eras, of which the first is 400,000 years long and a period of happiness; the second is 300,000 long and less good, the third is 200,000 long and still less good, and the fourth will last 100,000 years and is a time of evil and corruption, and that is the time we live in.[56] What he is describing is the four *yuga*s which make up a *kalpa* in the Vedic literature and which also went into Buddhism; but the scheme seems to be greatly simplified, and depending on precisely what he has in mind, the figures are either strikingly low or too high.[57] Bīrūnī observes that some Shamaniyya believe Adam to be the father of mankind while others hold different groups to have different ancestors, for reasons he finds silly. The Shamaniyya and the Indians have historical information about the first Buddha and the one after him, and how to reach the status of *bodhisattva* (*būdhāsafiyya*) and Buddha (*buddiyya*), through which we escape birth and death, that is reincarnation.[58] All this is recognizably about real Buddhism and could come from the same source that Khwārizmī was using, perhaps Īrānshahrī.

Bīrūnī knows more about the subject in his book on India. The Shamaniyya are closer to the Indians/Hindus than any others, though they detest the Brahmans, he says.[59] The book of *Gūrāman* (Sachau tentatively suggests *Gūḍhāmana*), meaning knowledge of the unknown (*'ilm al-ghayb*), was a book about augury composed by the Buddha, the founder of the Sumanī wearers of red robes (*al-budd ṣāḥib al-muḥammira al-shamaniyya*).[60] Bīrūnī also mentions a book of *Jin*, i.e. Jina (victorious), identifying *Jin* as the Buddha, and cites

---

[52] Bīrūnī, *Āthār*, 206.16.

[53] *Hind*, 53f/84f = i, 112.

[54] *Farkhār* is a Sogdian rendering of *vihāra* (pointed out to me by K. van Bladel and also noted in *Encyclopaedia Iranica*, 'Buddhism').

[55] Bīrūnī, *Āthār*, 206.18.

[56] Bīrūnī, *Āthār*, 206.20-22, with the continuation in J. Fück, 'Sechs Ergänzungen zu Sachaus Ausgabe von al-Bīrūnī's "Chronologie Orientalischer Völker"', in his *Documenta Islamica Inedita*, Berlin 1952, 74.

[57] Cf. W. M. McGovern, *A Manual of Buddhist Philosophy*, London 2000 (first publ. 1923), 45ff; A. Sadakata and H. Nakamura, *Buddhist Cosmology*, Tokyo 1997, ch. 4, esp. 106.

[58] Bīrūnī in Fück, 'Sechs Ergänzungen', 74.

[59] *Hind* 10/15 = i, 21.

[60] *Hind*, 75/122 = i, 158.

the book as denying that Mount Meru is round.[61] Nonetheless, he elsewhere says that he has not found a single Buddhist (Shamanī) book on the topic of Mount Meru or met a Buddhist who could explain their views on this subject, so he cites the further details from Īrānshahrī.[62] Maybe Jina here is the founder of Jainism, his identification as the Buddha notwithstanding. Bīrūnī also cites the *Bṛht Saṃhita* of the astronomer Varāhamihira (d. 589), which is still extant, but which is not a Buddhist book, on how to construct idols: Jina, that is the Buddha, should be depicted as extremely beautiful, with the lines of his palms and feet like a lotus, seated on a lotus, with a placid expression, and with soft (? *hashshāsh*) hair as if he were the father of creation.[63] The *arhant* was another form of the Buddha's body (but again it seems to be a Jain figure):[64] in that role he should be depicted as a handsome naked youth with hands reaching to his knees and his wife Śri under his left breast.[65] (Vishnu, of whom the Buddha was the ninth incarnation according to the Hindus, was also to be depicted with Śri under his left breast.)[66] The Shamaniyya looked after the idol of the Buddha, while the class known as Nagna looked after that of Arhant, he says, apparently on the authority of the same book.[67] (It also mentioned that the idol of the Maga in India was the sun.)[68] He knew of a book by a Buddhist astronomer called Sugrīm (Sugrīva according to Sachau) al-Shamanī;[69] and he had heard that when the Buddhūdan (Buddha?) addressed his adherents (*qawmihi*), the Shamaniyya, he called the three powers latent in matter *buddha*, *dharma* and *sangha*, meaning intelligence, religion and ignorance (*sic*).[70] Finally, we are told that the Shamaniyya cast their dead into the river, following an injunction of the Buddha, an odd piece of information, though this mode of disposing of the dead is in fact reported for Tibet.[71]

As Gimaret observes, Bīrūnī did not know much about Buddhism. It was clearly from Hindus that he derived most of his information about it, and what he describes is largely of doctrines that it shared with Hinduism. This is also true of Īrānshahrī's and Maqdisī's information, and it may reflect the state of Buddhism in India at the time.[72]

---

61 *Hind*, 121/201.1 = i, 243.

62 *Hind*, 124/206 = i, 249. He is not denying having seen any Buddhist book or met any Buddhist in general, as Gimaret, 'Bouddha', 294, takes it.

63 *Hind*, i, 57/91 = i, 119.

64 Thus M. Tardieu, 'La diffusion du bouddhisme dans l'empire kouchan, l'Iran et la Chine, d'après un kephalaion manichéen inédit', *Studia Iranica* 17, 1988, 173n.

65 *Hind* 57/91 = i, 119.

66 *Hind*, 56/89f = i, 118.

67 *Hind*, 59/93 = i, 121.

68 Bīrūnī, *Hind*, 58/93 = i, 121. He also mentions them at 11/16 = i, 21.

69 *Hind*, 74/120.-2 = i, 156.

70 *Hind*, 20/30 = i, 40 ("Buddhodana (*sic*)", with another *sic* after "ignorance").

71 *Hind*, 284/ = ii, 169 (it also puzzled Gimaret, 'Bouddha', 293); cf. D. J. Davies and L. H. Mates, *Encyclopedia of Cremation*, Aldershot 2005, 97.

72 Gimaret, 'Bouddha', 295, 299, 307.

THE HISTORY OF SUMANISM

If Bīrūnī did not know much about Buddhism, he knew more than most about Iranian paganism, and it is to his statements on this subject that we may now turn. In the passage with which this article began he says that the whole region from Khurasan through Fars, Iraq and Mosul to the border of Syria had once practised the religion of the Shamaniyya. This continued to be the case until Zoroaster appeared in Azerbaijan and preached in Balkh, where Gushtāsb and his son Isfandiyār adopted Zoroastrianism (*Majūsiyya*) and spread it by force and by treaty *(qahran wa-ṣulḥan)* in east and west alike (*fī bilād al-mashriq wa'l-maghrib*), setting up fire temples all the way from China to the Byzantine empire (*wa-naṣaba buyūt al-nīrān min al-Ṣīn ilā 'l-Rūm*). The later kings of Fars and Iraq, presumably meaning the Sasanians, also chose it as their religion, so the Shamaniyya withdrew to Balkh.[73] What Bīrūnī is saying here is not that the entire region from Khurasan to the Byzantine empire had once been Buddhist, but rather that it had once adhered to the same sort of paganism: it is only when the religion withdraws to Balkh that we have to understand it as Buddhism. One would assume Bīrūnī's statement to be indebted to Ḥamza and Khwārizmī on the aboriginal religion of mankind, called Sumanī in the east and Chaldaean/Sabian in the west. He quotes it in his *Āthār*, as seen already.[74] But he is not simply reproducing it here, using the eastern rather than the western term for the aboriginal religion, for what he is saying is not that all mankind had once adhered to the Shamanī religion, but rather that people had once done so in regions which add up to the former Sasanian empire. Unlike Ḥamza and Khwārizmī, moreover, he is making this point in connection with the history of Zoroastrianism, and what he tells us is that the original religion of the Iranians was forcibly suppressed by Zoroastrian rulers. He envisages these rulers as using compulsion in ways that included *jihād*: the new religion was imposed by force and by *treaty*. In short, Gushtāsb and his son Isfandiyār are here depicted as behaving much as the Safavids were to do some six centuries after Bīrūnī wrote, suppressing one religion current in Iran in favour of another and waging war in its name against their neighbours.

What lies behind this idea? Bīrūnī is not our only source for it. According to Masʿūdī, Vishtāspa/Gushtāsb made Zoroastrianism victorious by military force (*qātala ʿalayhā ḥattā ẓaharat*).[75] Thaʿālibī says that he forced people to adopt Zoroastrianism, slaughtering large numbers of his own subjects in that connection.[76] The third/ninth-century Zoroastrian Martan Farrukh informs us that his son and brother, Spendād and Zarēr, propagated the new religion all the way to the Byzantine empire and India together with other warriors.[77] But it is usually only against the Huns/Turks ("Turan") that Vishtāspa and his son fight in the Zoroastrian books and Muslim sources reflecting the Sasanian tradition,[78] and the idea of Vishtāspa/Hystaspes imposing the new religion by force seems to be unknown to

[73] *Hind*, 10f/15f = i, 21.

[74] Above, note 52.

[75] Masʿūdī, *Tanbīh*, 90.14.

[76] Thaʿālibī, *Ghurar akhbār mulūk al-furs wa-siyarihim*, ed. and tr. H. Zotenberg, Paris 1900, 257.

[77] P. J. de Menasce (ed. and tr.), *Škand Gūmānīk Vičār*, Fribourg en Suisse 1945, x, 65-68.

[78] Ṭabarī, *Ta'rīkh*, i, 676f; Yarshater, 'Iranian National History', 376; A. Shapur Shabazi, 'Goštāsp', *Encyclopaedia Iranica*.

the Greek tradition, reflecting the Hellenistic and the Parthian periods. This suggests that the image of the first Zoroastrian kings as religious tyrants was formed in the Sasanian period, reflecting Sasanian policies.

The Sasanian use of force on behalf of Zoroastrianism is known from numerous literary sources, mostly Christian, but also the ultimately Zoroastrian *Letter of Tansar* and, in a more legendary vein, the *Kārnāmag ī Ardaxšēr ī Pābagān*.[79] They say nothing about Sasanian *jihād* or measures against Buddhism. Both activities are mentioned in the famous inscriptions of the third-century priest, Kirdīr, however. Kirdīr boasts of having set up fires and priests throughout the empire, inflicting heavy blows on Buddhists (*shaman*), Hindus (*brāman*), Jews, Nazarenes, Christians, *maktak* (unidentified), and Manichaeans (*zandīk*), routing Ahriman and the demons (*dēvān*), and setting up fires and priests in the land of the non-Iranians, too, "where the horses and men of the king of kings reached".[80] The provinces affected by these measures, whether in the form of internal repression or external *jihād*, stretch from Syria, Cilicia, Cappadocia and Pontus in the west to "the Kushan country up to Peshawar" in the east: not quite Syria to China, as Bīrūnī says, but certainly Rūm to India, as Martan Farrukh puts it.[81] And here as in Bīrūnī, it is by the establishment of fire temples that Zoroastrianism is imposed. In line with this, archaeologists generally credit the decline of the Buddhist monasteries at Tirmidh to the Sasanian conquest of the region in the later third or fourth century;[82] and a shrine at one of these monasteries (Karatepe) seems hastily to have been converted into a Zoroastrian fire altar when Tirmidh was occupied by Sasanian troops, who left behind Persian graffiti.[83] These activities were hardly forgotten. Yet we do not hear anything about Sasanian kings waging *jihād* on behalf of Zoroastrianism in the standard accounts of the Sasanian kings. What we do hear is that the Pīshdādid kings engaged in it, thereby eliminating the Shamanī religion from an area corresponding to the Sasanian empire. In short, it seems that the Pīshdādids have been

[79] Cf. A. de Jong, 'One Nation under God? The Early Sasanians as Guardians and Destroyers of Holy Sites'. in R. G. Kratz and H. Spieckermann (eds.), *Götterbilder, Gottesbilder, Weltbilder*, i, Tübingen 2006, 233ff.

[80] D. N. Mackenzie (ed. and tr.), 'Kerdir's Inscription', in G. Herrmann, *The Sasanian Rock Reliefs at Naqsh-i Rustam* (*Iranische Denkmäler: Iranische Felsreliefs I*), Berlin 1989, 35ff; synoptic translation of the Naqsh-i Rustam, Sar Mashhad and Kaʿba of Zoroaster inscriptions by Ph. Gignoux, *Les quatres inscriptions du mage Kirdīr*, Paris 1991, 66ff.

[81] MacKenzie, 'Kerdir's Inscription', §§14f. The Kushan country has disappeared in Gignoux, *Quatres inscriptions*, 71, but "to Peshawar" remains. For the religious groups mentioned, see F. de Blois, 'Naṣrānī (*nazōraios*) and ḥanīf (*ethnikos*): studies on the religious vocabulary of Christianity and Islam', *Bulletin of the School of Oriental and African Studies* 65, 2002, 5ff.

[82] P. Leriche, 'Termez antique et médiévale' in P. Leriche and others (eds.), *La Bactriane au carrefour des routes et des civilisations de l'Asie Centrale: Termez et les villes de Bactriane-Tokharestan* (actes du colloque de Termez 1997), Paris 2001, 80; B. Stavisky, 'Le Bouddhisme à Taramita-Termez au IIᵉ-Vᵉ siècles' in the same work, 61.

[83] B. Stavisky, *La Bactriane sous le Kushans*, Paris 1986, 198; idem, 'Le problème des liens entre le bouddhisme bactrien, le zoroastrianisme et les cultres mazdéens locaux à la lumière des fouilles de Kara-tepe', in F. Grenet (ed.), *Cultes et monuments religieux dans l'Asie Centrale pré-Islamique*, Paris 1987, 51; cf. also the helpful discussion in M. G. Raschke, 'New Studies in Roman Commerce with the East', in H. Temporini and W. Haase (eds.) *Aufstieg und Niedergang der römischen Welt*, Berlin and New York 1975–91, II (Principat), ix/2, 808, 1058.

reshaped in the image of the later kings: the Sasanian assault on Buddhism was remembered as war against the Sumaniyya by Gushtāsb and his son. Compare Yarshater, 'Iranian National History', 402f, on the reshaping of the legendary kings along Sasanian lines.

It is not clear whether Kirdīr refers to the suppression of Iranian paganism: his measures against Ahriman and the demons (*dēvān*) could be understood in that vein, but they could also be read as mere recapitulation of his activities against the foreign faiths. Either way, it is hard to believe that he and/or his successors can have imposed what they took to be Zoroastrianism on Iran without using force against Iranian priests as well, for the diversity within the Iranian religious tradition must have been enormous, given that the priests in question had never been united in one organisation or subordinated to a single authority before. There are signs of diversity even in the Pahlavi books, though all they preserve is a single priestly tradition.[84] When Thaʿālibī describes Gushtāsb as slaughtering large numbers of his own subjects, one would once more assume the behaviour to be that of the Sasanians.

Bīrūnī has something interesting to say about the result as well. In his *Āthār* he tells us that the ancient Magians (*al-majūs al-aqdamūn*) were those who existed before Zoroaster; they no longer existed in the pure form: all of them were now of Zoroaster's people, or of the Shamaniyya, but they added some ancient things to their religion which they had taken from the laws of the Shamaniyya and the ancient Harranians.[85] By *majūs* Bīrūnī is not likely to mean priests (Magi), a sense the word never seems to carry in Arabic, but since his *majūs* predate Zoroaster, he obviously is not using the word in its normal sense of Zoroastrians either. He must mean something like adherents of Iranian religions. Shahrastānī, perhaps following Bīrūnī, also uses the word in this sense: he classifies the Zoroastrians (*al-Zardūshtiyya*) as a subdivision of *al-majūs*.[86] What Bīrūnī is telling us is that there used to be communities which practised pre-Zoroastrian forms of Iranian religion. They were pre-Zoroastrian in the sense of predating the forcible imposition of official Zoroastrianism credited to Gushtāsb and his son, so what Bīrūnī is talking about is really the different forms of Iranian religion encountered by the Sasanian kings. (How far they were pre-Zoroastrian in the sense of rooted in the traditions rejected by the adherents of the Gāthās rather than simply different developments of a common heritage is another question on which his information throws no light.) The ancient *majūs* must be the ancient Shamaniyya, and Bīrūnī confirms this in his account of how the Shamaniyya were suppressed: "the *majūs* have survived to this day in the land of India", he says.[87] Here he is telling us that they survived in Iran as well, not just as Buddhists (as we have learnt

[84] Cf. S. Shaked, 'First Man, First King: Notes on Semitic-Iranian Syncretism and Iranian Mythological Transformations', in S. Shaked, D. Shulman, and G. G. Strousma (eds.), *Gilgul: Essays on Transformation, Revolution and Permanence in the History of Religion dedicated to J. Zwi Werblowsky*, Leiden 1987, 252; idem, 'Some Islamic Reports concerning Zoroastrianism', *Jerusalem Studies in Arabic and Islam* 17, 1994, 46; idem, *Dualism in Transformation. Varieties of Religious Experience in Sasanian Iran*, London 1994, 71, 97f.

[85] Bīrūnī, *Āthār*, 318 (for *shamsiyya*, read *shamaniyya*).

[86] Shahrastānī, *Kitāb al-milal wa'l-niḥal*, ed. W. Cureton, London 1842-1846, 182, 185; tr. D. Gimaret and G. Monnot, *Livre des religions et des sectes*, UNESCO 1986, 635, 642.

[87] *Hind* 10/15 = i, 21.

already from Ḥamza and Khwārizmī), but also as Zoroastrians. They had retained some of their former beliefs, we are told, having taken something from the laws of the Shamaniyya and the ancient Harranians with them. This is precisely what one would expect to have happened when the Sasanians set about imposing religious unity: the diversity came to be represented within the official religion.

What was it that the ancient *majūs* had taken with them from Sumanism and ancient Harranian religion? Bīrūnī does not say. This is deeply disappointing. He seems to be the only pre-modern scholar to know about ancient Iranian religion living on within Zoroastrianism, just as he seems to be the only scholar before modern times to know (as will be seen) that Indians and Zoroastrians were divided over the status of the *dēvs*: it is impossible not to be awed by his learning and acumen. By the same token it is hard to forgive him his silence here. The information he had is not likely to turn up in any other source. Unfortunately, all we can do is try to guess what he had in mind.

One would assume the answer to be a cluster of features, and they could include worship of the astral bodies, which Bīrūnī identifies as the religion of the Pīshdādid kings before their acceptance of Zoroaster[88] and for which the Harranians were famed. But worship of the sun, moon, and other astral bodies was so intrinsic a feature of Zoroastrianism that he (or his source) can hardly have regarded it as special to some Zoroastrian priests rather than shared by all of them.[89] A more interesting answer would be worship of the *dēvs*. Bīrūnī mentions that the veneration of these beings (whom he equates with angels) was peculiar to the Indians, adding that "people say that Zoroaster made enemies of the Shamaniyya by calling the devils (*al-shayāṭīn*) by the name of the class which they consider the highest", and that "this (usage) has survived in Persian thanks to the influence of (*min jihat*) of Zoroastrianism (*al-majūsiyya*).[90] In other words, Zoroaster called the demons *dēvs*, or, as we would say, he demoted the *dēvs* from divine to demonic status. But the Shamaniyya who resented this demotion could simply be the Buddhists, who are well known to have revered the *devas*, bringing them with them to eastern Iran, and the fact that Bīrūnī is using *majūsiyya* in the sense of Zoroastrianism here suggests that he did not associate veneration of the *dēvs* with the ancient *majūs* in particular. A more plausible answer would perhaps be reincarnation, known to be a Sumanī belief and credited to the Sabians of Harran as well.[91] Among the Zoroastrians it is reported for Mazdak, Behāfarīdh and all Khurramīs.[92] Shahrastānī also reports it for the Kanthaeans,[93] whom some classified as

88 *Āthār*, 204.

89 Cf. M. Stausberg, *Zarathustra and Zoroastrianism*, London 2008, 31, 48.

90 *Hind*, 44/68f = i, 91.

91 Masʿūdī, *Murūj*, iv, 65ff/ii, §1396 (where only Greek authorities are cited); ʿAbd al-Jabbār, *Mughnī*, v, 152, citing the philosopher Sarakhsī; Shahrastānī, *Milal*, 249f; tr. ii, 169 (where most of the information actually paraphrases an account originally referring to the followers of ʿAbdallāh b. Muʿāwiya and other Khurramīs, cf. R. Freitag, *Seelenwanderung in der islamischen Häresie*, Berlin 1985, 9ff). It is also credited to the philosophers and Sabians by Shahrastānī, *Milal*, 133; tr. i, 511, where the Sabians could be the Harranians or pagans in general.

92 Abū Ḥātim al-Rāzī, *Kitāb al-iṣlāḥ*, ed. Ḥ. Minuchihr and M. Muḥaqqiq, Tehran 1377, 159, 169; cf. Abū ʿĪsā in Ibn al-Malāḥimī, *Muʿtamad*, 584.4; Shahrastānī, *Milal*, 133; tr. i, 511; W. Madelung 'Khurramiyya', *EI*².

93 Shahrastānī, *Milal*, 197; tr. i, 671f.

dualists and others as Sabians,[94] and who are said to have adopted fire-worship when the Sasanian king, Pērōz (459–87), prohibited all religions other than Zoroastrianism.[95] Bīrūnī's ancient *majūs* could have brought the doctrine into Zoroastrianism in response to such royal pressure too. But this is only plausible if Bīrūnī's statement about the ancient *majūs* is based on a literary source rather than personal observation, for he does not mention reincarnation as either a Sumanī or a Sabian/Harranian belief himself.[96] His source for the pre-Zoroastrian *majūs* could have been Īrānshahrī or Abū Bakr al-Rāzī, whose work he knew very well. The latter discussed the beliefs of the Harranian Sabians in a lost work of his[97] and seems to have believed in reincarnation himself.[98] But no doubt it could have been others too. Unfortunately, there does not seem to be any way of making up for Bīrūnī's silence.

PAGANISM AND ZOROASTRIANISM

One interesting feature to emerge from the accounts of the Sumaniyya is that Muslim authors distinguish sharply between paganism and Zoroastrianism. If by paganism we mean *dēv* worship, so too of course did the Zoroastrians, but Zoroastrianism was nonetheless in some ways a form of paganism itself. Most obviously, it was polytheist. This is not perhaps of great significance, for like Greek pagans before them and Arabian pagans after them, Zoroastrians would claim to worship one God, all the other deities being simply "the king's great men".[99] Even recast as a form of monotheism, however, Zoroastrianism was pagan in the sense of inseparable from its civic context. It was not formulated as a set of doctrines that could be presented to anyone regardless of who or what they were, in the "to whom it may concern" style; rather, it was the myths and rituals of a particular people, and its focus was on the cult that connected this people, or a particular subdivision of it, with the divine, above all sacrifice. Zoroastrianism did have something of a detachable "philosophy", as the Greeks would have called it, and it was also less tolerant in its attitude to other gods than most pagan religions: a whole range of deities were rejected as *dēvs*. But whatever exactly might count as a *dēv* in post-Avestic times, the Zoroastrians freely worshipped non-Avestic deities such as Sasan, Bagdana or Nana, who was as popular in

---

94 Abū ʿĪsā in Ibn al-Malāḥimī, *Muʿtamad*, 589.

95 Theodore Bar Koni, *Livres des scolies*, tr. R. Hespel and R. Draguet, Louvain 1981, §84f (255–57); cf. W. Madelung, *Religious Trends in Early Islamic Iran*, Albany 1988, 3.

96 Cf. his *Hind*, ch. 5, where he cites Plato, Proclus, Mani, and the Sufis for comparative purposes, without associating the two Greeks with Harran (contrast Masʿūdī, above, note 91).

97 Masʿūdī, *Murūj*, iv, 68/ii, §1397. Regrettably, all Masʿūdī says about the book is that it contained things too repugnant for him to mention them.

98 P. Kraus (ed. and tr.), 'Raziana I: al-sīra al-falsafiyya', *Orientalia* 4, 1935, 314f; tr. 328f (reprinted without the old pagination in Rāzī, *al- Rasāʾil al-falsafiyya*, ed. P. Kraus, Cairo 1939, 97–111); cf. E. A. Alexandrin, 'Rāzī and his Mediaeval Opponents: Discussions concerning Tanāsukh and the afterlife', in M. Szuppe (ed.), *Iran: Questions et Connaissances*, ii, Paris 2002, 397–407.

99 G. Hoffmann, *Auszüge aus syrischen Akten persischer Märtyrer*, Leipzig 1880, 42. The Zoroastrian gods other than Ohrmazd have been reduced to angels already in Abū ʿĪsā's account (in Ibn al-Malāḥimī, *Muʿtamad*, forthcoming, 639).

western Iran as she was at Panjikant,[100] for pagan deities were much like monotheist saints: their field was patronage, intercession, the passing of gifts and services between the divine and the human worlds, not the formulation of doctrines about the nature of reality.

To be a Zoroastrian was first and foremost to participate in the official cult, which functioned as a sign of loyalty to the Sasanian polity. When Kartīr boasts of having disseminated the religion, he says that he has set up fire temples and appointed priests all over the empire and beyond: of persuading people of the truth of Zoroastrian tenets there is no mention. When Pērōz prohibited all religions other than Zoroastrianism, the Kanthaeans added fire worship to their cult: they did not change their beliefs.[101] And when the Christians were asked to renounce their religion, what they were actually asked to do, according to themselves, was not to renounce anything, but rather to sacrifice to the gods, sun, moon, fire or the elements, in short to combine their Christianity with participation in the Zoroastrian cult:[102] here as in the Roman empire, all they were being asked to provide was a token of loyalty, an elementary assurance that they inhabited the same political and cultural universe as everyone else, which was of course precisely what they did not. Of abjuration formulas, demands for affirmation of belief in Ohrmazd, or recitals of a Zoroastrian confession of faith we do not hear a word.[103]

It is not surprising, then, that the Christians thought of Zoroastrianism as a religion of the same type as the Greek paganism they had fought against in the Roman empire. They often labelled the Zoroastrians pagans *(ḥanpe)*, argued against their worship of fire, derided their offerings to idols, and sometimes listed their many deities by the names of their Greek counterparts.[104] What is more surprising is that the Muslims consistently treat Zoroastrianism as a faith-based religion much like Christianity or Islam. It is possible that they had a different impression of it back in the days when the jurists debated whether or how the Zoroastrians were entitled to *dhimmī* status.[105] But though the heresiographers, writing from the third/ninth century onwards, complain that Zoroastrianism is full of errant nonsense (meaning myths) and lacking in uniformity,[106] they do not classify it as polytheist, argue against its worship of fire, deride its offering to idols, or even mention the Zoroastrian habit of calling fire the son of God.[107] The main reason for this difference must be that the Muslims did not have to establish themselves in Iran by laboriously converting Zoroastrians on the ground, venturing into their villages or towns to persuade them that fire worship, polytheism or libations were wrong. As conquerors they could

[100] M. Stausberg, *Die Religion Zarathustras*, i, 2002, 249, 253; Hoffmann, *Auszüge*, 130ff.

[101] Cf. above, note 95.

[102] E.g. Hoffmann, *Auszüge*, 24, 29, 53, 79f.

[103] Hoffmann, *Auszüge*, 51; J. Walker, *The Legend of Mar Qardagh*, Berkeley and Los Angeles 2006, 57, cf. 58.

[104] M. G. Morony, *Iraq after the Muslim conquest*, Princeton 1984, 292n; J. Walker, *The Legend of Mar Qardagh*, Berkeley and Los Angeles 2006, 23; G. Hoffmann, *Auszüge*, 29, 42, 71, 72, 74.

[105] Cf. Y. Friedman, 'Classification of Unbelievers in Sunnī Muslim Law and Tradition', *Jerusalem Studies in Arabic and Islam* 22, 1998, esp. 179ff.

[106] E.g. Abū ʿĪsā in Ibn al-Malāḥimī, *Muʿtamad*, forthcoming part, 641 (*al-sukhf wa'l-khurāfāt*); Maqdisī, *Badʾ*, iv, 26 (more *hawas* and *takhlīṭ* than any other people).

[107] Cf. R. C. Zaehner, *The Dawn and Twilight of Zoroastrianism*, New York 1961, 59. For examples, see Yasna 1:12, 17:11; Hoffmann, *Auszüge*, 53 (also water).

ignore the *pagani*, the rural people who came to be a byword for heathen ways, until the *pagani* came to them, having converted of their own accord and/or acquired enough knowledge of Islam to present Zoroastrianism as a faith intelligible to them. Paganism was no longer dangerous. What preoccupied the Muslims were the earlier recipients of revelation, who offered what were rival constructions of the same religious space: there was no question of remaining silent when *they* talked about sons of God. But Zoroastrianism did not matter except in so far as it recast itself as a set of doctrines defensible in terms of *kalām*, the form in which the heresiographers confronted it.

It was not until they got to India that paganism became a real problem to the Muslims. They deemed some of the philosophical views of the Sumaniyya sufficiently unsettling to pay some polemical attention to them, as we have seen, but they merely reported on their idolatry, and of their gods they say nothing at all, except for Bīrūnī's comment on their reverence of *dēvs*. There was more interested in the pagans of Harran, partly because they were closer to the metropolis and partly because they were reputed to combine their polytheist cult with Greek philosophy of the most prestigious kind. They were treated as an object of curiosity rather than horror. Like other pockets of genuine paganism, they had the appearance of archaic survivors from a bygone age, much as hunter-gatherers were to look in a world of steam-engines and factories; and since they did not pose a threat, the Muslims were free to reflect on them with scholarly detachment and use them, as the hunter-gatherers were also to be used, as evidence for the bygone days in question. It was in this speculative vein that they cast the Sumanīs and the Sabians as representatives of the earliest stage in the history of human religion, an initial era of error explicable in terms of purely human developments before the sequence of divine revelations began.

4

Eastern Sources on The Roman and Persian War in the Near East 540–545

Michael R. Jackson Bonner

INTRODUCTION

Historians of Sasanian Iran are faced with an almost complete lack of contemporary material in Middle Persian. The monumental inscriptions of the Persian kings are, of course, primary sources which the historian must take into account; but these are not numerous, and were produced only in the early centuries of the dynasty. An historian looking at the middle or late period of the Sasanian era simply has no literary primary sources to work with. Scholars have therefore looked elsewhere for relics of indigenous Iranian history and the most impressive yields have come from Muslim histories.

Theodore Nöldeke's nineteenth-century study of the Sasanian material in Ṭabarī's *Annals* traced all later Muslim accounts of Iranian history to an official, dynastic chronicle, the so-called *Khwadāynāmag*, now lost and known only through derivative texts.[1] The Byzantine historian Agathias is supposed to have drawn on this ancient source in translation, Ibn al-Muqaffa', a Zoroastrian convert to Islam of doubtful sincerity, is said to have translated it into Arabic, and the universal annalists who used this translation form "a virtually complete roll-call of noted historians at work in the early medieval heyday of Islam."[2] But the sources said to derive from the *Khwadāynāmag* are in many ways disappointing: Ṭabarī's *Annals* and Firdawsī's *Shāhnāma*,[3] often considered the best repositories of Sasanian material available, are late, derivative, incomplete, anecdotal, and often downright whimsical.

[1] Th. Nöldeke, *Die Geschichte der Perser und Araber zur Zeit der Sasaniden*, Leiden 1879: pp. xv–xvi. Many criticisms of Nöldeke's theory can be made, as I did in my M.Phil thesis, *A Study of Three Neglected Sources of Sasanian History in the Reign of Khusraw Anushirvan* (M.Phil Oxford 2010), pp. 3–12, but this topic cannot be taken up again here.

[2] J. Howard-Johnston, *Witnesses to a World Crisis*, Oxford 2010: p. 342. The annalists invoked are Dīnawarī (d. 891), Ibn al-Qutayba (d. 899), Ya'qūbī (d. *c.* 900), Ṭabarī (d. 923), Mas'ūdī (d. 955), Hamza al-Isfahanī (d. 970), Bal'amī (fl. 963), Tha'ālibī (d. 1038), Bīrūnī (d. *c.* 1050).

[3] The Iranian national epic, the Shāhnāma, is also said to be founded on the Khudāy-Nāma, but its author, Firdawsī, did not use the Arabic translation of Ibn al-Muqaffa'. Firdawsī's epic is said to descend from the Khudāy-Nāma collaterally (Nöldeke, *Die Geschichte*, p. iv).

The surest test of a source's worth is its comparison to other texts of known value. In the case of Arabic documents dealing with Sasanian Iran, the ideal test involves weighing the later texts against contemporary accounts from the Roman, Syrian, and Armenian *milieux*. But this is often impossible. For the most part, only when the doings of the Sasanian Empire impinge directly on the Roman world do western sources take notice of them. This state of affairs leads the historian to one obvious topic: war. For it was war that brought the Great Powers together in a way that nothing else did, and it was war that made perhaps the deepest impression in their respective annals. It can be said, perhaps, that Roman and Persian warfare affords the ideal context in which to compare Sasanian and foreign sources.

The following short essay is excerpted from my M.Phil thesis, and it is restricted both in terms of the sources used and its chronological extent. Three eastern sources form the backbone of the investigation: Dīnawarī's *al-Akhbār al-Ṭiwāl*,[4] the so-called *Sīrat ānūshīrwān* imbedded in Ibn Miskawayh's *Tajārib al-Umam*,[5] and Firdawsī's *Shāhnāma* – all said to be derived, in one way or another, from indigenous Sasanian sources. This is not the place to dilate on the reasons for selecting these texts, as I have done so at length elsewhere.[6] But some cursory remarks should be made. Dīnawarī (d. 896) is one of the earliest Muslim authors to use Sasanian material from the putative *Khwadāynāmag*. Dīnawarī resembles Ṭabarī in his presentation of annalistic history in prose, and agreement of these two sources suggests that a common tradition has been transmited faithfully. Dīnawarī, nevertheles, often presents data in a manner peculiar to himself, and offers much that is not found in Ṭabarī. The *Sīra* is the autobiography, or rather the *fragments* of the autobiography, of Khusraw I, and is therefore unlike any other source involved in the present study. The *Tajārib al-Umam* cannot have been published later than 1030, when its author died, and this must give us some notion of the age of the *Sīra* also, though it cannot be dated with certainty.[7] The *Shāhnāma*,[8] the Iranian national epic completed in 1010, is perhaps the most controversial text that I have chosen. At the very least its prodigious length should have suggested that it might contain a good deal of valuable material, but few have attempted to analyse it or use it in earnest as a historical source.[9]

---

[4] Dīnawarī, *Kitāb al-Akhbār al-Ṭiwāl*, Wladimir Guirgass and Ignatij Kratchkovsky (eds.), Leiden 1888.

[5] Ibn Miskawayh, A. I. M., and Caetani, L., *The Tajārib Al-Umam* or *History of Ibn Miskawayh*, reproduced in facsimile from the Ms. at Constantinople in the Ayā Sūfiyya library, by Leone Caetani, principe di Teano ... Vol. VI, A.H. 326–369, Leiden 1917 [=*Tajārib al-Umam*]; and M. Grignaschi, "Quelques Spécimens de la littérature sassanide conservé dans les bibliothèques d'Istanbul", *Journal Asiatique* 254, 1966, 1–142.

[6] Bonner, *A Study*, 13–26.

[7] The *Sīra* is best known to scholarship in Grignaschi's French translation, as the whole text of the *Tajārib al-Umam* has not been published (to the best of my knowledge) in a modern edition. I rely on the French translation for the most part, and cite Caetani's Arabic facsimile only when I found it clearly legible. See note 5.

[8] Firdawsī (ed. Khaleghi-Motlagh, Dj., Omidsalar, M., and Khatibi, A.), *Shāhnāma*, New York 1987, v. 7 [=*Nūshīn-Ravān*].

[9] Rubin, Z. "The Reforms of Khusraw Anūshirwān," in Cameron, A. (ed.) The Byzantine and Early Islamic Near East III: States Resources and Armies. Princeton 1995, 234–236.

The period of time in question is the fourth decade of the sixth century, and the relevant war was that which terminated the so-called Endless Peace: the first conflict between Justinian and Khusraw I.[10] I have chosen the Near Eastern war of 540–545 not only because it was the first martial undertaking of Khusraw I, whose reign is perhaps the best point at which to begin any investigation of Sasanian history,[11] but also because Procopius, the great Byzantine historian of the age of Justinian, was an eyewitness to relevant events in the Neat East. There will, therefore, be ample data against which to test our Sasanian material, and the context chosen will be significant for scholars of the Late Roman Empire and Orientalists alike.

THE OUTBREAK OF WAR

All Arabic and Persian sources offer meagre treatment of the outbreak of war in 540. Ṭabarī offers only the vaguest reference to the Eternal Peace,[12] and there is no hint of the Armenian Question in any source. Khusraw's campaigns in Syria, though narrated in a somewhat haphazard and imprecise manner, are nevertheless dwelt on with particular relish, and his destruction of Antioch and its memorable aftermath are emphasised heavily. The war in Lazica is not mentioned in any eastern source. Procopius and Agathias must therefore remain the best sources for this conflict. The Oriental sources seem to rest not on sound military intelligence, but rather on domestic propaganda, but they nevertheless contain valuable material. Dīnawarī and Firdawsī describe in detail Khusraw's illness and the revolt of his son Nūsh Zād – two occurrences that receive attention in Procopius. Firdawsī contributes the names of Khusraw's generals,[13] unknown to any other source. But the most

---

[10] Other military engagements in other periods of Sasanian history might have been chosen. In fact, eastern accounts of the entire Roman and Persian war from 540 to 562 could be compared to the relevant treatments by many western historians, but this would be too long an undertaking for a brief article. The Near Eastern front, opened in 540 and shut down in 545 because of an outbreak of the plague, forms a discrete and more manageable episode in that much longer conflict.

[11] The reign of Khusraw is the ideal place to begin any study of Sasanian Iran. Remembered to this day as a golden age, Khusraw's reign lasted 48 years and dominated nearly half of the sixth century. An age of reform in Iran, as it was in New Rome, this century saw a massive increase in the fire power of the Iranian state, showcased in Khusraw's extraordinary conquest of Antioch in 540. Lazica was reduced, albeit briefly, to a Persian protectorate, and Yemen became an Iranian dominion. The military reforms in the sixth century made possible Khusraw II's rapid conquest of Roman territory in the seventh. Khusraw's tax reforms were adopted by the Muslim Caliphate, and remained almost unchanged. The disorders wrought by the Mazdakite heresy had plagued the Iranian state from the end of the fifth to the early sixth century, but it was in Khusraw's reign that they came to an end. His reign saw the rise of the Turks, and the annihilation of the Hephthalite empire, which had menaced Iran since 484. It was in Khusraw's reign too that Muhammad was born. In short, to understand the reign of Khusraw I is to understand a great portion of Sasanian and Late Antique history.

[12] "There was, as it is related, an agreement and a truce between Kisrā Anūsharwān and Yakhtiyānūs, king of Rome" (Ṭabarī, *Taʾrīkh al-rusul waʾl-mulūk*, ed. M. J. de Goeje and others, Leiden 1893 [=Ṭabarī], 958: ll. 11–12).

[13] Before plunging us into the mire of hyperbole, Firdawsī presents with perfect credibility the

significant element of our Persian and Arabic sources concerns Sasanian *attitudes* to the war with New Rome, and the domestic portrayal of this conflict.

Sasanian propaganda blamed the Roman emperor for the outbreak of war. Ṭabarī, Dīnawarī, and the *Shāhnāma* are unanimous: the pro-Roman Saracens attacked Khusraw's Lakhmid vassal Mundhir.[14] The *Sīra*, without discussing Saracen affairs, ascribes the outbreak of war to Caesar's perfidy,[15] and we can well infer that much the same scenario is implied. Procopius, perhaps unsurprisingly, presents exactly the opposite scenario. Khusraw is said to have commanded Mundhir to "assist in the invention" of a reason for breaking the truce, and a conflict over boundary lines was concocted.[16]

Whatever the nature of the Saracen conflict may have been, it was not the only stimulus to war. Trouble in the Caucasus was a major factor. Complaints of the Armenians are said to have urged Khusraw to action,[17] and their harangue before the Persian king, which we find in Procopius, though probably an invention, may represent real grievances. The Persian and Arabic consensus fits well with the Armenians' claim that Justinian had attempted to pervert the loyalty of Mundhir, and incite the Huns (presumably those in the Caucasus) to attack Iran.[18] But we hear of no other reasons in the eastern sources.

It is not difficult to imagine that Armenians, discontented with Roman rule for the reasons given by Procopius, would side with Persia. Much the same may be said for the Laz. Procopius claims that Justinian's interventions were a major source of discontent in Lazica,[19] and that the imposition of Christianity infuriated the votaries of Zoroaster, and

---

names of Khusraw's commanders. Shērōy son of Bahrām, Farhād, Āshtād-Pērōz, Gurshasp, and Hurmazd son of Kharrād (*Nūshīn-Ravān*: ll. 546–550) are the six Persian generals who led the invasion. Given the recent developments in Iranian sigillography, it is not impossible that the existence of these men will be confirmed, but this subject cannot be pursued here.

14 "Khālid [*recte* "Hārith" (C. E. Bosworth (tr.), *The History of al-Ṭabarī, v, The Sasanids, the Byzantines, the Lakhmids and Yemen*, New York 1999, p. 252, n. 611)] son of Jabala made a raid on Mundhir's domain, and killed some of his companions with great butchery, and plundered much of his property" (Ṭabarī, p. 958: ll. 16–17). "They say verily that Khālid son of Jabala, the Ghassānid, made a raid on Nuʿmān son of Mundhir ... and he killed some of his companions with great butchery, and he drove away the camels of Mundhir and his horses" (Dīnawarī, 70: ll. 3–8).

In the Shāhnāma the complaints are put into the mouth of Mundhir, who addresses himself to Khusraw: "... if thou art Shāh of Īrān, protector, and supporter of the brave, why do the Romans lord it over us, and ride throughout the horsemen's desert? If the Shāh were on the throne of the Caesars, it would be fitting if the arrogant became headless. If the noble Shāh give leave, they will see us seek redress! The riders of the desert, when they find the Roman horsemen, shall be furious in battle" (*Nūshīn-Ravān*: ll, 436–40).

15 "When Caesar and his attack double crossed me" (*Tajārib al-umam*, 189).

16 "Having conferred with Alamundarus, Chosroes ordered him to assist in providing causes for war. He [i.e., Alamundarus] accused Arethas of wronging him with regard to border lands, and, while the truce held, came into conflict with him, and on this pretext began to overrun the land of the Romans" (Procopius, ed. & trans. H. B Dewing, Cambridge, Mass. 1914–1928, *Bellum Persicum* II.i.1–3).

17 Procopius, *B.P.* II.iii.34–53.

18 Procopius, *B.P.* II.iii.47.

19 Braund, D. Georgia in Antiquity: A History of Colchis and Transcaucasian Iberia, 550 BC–AD 562. Oxford 1994, 290.

that the presence of the Roman army[20] in the wake of Gourgen's flight[21] was intolerable. Procopius also accuses two very unpopular generals, Peter and John Tzibus, whose appalling conduct eroded Lazian loyalty to Rome.[22] Nevertheless, very little of the Great Game that had evolved between the two powers is mentioned in Persian and Arabic sources. No attempt is made to understand the trouble in Armenia and Lazica: only the contest played out in Arabia receives attention, but even this is meagre. Our Oriental sources allege either a letter from Mundhir to Khusraw,[23] or a personal interview,[24] in which the Persian king is urged to induce Caesar to punish his refractory vassal. The war in Lazica, though initially successful, did not end in Iran's favour, and this helps to explain the silence of our sources in this connexion. Khusraw's assistance to Mundhir is emphasised because the anecdote suggests an honourable beginning to the war.

This theme takes a religious turn in the *Shāhnāma*. According to Firdawsī, military action was not immediate. Instead Khusraw procceeded directly to Azarbayjan,[25] the heartland of the Zoroastrian religion, where certain rites were performed within the fire temple there. Firdawsī's description implies that Khusraw's prayers for victory[26] involved a *written* Avesta which was recited by a mōbed.[27] Khusraw's attack on New Rome appears as something of a holy obligation, for which the blessing of heaven was sought. In this connexion, it is

---

[20] "Roman soldiers began to frequent [Lazica], and these barbarians were annoyed by them" (Procopius, *B.P.* II.xv.6).

[21] Procopius, *B.P.* I.xii.4.

[22] For the crimes of John Tzibus, see Procopius, *B.P.* II.xv.9–11. Procopius accuses Peter of having set up a monopoly that had a disastrous effect of the economy (Procopius, *B.P.* II.xv.6; 8).

[23] "Mundhir wrote to Kisrā telling him what Khālid b. Jabala had done to him. And Kisrā wrote to Qaysar that he demand payment from Khālid to Mundhir, as he had not killed any of Khālid's companions, and to return what he had taken of his chattels" (Dīnawarī, 70: ll. 8–11). The salient portion of Firdawsī's version of Mundhir's communication is quoted in n. 124.

[24] In his second narrative, Ṭabarī makes Mundhir approach Khusraw and demand that he write to Justinian, so that he might punish the offending Arab, force him to return the booty taken, and pay the "wergeld" for the Arabs whom he had killed (Ṭabarī, 959: l. 5).

[25] "Then with nobles before and behind him he went quickly to Āzar-Ābādagān" (*Nūshīn-Ravān* l, 522).

[26] *Nūshīn-Ravān* l, 530.

[27] "He sought the barsam-twigs from the pure dastūr; he washed his two cheeks in the water of his two eyes. He entered the fire temple in holy silence. A seat embroidered with gold was set down, [and] upon it was placed the book of the Zand-u-Ust. The mōbed chanted accurately with his voice" (*Nūshīn-Ravān* ll, 524–526). The priests rend their shirts (*Nūshīn-Ravān* 1, 527), and grandees cast jewels and mutter praises (*Nūshīn-Ravān* 1, 528). Exactly when the writing and codification of that book happened is a vexed question that cannot be addressed fully in the present work. Suffice it to say, though, that the Sīra also assumes a written Avesta in the reign of Khusraw. At one point in his reign, Khusraw was attacked by an assassin (Grignaschi, "Quelques Spécimens", 16–17), who was a votary of a fanatical sect possessed of "a book and a revelation" (Grignaschi, "Quelques Spécimens", 29, n. 5). If these were known to differ in some way from the orthodox revelation, and the Sīra implies that they were, we must infer that the Avesta had been committed to writing in or before the reign of Khusraw I (Grignaschi, "Quelques Spécimens", 29, n. 5). This accords with a ninth-century tradition, endorsed by Boyce, that Khusraw I ordered the writing of the Avesta (M. Boyce, *Zoroastrians: Their Religious Beliefs and Practices*, London 1979, 135).

probably significant that the fire temple in Azarbayjan was dedicated to Adur-Gushnāsp, the god and patron of war.[28] But two foreign notices seem to shed more light on Khusraw's ritual. First, we have Ammianus' claim that Shāpūr, according to Persian custom, took auspices before crossing the Tigris to make war on the Romans.[29] The ritual described in the *Shāhnāma* probably involved such auspices, and the Avesta may have been used for a kind of bibliomancy. Second, we have Procopius' notice regarding an "oracle" in Azarbayjan, consulted on all important matters, to which Khusraw repaired before invading the Near East.[30] There is no explicit statement that this was Khusraw's reason for going to Azarbayjan, but the suggestion is strong, and Procopius' report of the oracle would otherwise appear to have no purpose. Firdawsī seems, therefore, to have correctly reported Khusraw's location and activities in Azarbayjan. Finally, we might infer that Khusraw's sacrifices and prayers to the sun and other divinities, performed at Seleucia,[31] represent a thanksgiving after the success of the holy obligation undertaken in the temple of Adur-Gushnasp.

Khusraw's invasion follows the ritual. We can get a sense of the Sasanian perception of the war by noting the difference between the Oriental accounts of the invasion and the narrative of Procopius. Ṭabarī and Dīnawarī are clear: in his progress towards Antioch, Khusraw *conquered* many cities and the Roman fortress at Dara.[32] Firdawsī goes even further, adding that cities which he names Surab, Arayish-i-Rum, and Qaliniyus were not merely plundered but levelled with the ground, and every living thing within Arayish-i-Rum was destroyed.[33] In any case these lists of cities captured or plundered are uncorroborated by Procopius' detailed treatment.[34] Its seems therefore that Sasanian propaganda exaggerated the subordinate status of any city or state that paid tribute to Iran. Apart from Antioch, it did not matter to the Persians which cities were involved, provided that their forced submission was emphasised. It was probably because of the tribute paid that even Rome

---

[28] M. Boyce, *Zoroastrians*, 124.

[29] The Romans were waiting, "whilst the king delayed on the other side of the Tigris, until the auspices allowed [him] to advance" (Ammianus Marcellinus, *Res Gestae*, ed. & tr. Rolfe, J. C., Cambridge, Mass. 1935–1939, v. ii: xxi.13.2), which in the event were unfavourable (Ammianus, *Res Gestae*, xxi.13.8).

[30] "There [i.e., in Adarbiganōn] is the great fire shrine, which the Persians venerate most among gods, where indeed the magi who tend the inextinguishable flame perform with precision many rites, but in particular they consult an oracle on very important matters" (Procopius, *B.P.* II. xxiv.2).

[31] "Chosroes came...to Seleucia .. .and having sacrificed to the sun and to whichever other [gods] he wanted, and having called upon the gods many times, went away" (Procopius, *B.P.* II.xi.1).

[32] Ṭabarī, 898: ll. 5–6; 959: ll. 9–12; Dīnawarī, 71: ll. 12–14.

[33] "Not one noble remained [alive] in the army; in countryside not even a thorn remained in the earth." (*Nūshīn-Ravān* l, 607). Surely this was an outrage that not even Procopius would have concealed. Firdawsī's entire treatment of this episode is found in *Nūshīn-Ravān*: ll. 589– 660. The names of the cities mentioned seem to be corruptions of Sura, Hierapolis, and Callinicum.

[34] Procopius mentions that tribute was paid by Sura, though Khusraw sacked it regardless (Procopius, *B.P.* II.v.13–27), by Sergiopolis, though payment was deferred by a year (Procopius, *B.P.* II.v.29–33), by Hierapolis (Procopius, *B.P.* II.vi.21–25), and by Beroea, which was also attacked savagely (Procopius, *B.P.* II.vii.4–13). The siege of Antioch follows (Procopius, *B.P.* II.viii–ix).

itself was depicted as an Iranian province in the *Shāhnāma*[35]– surely a piece of propaganda which Firdawsī found in his sources.

The issues surrounding the Roman tribute help to clarify two difficult passages in Ṭabarī. First, Ṭabarī's treatment of the war draws to a close with a statement that Justinian was forced to pay a massive sum to buy the freedom of "the rest of the towns of Syria and Egypt."[36] Egypt, of course, was untouched by this war, and this seeming anachronism suggested to Bosworth that the campaigns of Khusraw II, which did involve Egypt, were conflated with those of Khusraw I.[37] Ṭabarī, though, may have actually preserved a piece of Iranian propaganda, whereby the Roman tribute was represented as preventing Khusraw's threatened advance deeper into Roman territory. The Sasanian dynasty probably laid claim to Egypt on the grounds that it had belonged to the Achaemenids. It is not, therefore, necessary to infer that a reference to Egypt is out of context in a treatment of Khusraw's first war with New Rome, and we need not infer an elementary mistake on Ṭabarī's part in order to explain its inclusion here. In any case, the rest of Ṭabarī's treatment in this connexion proves that he was not confused about which ruler and which war he was dealing with. Second, Ṭabarī's final notice[38] on this war, though it is not explicit, must deal with the armistice of 545, which shut down the front in the Near East, and by virtue of which the Romans agreed to an annual payment.[39] The same story is reported by Dīnawarī and Firdawsī. Dīnawarī also records the fixed annual payment, but does not say how much it was, and adds that Sharwīn al-Dastabāy and Khurrīn, his slave, were appointed not only to oversee it, but also to live with "the king of Rome."[40] In the *Shāhnāma,* we hear of Caesar's embassy, led by someone called Mihrās,[41] sent to bestow tribute which is valued rather absurdly at ten ox-hides full of dinars.[42] These notices must be discarded in favour of Procopius' more thorough testimony, but they do give some hints that the Roman tribute was, according to Iranian perception, surrounded with an official and ceremonious aura.

THE TAKING OF ANTIOCH

Khusraw's taking of Antioch was a massive blow to Roman prestige, and seems to have been the highlight of the war. All sources report Khusraw's conquest in nearly the same way, though Procopius' treatment is best. There are, however, some noteworthy differences

[35] This line appears in the context of Khusraw's quadripartition: "Iraq and the land of Rome came fourth" (*Nūshīn-Ravān* l, 76).

[36] "As for the remaining cities of Syria and Egypt, Yakhtiyānūs bought them from Kisrā for a great sum, which he made over to him" (Ṭabarī, 960, l. 3–4).

[37] Bosworth (tr.), *The History of al-Ṭabarī,* 255, n. 617.

[38] An agreement was reached, whereby Khusraw agreed not to attack Roman territory, and Justinian agreed to an annual payment, but no amount is specified (Ṭabarī, 960: ll. 5–7).

[39] Procopius, *B.P.* II.xxviii.3–11.

[40] Dīnawarī, p. 71: ll. 2–6. The final detail is uncorroborated by Procopius.

[41] *Nūshīn-Ravān* l, 714.

[42] "Tribute and toll were levied on Rome: ten ox-hides full of dinārs" (*Nūshīn-Ravān* l, 729).

in details of the aftermath of the city's capture and the deportation of its people to a new city near Ctesiphon.

Firdawsī calls Khusraw's second Antioch *Zēb-i-Khusraw*,[43] a name which sounds eerily like Dīnawarī's *Zabr-Khusrū*[44] – another sign of a common source that was unfortunately misread in this case. Ṭabarī, of course, calls it *al-Rūmiyya*,[45] and this (as has already been noted above) probably descends from another tradition. All of our sources – even Procopius who calls it *Khusraw's Antioch*[46] – report the name incorrectly. Sebeos reports what was probably the true name of the new city, *Veh Anjatok' Khosrov*, but adds that it was also called *Shahastan-i Nok-noy*.[47] All narratives apart from Dīnawarī report that the captives deported to the new city were well provided for.[48] Perhaps Dīnawarī omitted a detail which, in his opinion, was unnecessary to repeat or obvious to his reader, or perhaps he was careless in his abridgement. Unlike Ṭabarī and Dīnawarī, Firdawsī and Procopius do not mention that that the New was an exact copy of the Old Antioch.[49] All sources apart from Procopius make the overseer of the city a Christian, though each reports his name differently. Firdawsī does not name him,[50] Dīnawarī calls him Yazdfanā,[51] and Ṭabarī calls him Barāz.[52] As far as Procopius is concerned, there was no overseer of New Antioch: Chosroes is said to have thought it right that the Antiochenes be called royal subjects, "that they be subject to no authorities but the king alone."[53] Perhaps Procopius omitted this fact in order to avoid embarrassing Justinian, or perhaps his information was deficient and this comment is merely an extrapolation. In any case, it seems likely that Ṭabarī and Dīnawarī are closer to the truth.

---

43 *Nūshīn-Ravān* l, 681.

44 Dīnawarī, 71: l. 17.

45 Ṭabarī, 898: l. 9; 959: l. 16.

46 Procopius, *B.P.* II.xiv.1.

47 "Veh Anjatok' Khosrov, which they named and called Shahastan-i Nok-noy" (Sebeos (ed. Abgaryan, G. V.). Patmut'iun Sebeosi. Yerevan 197 [=Sebeos], 69: ll. 23–24).

48 Chosroes provided them with a bath, an hippodrome, along "along with other luxuries," as well as charioteers and musicians (Procopius, *B.P.* II.xiv.1–2). Procopius, *B.P.* II.xiv.1–2; *B.P.* II.xiv.2. The citizens were provisioned by Chosroes at the public expense (Procopius, *B.P.* I.xiv.3). Ṭabarī mentions the allocation of stipends (Ṭabarī, 959: l. 19). Firdawsī is unusually laconic: "He apportioned necessities to everyone" (*Nūshīn-Ravān* l, 687). Dīnawarī is silent.

49 Dīnawarī, 70: ll. 15–17; Ṭabarī, 898: ll. 6–9; 959: l. 15. There is no direct mention of this identity in the Shāhnāma, but there is an anecdote about a man who missed the mulberry bush that had stood outside his house before his capture. Khusraw is said to have given him a new tree (*Nūshīn-Ravān* ll, 691–92). Procopius has nothing to say on this matter.

50 *Nūshīn-Ravān* l, 693.

51 Dīnawarī, 71: l. 1.

52 Ṭabarī, 960: l. 2.

53 Procopius, *B.P.* II.xiv.3.

THE INSURRECTION OF NŪSH ZĀD

In the midst of war with New Rome, Khusraw and his entire army came down with the plague in 543, and retired either to Azarbayjan,[54] as Procopius suggests, or to Hims,[55] as Dīnawarī claims. This difference is only of minor significance, as nothing else depends upon Khusraw's location whilst ill. Part of the Iranian army, which had already been divided to fight on two fronts, probably lingered in the Near East when that front had been shut down after the outbreak of bubonic plague. Dīnawarī may have simply guessed where Khusraw was. In any case, Procopius' placement of Khusraw further north should probably be preferred, as Azarbayjan was probably untouched by the plague, and his testimony is contemporary to the events in question. Procopius, Dīnawarī, and the *Shāhnāma* report that whilst Khusraw was ill, his son, Nūsh Zād rebelled, and made a bid for the throne.[56]

Procopius proves that the revolt actually happened. His *Bellum Persicum* merely introduces the revolt of Nūsh Zād,[57] but the full story is narrated in the *Bellum Gothicum*. Here, Khusraw's eldest son is named "Anasozadus," which clearly answers to Dīnawarī's "Anūsh Zādh" and Firdawsī's "Nūsh Zād."[58] He was exiled by his father, for many transgressions, chief amongst which was philandering with his father's wives.[59] Hearing of his father's illness, Anasozadus raised up a revolt, which Khusraw's general "Phabrizus" put down: Anasozadus is taken captive and his eyelids are disfigured.[60] So runs Procopius' account.

Though we may well praise Procopius' treatment of the revolt for its sobriety and accuracy, his presentation creates a strange chronological difficulty. The *Bellum Persicum* places the revolt in the midst of Khusraw's war with New Rome in about 543,[61] but the *Bellum Gothicum* makes it happen in about 550, the final year of the five-year truce agreed in 545.[62] This discrepancy led Börm to suggest, albeit hesitantly, that there were in fact two revolts.[63] But this is an inadequate explanation for what actually happened. The chronological problem will be addressed below, but for now it suffices to observe that Procopius makes no suggestion that he is describing two different revolts, and Dīnawarī and Firdawsī report only one.

---

54 Procopius, *B.P.* II.xxiv.1. Procopius does not state explicitly that Khusraw went to Āzarbāyjān in order to recover his health, but, although the rumour of his illness is reported after his journey northward, it is clear that he was infected whilst in the Levant and that the disease left him whilst in Āzarbāyjān.

55 Dīnawarī, 71, ll. 7–8.

56 This insurrection is mentioned in passing in Christensen, *L'Iran sous les Sassanides*, Copenhagen 1944, 383, but the author offers no serious discussion.

57 Procopius, *B.P.* II.xxiv.8.

58 "... among his sons the eldest was named Anasōzados." (Procopius, *B.G.*, VIII.x.8).

59 The son was punished "by exile," because "in his lifestyle he had erred in many ways contrary to established custom, having with no hesitation copulated with his father's wives." (Procopius, *B.G.*, VIII.x.8).

60 Procopius, *B.G.* VIII.x.17–22.

61 Procopius, *B.P.* II.xxiv.1.

62 Procopius, *B.G.* VIII.xi.1.

63 Börm, H. *Prokop und die Perser: Untersuchungen zu den römisch-sasanidischen Kontakten in der ausgehenden Spätantike*. Stuttgart 2007, 127.

The *Shāhnāma* offers what is by far the fullest, to say nothing of the longest, account, but Dīnawarī's much shorter treatment is almost identical to it in substance until the story's climax. In both sources, we are clearly dealing with an epic. It is tempting to infer, as Nöldeke and Börm have done, that the epical quality of Nūsh Zād's insurrection was added by later authors, and that the account of his martyrdom was a poetic fantasy generated by Firdawsī.[64] An examination of the contents of the *Shāhnāma*'s treatment of the revolt, however, shows that this view is mistaken. This is not by any means to suggest that the revolt of Nūsh Zād, as narrated in *al-Akhbār al-Ṭiwāl* and the *Shāhnāma*, is as sober an account as that of Procopius. On the contrary, we are indeed faced with a highly elaborate version of history, but the qualities of an epic were already mature and fully developed in the source used by Dīnawarī and Firdawsī.

A review of Dīnawarī's and Firdawsī's treatment suffices to show this. Khusraw's son Nūsh Zād, both Dīnawarī and Firdawsī agree, was born to a Christian mother, who had refused to become a Magian.[65] Though Dīnawarī says only that Nūsh Zād *differed* from his father in religion,[66] Firdawsī confirms that he was indeed a Christian.[67] The youth had been confined to gaol in Junday Shapur,[68] but when news of Khusraw's illness reached him, Nūsh Zād escaped, recruited an army of Christians, threw his father's deputies out of Ahwaz, and began preparations to march on Ctesiphon.[69] Apart from mentioning the capture of Nūsh Zād and the restoration of Khusraw's dominions,[70] Dīnawarī does not explain how this insurrection was dealt with. The rest of the episode is narrated only by Firdawsī.

Many were involved in Nūsh Zād's rebellion. For Firdawsī, the insurrection begins when Nūsh Zād frees the madmen imprisoned at Junday Shapur, and all Christians – even prelates – flock to his banner.[71] Some of the nobility were also involved – such, at least, is implied by Khusraw's command to kill the implicated nobles.[72] The dissidents may well have been very numerous, but it is difficult to believe that Nūsh Zād's army numbered 30,000 men: this may be an error for 3000. A line that Khaleghi-Motlagh deleted on no easily discernible grounds makes Nūsh Zād's mother the financier of the coup.[73] This claim is curiously reminiscent of Procopius' report that Nūsh Zād had taken to bed some of Khusraw's wives. A rebellious alliance between mother and son might well have provided grounds for such slander.

News of the insurrection reaches Khusraw, who then writes a doleful letter to his

[64] Nöldeke, *Die Geschichte*, 473.

[65] Dīnawarī, 71, l. 9–11; *Nūshīn-Ravān* l. 748–51.

[66] Dīnawarī, 71, l. 12.

[67] *Nūshīn-Ravān* ll. 753–55.

[68] *Nūshīn-Ravān* ll. 756–58

[69] Dīnawarī, 71, ll. 12–17.

[70] Dīnawarī, 72, l. 18–19.

[71] *Nūshīn-Ravān* ll. 784–88. In the first hemistich of the final line, we may suspect that the number 30,000 is a mistake for 3000, a more realistic number.

[72] *Nūshīn-Ravān* ll. 872–74. This command is also found in Dīnawarī; likewise the notion that any one that curses Nūsh Zād curses Khusraw also (*Nūshīn-Ravān* ll. 878–79).

[73] "[His] mother gave him many provisions, for her treasury was adorned by the king." This line appears among Khaleghi-Motlagh's notes (*Nūshīn-Ravān*, 149: n. 7).

lieutenant at Ctesiphon, Rām Barzīn,[74] whose name Procopius seems to have transcribed incorrectly. Much of this is familiar from Dīnawarī's account. Khusraw expresses his rage,[75] and expounds a rather dim view of Christians,[76] who are said to be cowardly, but there is nothing about "turning the other cheek" as in Dīnawarī.[77] Khusraw's suspicion that his son had formed an alliance with the Roman emperor, unique to Firdawsī,[78] is not true, despite representing a realistic fear. The king urges his lieutenant not to kill Nūsh Zād, who is rather to be captured,[79] and held in the palace and treated with respect and generosity, but the nobles who follow Nūsh Zād, as has been seen, are to be put to death.[80] The end of the story, found only in Firdawsī, involves a battle between the armies of Nūsh Zād and Rām Barzīn, and the rebel dies the death of a Christian martyr, and is buried accordingly.

Apart from Nūsh Zād's martyrdom, the details rehearsed above are not in themselves unbelievable, nor do they actually *contradict* Procopius' account. Procopius, however, neglects to mention that Nūsh Zād was a Christian. But Procopius is not the only author to have omitted elements of the story. Dīnawarī ends his account abruptly, after Khusraw's letter is quoted. Neither Ṭabarī nor the *Sīra* include a mention of the story at all. In short, every source apart from the *Shāhnāma* lacks important details or omits the story altogether. Why is this the case? Why is the coverage of this revolt so uneven, especially in Dīnawarī and Firdawsī, whose accounts are obviously grounded in the same source?

Speculation on whether the original *Sīra* included the revolt of Nūsh Zād may well be pointless. But in a curious passage Khusraw demands that his relatives and courtesans respect his religion,[81] as though alluding to earlier trouble, and we may be tempted to link this with the insurrection of his son. As for our other texts, we can venture more secure inferences. The silence and confusion of Procopius are perhaps easiest to explain. Rumours of Khusraw's illness and his son's revolt did not fail to reach the historian. They came from the highest levels of the Armenian church and from a Christian advisor to Khusraw, and this by a somewhat circuitous route which is not concealed.[82] The Christianity of Nūsh Zād must have been the reason why these officials, and *Christian* officials at that, transmitted

---

74 *Nūshīn-Ravān* ll. 793–800.

75 *Nūshīn-Ravān* l. 817.

76 *Nūshīn-Ravān* ll. 822–23. "Such is the religion of Christ, that if one moment thou strikest hard, anyone will turn from it dejected: he will quit the faith of Christ [and] in the end the cross will be his enemy" (*Nūshīn-Ravān* ll. 822–23).

77 "How shall the Christians remain, when in their religion a man among them must offer his right cheek when his left cheek is struck?" (Dīnawarī, 72: ll. 7–8).

78 *Nūshīn-Ravān* l. 836–37.

79 *Nūshīn-Ravān* l. 843.

80 *Nūshīn-Ravān* ll. 872–74.

81 «Il est naturel que les parents du roi et ses courtisans soient puissants et forts. Mais si le souverain néglige de les contrôler, ceux qui ont le droit de lui adresser la parole deviennet avides, à l'exception de ceux qui suivent l'«adab» de leur roi, qui respectent sa religion» etc. (Griganschi, "Quelques Spécimens", 22).

82 Procopius claims that his information on Khusraw's illness and Nūsh Zād's rebellion was communicated to the Armenian general Valerian by a secret envoy who heard the story from the brother of the Bishop of Dvin (Procopius, *B.P.*, II.xxiv.8).

the rumour. Nūsh Zād's faith, we should infer, is not an invention of a later time. It is difficult to imagine why this detail would have been made up, but it is not hard to see why Procopius would have concealed it. If Justinian had heard of the insurrection, he took no action, and this must have proved an embarrassment; but if word of the rebellion had *not* reached him, to be informed of it too late would have infuriated the emperor. Procopius had good reason to reduce the story, in his *Bellum Persicum* at least, to the bare facts and minimise the detail that was likely to give offence.

The situation is different in Procopius' *Bellum Gothicum*, where the revolt is given fuller treatment. The story reached him, once again, from a Christian: this time Khusraw's physician Tribunus,[83] and this fact also allows us the inference that Nūsh Zād's Christianity was the point of interest. Nevertheless, the faith of Nūsh Zād is still missing. We have already noted that the story has also been dislodged from its proper context and moved seven years later. Furthermore, the book in which we find this longer treatment is the eighth in Procopius' *History*, separated from the first mention of Nūsh Zād's revolt by five volumes. This temporal and spatial displacement may have been the result of sheer carelessness, occasioned by the arrival of new and perhaps startling information long after Procopius had written his treatment of the war in the Levant. But this is unlikely: Procopius must have known the full story from the beginning, and his delay in reporting the revolt signifies a hesitance to reveal sensitive information. The chronological error is deliberate. Procopius moved the revolt to 550, when it would have been impossible for Justinian to take advantage of it: the Goths had taken Rome, Italy demanded intense military action, and warfare raged in Lazica. Roman support for a Persian coup would have been impossible at this time.

Ṭabarī omitted the revolt not because he chose to excise it, but rather because his sources did not include it. This can be inferred from the silence of Eutychius and Ibn Qutayba, who also omit the revolt. The story of Nūsh Zād must therefore come from another source, one preoccupied with Christian affairs, probably composed in Syriac, and only written into the texts supposedly derived from the *Khwadāynāmag*[84] by Dīnawarī's source and Firdawsī by way of an Arabic translation.

How can these inferences be justified? The episode would not have been interesting to Zoroastrians, it is full of Christian imagery, the narrator is sympathetic to Nūsh Zād, who dies a martyr for the Christian faith, and Syrian ecclesiastical vocabulary abounds.[85] But

[83] This physician was sent to Khusraw by Justinian (Procopius, *B.G.* VIII.10–16).

[84] This source found its way into both *al-Akhbār al-Ṭiwāl* and the *Shāhnāma*, but, as we have seen, Dīnawarī does not narrate the entire episode. The same incomplete narrative, nearly identical to that of Dīnawarī, is found also in Nihāyat al-Irab (E. G. Browne, "Some Account of the Arabic Work Entitled "Nihāyatu'l-irab fī akhbāri'l-Furs wa'l-'Arab," Particularly That Which Treats of the Persian Kings", *Journal of the Royal Asiatic Society of Great Britain and Ireland*, 1900, 231).

[85] Syrian ecclesiastical terms appearing in this episode are given in Arabic transliteration: *jāthalīq* (*catholicos*) and *biṭrīq* (patriarch) (*Nūshīn-Ravān* l. 895), and *suquf* (*Nūshīn-Ravān* l. 963). These are clearly Arabicised forms of the Syriac *qathūlīqā* (or *qathlīqā*), *pāṭaryarqā*, and *afesqūfā*, recognisable by the change of the Syriac q and p to j and b, and so forth, in Arabic. *Sukūbā* (bishop) (*Nūshīn-Ravān* l. 957) seems to be derived from *afesqufā* also. However, the fact that these terms have been arabicised suggests that the source had not been translated into Pahlavi – an observation which refutes Nöldeke's claim that Firdawsī used no Arabic sources (Nöldeke, *Geschichte*, xxiii).

the most convincing evidence that the source was Syrian is the emphasis on Christian burial. Inhumation, so deeply offensive to Persian sensibilities,[86] was attacked in the persecutions under Bahrām V, whose chief *mōbed* ordered the disinterment of all buried Christians.[87] Burial and the rites associated with it must, therefore, have been something of a cultural shibboleth for Iranian Christians. Nūsh Zād, accordingly, when on the point of death, specifically eschews the *dakhma*, the aromatic balms, and all other trappings of a Zoroastrian funeral, and requests Christian rites.[88] It is hard to imagine that such a story was composed by a Zoroastrian, and a Christian, probably Nestorian, Syriac origin seems a reasonable inference.

That the earliest recension of this hypothetical Syrian source omitted the conclusion of Nūsh Zād's revolt appears unlikely. Dīnawarī seems to have had a taste for the dramatic, and it is very surprising that the most entertaining part of Nūsh Zād's revolt is absent from his narrative. Dīnawarī must have deleted it himself, and it is not hard to see why. The anti-Christian speech which Firdawsī puts into the mouth of one of Rām Barzīn's warriors is an inflammatory attack not on the Christian religion, but rather on Christ himself.[89] The speech is redolent of Zoroastrian anti-Christian invective, such as we find reported in Armenian sources,[90] and we need not doubt its authenticity. Iranian Christians

---

[86] Procopius reports that one of the charges against Seoses, a high-ranking Persian at whose execution Kavād connived, was "to have buried his wife," though "hiding in the earth the bodies of the dead" was forbidden (Procopius, *B.P.* I.xi.35). Agathias claims that the Persians strictly forbade the use of tombs or coffins, and even covering the dead with earth was for them "hardly lawful" (Agathias Scholasticus, *Historiarum libri quinque: Recensuit Rudolfus Keydell*, Leiden 1967, B.23.1).

[87] The order was given by Mihr-Shabūr, the chief *mōbed*, and "the dead that had been buried from the years of his fathers were brought out before the eyes of the deacons" (*Acta Martyrum et Sanctorum*, iv, ed. Bedjan, Paris 1894, 254). This persecution is discussed in S. Brock, "Christians in the Sasanian Empire: A Case of Divided Loyalties", *Byzantine and Modern Greek Studies* II, 1976, 9: n. 37.

[88] "Make no dakhma or bier or great lamentation; prepare a grave according to Christian usage: there is no need of camphor, musk, or ambergris" (*Nūshīn-Ravān* ll. 951–52).

[89] An old man calls out to Nūsh Zād, and amongst many threats and boasts utters what is surely an orthodox Zoroastrian attack on Christianity: "Christ the deceiver himself was slain, because he had eschewed the faith of Yazdān. Among those who teach religion choose not him, who knew not his own face. If the glory of Yazdān had shone upon him, how could the Jews have got the better of him?" (*Nūshīn-Ravān* ll. 908–10). The whole battle is narrated in *Nūshīn-Ravān* ll. 888–980. Nūsh Zād responds to the "doting airhead," but to no avail (*Nūshīn-Ravān*: l. 927ff).

[90] The letter of Mihrnerseh, who is called "The Great Framadar of Iran and Aniran," addressed to "Greater Armenia," quoted in Ełiše's History (Ełiše, *The History of the Armenian War: a facsimile Reproduction of the 1957 Yerevan Edition with an Introduction by R. W. Thomson*, New York 1993 [=Ełiše], 24–27), proves that the Zoroastrian hatred of Christianity was organised by the highest orders of church and government. Several theological grievances are listed, and the mere humanity of Christ is strongly asserted. The torture, crucifixion, death, and burial of Christ are said by Eghishe to have infuriated Yazdgard (Ełiše, 12: l. 20–13: ll. 1–2), presumably because these indignities were unfit for one who was believed to be a god. The letter of Khusraw II to Heraclius, quoted in Sebeos, is accordingly explicit in ascribing imposture to Christ, who died an ignominious death at the hands of the Jews: "this Christ, who could not save himself from the Jews, they slew by hanging [him] on the cross." etc. (Sebeos, 123: ll. 30–31).

would have been familiar with such rhetoric. But this speech, and especially its implication that Christ was crucified by the Jews, must have struck a Muslim audience as an extraordinary and outrageous blasphemy.[91] The public and maudlin display of grief when Nūsh Zād's body is returned to his mother[92] must have seemed no better than idolatry. The *Shāhnāma*, finally, clearly depicts Nūsh Zād as a Christian martyr[93] – another offence to Muslim sensibilities. Firdawsī's task was to glorify the reigns of the kings of Iran for the entertainment of the nobility, and he achieved this by versifying his sources faithfully without major expurgation. But Dīnawarī's readers were clerics and theologians, who would have looked with suspicion on a text too heavily laden with pre-Islamic tales cherished by a subjugated religious minority.

The revolt of Nūsh Zād dominates Firdawsī's account of Khusraw's first Roman war. The story is strangely reminiscent of what is perhaps the finest portion of the *Shāhnāma*, the story of Suhrāb and Rustam, in which father and son do battle and the son is slain. Could this parallel be the reason why the revolt was embellished by Persian Christians, who sought, as it were, to christen Iranian history? The epic of Nūsh Zād, a Christian martyr of royal blood, must also have filled the Christians of Iran with hope that a follower of Christ might one day sit upon the throne of Cyrus and Ardashīr. It was surely this very hope which gave rise to the rumour, diffused throughout the Christian Orient, and reported by Sebeos, that Khusraw himself had both converted to Christianity at the end of his life, and been given a Christian burial.[94]

CONCLUSION

The sources selected for this study were clearly not interested in a sober, blow-by-blow portrayal of the war in the Levant. Nor were they concerned with its real causes. The eastern sources are interested in effects and results, and their chief aim was to depict Iran as stronger, more agressive, and more successful than Rome, and Khusraw as superior to Justinian. This state of affairs raises questions about Persian self-image and ideology of state. If royal prestige was tied to belligerency and the wounding of Roman pride, the taking of Antioch is surely the greatest Sasanian achievement before the conquests of Khusraw II, and it is not surprising that our sources emphasise this more than any other element of the war.

In reality the insurrection of Nūsh Zād must have been simply another attempted *coup* by the king's son at a weak point in his reign. But this *coup* was perceived differently because the pretender was Christian. This is why the story was transformed into a romance.

---

[91] Quran 4, 157–58.

[92] *Nūshīn-Ravān* ll. 965–73.

[93] *Nūshīn-Ravān* ll. 963–64.

[94] "... in the hour of death, the light of the divine word shone and flashed around him" (Sebeos, 69: ll. 26–27), and Khusraw then makes a profession of his faith (Sebeos ll. 27–31), and is baptised by the Catholicos of Iran (Sebeos, 70: l. 2). A few days before his death, "he partook of the life-giving body and blood of the Lord" (Sebeos ll. 4–5). Finally, when Khusraw died, "the Christians, having taken up his body, put it in the royal tombs" (Sebeos ll. 8–9).

If my inference of a Syriac origin for this romance is correct, a heretofore unknown strain has been revealed within the *Khwadāynāmag* tradition. Future research, it is hoped, will put my claim to the test, and perhaps reveal within later Arabic and Persian histories further evidence of the Syriac source which I have inferred.

Normally western sources offer us only the merest glimpse into Sasanian affairs, as though gazing into Iran at a distance from the parapet of an Anastasian or Justinianic fortress. Likewise the view afforded by later Arabic and Persian sources is often equally obscure. But when the two perspectives are coincidentally trained on the same target, like two equal but intermittent lights, more of the relevant picture is revealed. Comparison of the relics of Sasanian history in later texts with western sources is unlikely to trigger a radical change in our knowledge of Late Antiquity. But it may add subtlety and nuance to our perspective, as I hope it has done here.

5

Collaborators and Dissidents: Christians in Sasanian Iraq in the Early Fifth Century

Philip Wood

Late Antiquity is more than just a chronological unit. For Peter Brown, in his *World of Late Antiquity*, the phrase emphasizes both the cultural efflorescence of the late Roman world as it re-examined its own past and the interconnections between the Roman world and its neighbours and successors, most notably Sasanian Persia and the Arab caliphate. But 'Late Antiquity' in this formulation remains focused on the Roman Empire and on texts in Latin and Greek. While there is much to be gained from emphasizing the connections between the Roman and Sasanian worlds (not least in the spread of Christianity and rabbinic Judaism) and on reflecting on the culture of Iraq as a Hellenistic off-shoot, we should also realize that there was considerable variety in the way that ideas from the Mediterranean were received and re-used further east. Most importantly, this process of reception was often mediated through Syriac, a language that was identifiably Christian before it was Roman, and the interaction of Syriac sources with those other traditions presents a rich, barely tapped vein of Sasanian cultural and political history. What follows is an attempt to read just one of a large corpus of Syriac martyr acts from the fifth century against the testimony of the Syriac synodica and the Persian historical tradition. Above all, I hope to emphasize that the East Syrian church, active outside the state Christianity of the Roman Empire, faced very different problems from the Roman church as it orchestrated its own relationship to the state and to internal dissidents.

The fourth century was typified by a series of persecutions against Sasanian Christians by their temporal rulers. Though these demonstrations of public violence may have only been directed against a small number of prominent trouble-makers, the deaths of men such as the bishop of the Sasanian capital of Ctesiphon, Simeon bar Sebbāʿe, provided the core of a later martyr literature that made the Church of the East a church of the martyrs.

However, we should also be aware that the bishops of Ctesiphon had no continuous history as rulers of the Church of the East. This impression, which is created by later medieval compilations such as the *Chronicle of Seert*, is, in effect, a back-projection of a situation that only arose in the fifth century, when bishops of Ctesiphon asserted their importance as servants of the shāh and as beneficiaries of a special relationship with the Christian Roman Empire. The peace negotiations between Rome and Iran at the beginning of the fifth century provided an opportunity for Ishaq, bishop of Ctesiphon, to assert his importance as 'catholicos'.

Ishaq's coup is visible from the Syriac *Synodicon Orientale*, a compilation of the synods of Ctesiphon that allows us an insight into the ambitions and limitations of the Church of the East as an institution. But, at the same time, the *Synodicon* also shows us the existence of a dissident tradition, of bishops who were excluded from the court influence that the catholicos and his allies claimed for their own. In addition, the martyr acts composed around contemporary holy men show that many did not respect the ranks of clerical hierarchy or the spirit of cooperation with the state that Ishaq emphasized at his synod in 410. The religious vandalism of these holy men, coupled with the dissatisfaction of many bishops, underlay the disintegration of catholical authority under Ishaq's successor Dadisho in 424, when the Sasanian state removed its support for an ineffectual institution and returned to the persecution of the Christians.

THE 410 SYNOD OF SELEUCIA-CTESIPHON

Under the ninth-century patriarch Timothy I the records of the earlier synods convened by the Church of the East were collected into a single *Synodicon*. Though the titles of earlier bishops of Ctesiphon were inflated to match ninth-century expectations, these alterations were both inconsistent and do not seem to have involved alteration of the rest of the text.[1] The first of these synods, convened under the auspices of the shāh Yazdegird I, the Roman emissary Marutha of Maypherkat, and the 'grand metropolitan' of Ctesiphon Ishaq, sought to transform the Church of the East along the same lines as the Roman world.

Importantly, this synod was also convened in the context of broader Persian-Roman diplomacy, which sought to scale down confrontation on Rome's eastern border. Following an initial treaty in 399, Marutha made a first visit in 402, in the context of diplomatic overtures between the court of Arcadius and the Persians, which was followed by Yazedgird's declaration of religious toleration. This was followed by a second visit in 409, probably the result of internal strife within the church in Iraq, to confirm Ishaq's prominence.[2]

The initial session of the synod articulated the relationship between the shāh, the Church of the East and the other dignitaries. Yazdegird is called 'the victorious king of kings, on whom the churches rely for peace' and he is praised for putting a stop to the persecutions of earlier years. Ishaq is honoured as catholicos (the first use of the title), 'judged by God worthy of a place at the head of the East' and Marutha is called 'the mediator

[1] V. Erhart, 'The development of Syrian Christian canon law in the Sasanian Empire, in R. Mathisen (ed.), *Law, Society and Authority in Late Antiquity*, Oxford 2001, 115–30, provides an introduction to the *Synodicon*.

[2] M. Higgins, 'Metropolitans of Seleucia-Ctesiphon', *Traditio* 9, 1953, 46–99, at 77–83 reconstructs the events, which have been compressed in the sources. The references to internal strife come from the 424 synod, but have been suppressed in the earlier synodica.

of peace between east and west'.[3] This preamble also notes the presence of the bishops of Antioch, Aleppo, Edessa, Tella and Amida, that is, of a sizeable delegation from the Syriac-speaking sections of the Roman world, and the metropolitans of Nisibis, Adiabene, Beth Garmai, Khuzistan, Maishan and Kashkar: the leaders of the church in Iraq (though not of Christian leaders further to the east).[4]

The preamble goes on to demand that each city should only have a single bishop and that all should have the same sacred days that were established in the Nicene canons, 'as was established under the victorious and God-loving emperor Constantine'. This text ends with a prayer for the king and for all the notables 'who wish to live in peace with the church of God'.[5]

This opening text presents an image of unity between the church in the east and in the Roman Empire, emphasized by the physical presence of the Roman bishops, and employs the rhetoric of peaceful co-operation while presenting Yazdegird's involvement in the synod as a sign of his victory, on the model of Constantine. Constantine's claim to rule over all Christians had been seen as a threat in the previous century during the Shāpūrian persecutions, so the presentation of Yazdegird as 'a new Constantine' and the shāh's self-presentation as a 'ruler over the whole world, east and west' might be seen as the adoption of Constantinian claims to universal rule by a Persian shāh. Shāpūr I's claims on his inscriptions to be ruler of *Ērān* and *an-Ērān* had themselves carried a claim to universal rule, but here we have Yazdegird making these claims, and having claims made for him, in the context of a Christian synod. Shāpūr I's inscriptions had been addressed to Middle Persian and Parthian-using elites and carried a sense of ethnic difference, but Yazdegird's claims are aimed towards, and re-echoed by, a new interest group, whose declarations were also heard by the Roman delegation.

The image of Yazdegird's victory may have also been important in the context of the need of both Rome and Persia to re-orientate themselves away from war with one another and towards the Huns. This diplomatic re-orientation may explain both the Romans' willingness to allow Yazdegird to employ the terms of Constantinian universal rule and the emphasis on Yazdegird the peacemaker as victorious, an image that was also intended for the shāh's notables. They are the principal targets of the magnification of the shāh and they are enjoined to align themselves to the shāh's policies by 'living in peace with the church of God'.[6]

This initial session was followed by an agreement on the creed and on the disciplinary canons of the Roman world of the fourth century (Ankara, Neocaesarea, Antioch, Gangra and Laodicaea). The *Synodicon* reports that the agreed formula for the creed was the Nicene creed, but texts of the *Synodicon* preserved in the western tradition show that another older creed was employed at this stage: Marutha and his companions seem to have judged this orthodox and it was only later generations' concern to demonstrate their own

[3] *Synodicon Orientale*, ed. J.-B. Chabot, Paris 1904, 18–9.

[4] *Synodicon Orientale*, 19.

[5] *Synodicon Orientale*, 20.

[6] Yazdegird is also called the 'peacebringer' (*rāmshahr*) in the Middle Persian inscriptions of his coins. T. Darayee, 'History, epic and numismatics. On the title of Yazdegird I', *American Journal of Numismatics* 16, 2004, 89–92.

unimpeachable orthodoxy that caused this later alteration.[7] In a similar vein, the western disciplinary canons included bans on heresies never known in the east: the issue at stake was uniformity as part of a universal communion, rather than the actual function of the canons *per se*.

The final session of the synod issued the new disciplinary canons of the Church of the East. They show that while the hierarchy of a church existed, and that its delegates could agree on a single creed, there were few norms about the 'abuse of office', the election of bishops or the relationship between bishops and institutional property. These canons articulate a centralized church, where all elected bishops must be 'perfected' by the catholicos in a secondary ordination and be gathered at a bi-annual synod at Ctesiphon to 'honour the [catholicos]'.[8] Bishops could not ordain one another alone, nor could an anathematized bishop be replaced without the agreement of the catholicos or a metropolitan. Additionally, it was the catholicos who could determine the liturgical year.[9]

The canons present the image of a clergy and episcopate that had been unregulated and that lacked guidelines for 'proper behaviour': they legislate against dishonest and illiterate clergy, against the ordination of deacons who do not know the Psalms and against violence between bishops.[10] These declarations on 'proper behaviour' flow from the general prescriptions of the first canon, which sets out the qualities of a bishop: 'to receive strangers, feed the poor, aid the oppressed, nourish orphans, refuse presents and to meditate on the scriptures'.[11] But as much as this image of a disorganised church probably does reflect the pre-410 reality, we should remember that it was also the excuse of the council's conveners to arrogate great powers to themselves, an alliance between the catholicos and his metropolitans that was confirmed by the presence of the westerners and the power of the shāh rather than being a 'bottom-up' wish for the regulation of the church. The shāh himself asserted that the wishes of the catholicos be regarded as laws, and he personally claimed the right to summon bishops, enforce church discipline and to nominate the catholicos, theoretical powers that he would try to use in future years.[12] Similarly, the bishops of the major sees of Iraq benefited from their status as the great men of the church, while the bishops of congregations further east, including the leaders of prestigious communities of Roman exiles, gained no such recognition. Before we accept too readily the claims of Ishaq as 'grand metropolitan and head of all bishops' (limited only by an abstract appeal to 'justice')[13] we should remember how much the shāh, the Roman bishops and the six metropolitans of Iraq stood to gain from such an arrangement.

One example of how the 'reform' of ecclesiastical organization might have benefited the catholicos is provided by the canon against multiple holders of sees: the synod demanded in these instances that there could only be a single bishop. Yet only two bishops, Batai of

[7] D. Winkler and W. Baum, *The Church of the East: A Concise History*, London 2003, 16.

[8] Canons 1 and 6.

[9] Canon 11, 17 and 13.

[10] Canons 4, 16 and 19.

[11] Canon 1.

[12] Canons 20, 21, and 25.

[13] Canon 21.

Meshmahig and Daniel, were removed from their sees. In the province of Khuzistan, which seems to have had many more than its fair share of incumbents, four men, Barsaiba, Agapetus, Shila and Mari, were all allowed to retain their positions as long as the catholicos could appoint their successors. As Labourt observed, this may reflect their influence at court, but the reticence of Ishaq and the synod also shows the wish to centralize decision-making on the person of the catholicos, rather than to local election.[14] The reversion of powers to the catholicos shows at least that such favours were temporary, and that the interests of shāh and catholicos were aligned in the centralization of church authority.

Ishaq's successors Ahai and Iaballaha benefited from this period of entente between the shāh and the Romans. The *Chronicle of Seert* reports that Ahai was selected by Yazdegird to investigate false claims by his nephew Nahrouz in Fars that a state shipment of pearls had been captured by pirates, and that Iaballaha was chosen to make diplomatic overtures to the Romans after receiving a Roman embassy from one Acacius of Amida – where he was given impressive presents at the court of Theodosius II, which he used to build and restore churches.[15] Iaballaha received, in turn, a second visit from Acacius in 420, when he convened a second synod to hear his letter of greeting and to re-affirm the disciplinary canons of the Anatolian councils.[16] The traditions embedded in the *Chronicle* seem to reflect a closer relationship between shāh, catholicos and the Romans, where peace negotiations revealed the potential of charitable donations from the Roman church and where a catholicos based in the shāh's Iraqi capital could monitor his allies in the Sasanian military heartland of Fars.

However, the profitable relationship did not imply that the rest of the ecclesiastical hierarchy was complicit with the behaviour of the catholicoi. Quarrels over the treatment of religious minorities in both empires and the Christian self-representation of the Theodosian court led to a brief war in 421–2 and a renewed spell of persecution under Yazdegird I and his successor Bahrām V.[17] The acts of the synod of 424, held under the catholicos Dadisho, give a different perspective on the stability of the reigns of Ishaq, Ahai and Iaballaha, as the smokescreen of earlier rhetoric is dropped to reveal the cracks in Ctesiphon's authority over other bishops. It follows the theme of earlier synods by issuing a preamble in which the signatories profess their loyalty, but it also reveals the existence of a party of dissidents, of which eleven are named, who, it is now revealed, were condemned by both Ishaq in 410 and by Iaballaha at a second synod in 420.[18] These men include Batai

[14] J. Labourt, *Le christianisme dans l'empire Perse*, Paris 1904, 98-9.

[15] *Chronicle of Seert*, ed. A. Scher, *Patrologia Orientalis* V, LXIX, 324, 324; LXXI, 326–7.

[16] *Synodicon*, 39.

[17] For this war and its causes see O. Schrier, 'Syriac Evidence for the Romano-Persian War of 421–422', *Greek Roman and Byzantine Studies* 33, 1992, 75–86, who emphasises that the Romans only declared war after Bahrām's succession and that conciliatory diplomacy was still attempted by Acacius in 420. Also see K. Holum, 'Pulcheria's crusade AD 421–2 and the ideology of imperial victory', *Greek, Roman and Byzantine Studies* 18, 1977, 164–71 on the treatment of Zoroastrian minorities in Anatolia and G. Greatrex, 'The two fifth-century wars between Rome and Persia', *Florilegium* 12, 1–14 on the course of the war.

[18] *Synodicon orientale*, 44. 11 dissidents are named compared to 36 signatories at the council of 424, though there were only 12 signatories at its predecessor in 420.

of Hormizd-Ardashīr, possibly the same Batai who was condemned by Ishaq, and one Pharabokht of Ardashir-Khurrah, who had previously been nominated as catholicos.[19] The sees of these dissidents are weighted towards the 'new cities' of Fars that had been founded in the previous two centuries, such as King's Dasqart, Belashparr, Darabgerd, Hormizd-Ardashir and Ardashir-Khurrah, possibly implying that some of them shared court connections that encouraged them to act in concert against the catholicos and his allies. At least one of these men, Abner of Kashkar, seems to have been a 'dual-incumbent' displaced from his see by an alternative line of episcopal succession.

So the impression of unity and centralization that we receive from the synods of Ishaq and Iaballaha is a work of rhetoric aimed to impress the dignitaries who were present that aimed for short-term diplomatic gains from the upper echelons of Roman and Persian administration, but which ignored grievances and alternative lines of patronage in the provinces, even if we cannot reconstruct these in detail. If the decade of 410–20 had brought the rewards of high level cooperation, then the final year of Yazdegird's reign would bring an end to 'the peace of the church' and to peace with Rome.

THE WAR OF 421 AND THE NEW PERSECUTIONS

The end of Yazdegird's reign saw a major volte-face by the shāh in which he resumed persecution of the Christians. This event was associated with Yazdegird's own weakness *vis à vis* his notables, who ultimately arranged his assassination and then killed his son Shāpūr. The throne was initially given to Shāpūr's cousin, Khusraw, until he was challenged by another son of Yazdegird, Bahrām, who, ruled as Bahrām IV with the aid of his Arab Lakhmid allies.

The Persian royal tradition, the *Khwadāynāmag*, embedded in later Arab histories such as Ṭabarī and in the New Persian *Shāhnāma*, may illustrate some of this uncasc at Yazdegird's behaviour. Ṭabarī reports that Yazdegird was known as 'the sinful one', possibly reflecting his support for Christianity, and complains that he did not trust those who spoke out for the oppressed, putting his trust only in foreign ambassadors and imposing monetary penalties and physical punishment on aristocrats. In this tradition, Yazdegird was killed by being thrown from a white horse, symbolizing his failure to fulfill his divine mandate for kingship.[20] By contrast, Bahrām V denounces his father's evil and is crowned by the chief *mōbed*, proving his right to rule by struggling for his crown set between two lions and by his adventures in India.[21] Much of this tradition is clearly legendary, but it does suggest that the attitudes of certain Persian elites towards the shāhs differed greatly and that they expressed this in terms of heroic myth and Zoroastrian mythology. Importantly,

---

[19] Pharabokht is mentioned in Mari, *Historia Ecclesiastica*, ed. and tr. H. Gismondi, *Maris, Amri, et Salibae: De Patriarchis Nestorianorum Commentaria II: Maris textus arabicus et versio Latina*, Rome 1899, 31/ 26.

[20] Ṭabarī, *Taʾrīkh al-rusul waʾl-mulūk*, ed. M. J. de Goeje and others, Leiden 1879–1901, i, 849–50 and tr. C. E. Bosworth, *The History of al-Ṭabarī, V. The Sasanids, the Byzantines, the Lakhmids and Yemen*, Albany 2000, 73.

[21] Ṭabarī, *Taʾrīkh*, i, 854–70.

Yazdegird is portrayed rejecting the advice of his aristocrats and using the state's power against them, while Bahrām is praised for lowering taxes and courting the *mōbeds*, especially his chief *mōbed* Mehr-Narseh, who, the tradition reports, acquired extensive landed property during his reign.[22]

The analogue to these accusations is provided by the Christian historical traditions. Not only did Yazdegird use Ahai and Iaballaha to monitor his relatives and conduct diplomacy, but Roman ecclesiastical history also emphasises the proximity of Marutha to Yazdegird. Socrates Scholasticus, writing in the 430s, narrates that 'the king loved Marutha' and that he detected the tricks of the Magi, who claimed that their god could speak to the king out of the flames, and that Marutha expelled demons from the king's son.[23] While neither the Roman ecclesiastical history nor the Arabic recensions of the Persian royal annals is a precise source, they present a relatively unified image here of a shāh content to use foreign advisors, to create institutions and to challenge the governance of local aristocrats.

Scott McDonough has usefully placed both Yazdegird's reign and that of his 'persecuting' successors Bahrām V and Yazdegird II into the context of the reform of the Sasanian state, where the personal rule of earlier shāhs was gradually and experimentally replaced by more stable structures. The period 350–480 saw the replacement of regional sub-kings with government-appointed *marzbān*; the centralization of silver manufacture (an important vehicle for royal propaganda); the issuing of mint-marked coins and an appeal to 'ancient' Kayanid myths as part of royal self-presentation.[24] These observations built on earlier studies of the government seals by Rika Gyselen that saw the fifth century as an era of bureaucratic expansion in the Sasanian world and as the period when *mōbeds* were regularly given government functions.[25] It is also important to remember that men like Kartir, the third-century *mōbed* who celebrated his persecutions in rock inscriptions that rivaled those of the shāh, was an exceptional figure, and that a permanent 'chief *mōbed*' probably only existed in the fifth century.[26]

This focus on centralization is important because it allows us to understand the

---

[22] For tax relief under Bahrām see Thaʿālibī (ed. and tr. H. Zotenberg, L'histoire des rois des Perses, Paris 1900, I, 555. For Mehr-Narseh's wealth, see Ṭabarī, *Taʾrīkh*, i, 870–1.

[23] Socrates, *Ecclesiastical History*, vii, 8, ed. G. Hansen, Berlin 1960, GCS 50 NF 4.

[24] S. McDonough, *Power by Negotiation: Institutional Reform in the Fifth-Century Sasanian Empire*, UCLA 2002 unpublished PhD, 136–65. Also see R. Gyselen, 'New evidence for Sasanian numismatics' in idem (ed.), *Contributions à l'histoire et géographie historique de l'empire sasanide*, Bures-sur-Yvettes 2004, 52–67 at 52–62 for the dating of mint marks.

[25] R. Gyselen, *La géographie administrative de l'empire sasanide*, Paris 1989, 30–5 on the development of the *mōbeds* and the office of '*mogbed*' as a land administrator for the Magi and eadem, 'Empreintes des sceaux sasanides', *Studia Iranica* 93 (1992), 53 for the association of magi with specific towns and provinces. However, this was only the beginning of this process: E. Venetis, 'The *Zoroastrian priests and the foreign* affairs of Sasanian Iran and the Later Roman Empire (5th Cent.)', *Nāme-ye Irān-e Bāstān* 3, 2003, 47–78, esp. 52 over-emphasises the early *effects* of these reforms, which we cannot assess for this early date.

[26] S. Wikander, *Feuerpriester in Kleinasien und Iran*, Lund 1946, 51 for the 440s as the institution of the first *mōbedan mōbed. Also note* P. Gignoux, 'Une categorie de mage a la fin de l'époque sasanide: le mogveh', *Jerusalem Studies in Arabic and Islam* 9, 1987, 19–23, an office he dates to the fifth century.

experimentation of Yazdegird and later shāhs with Christian institutions in terms of the Sasanian state, rather than purely from the perspective of churchmen. What Yazdegird shared with his successors was the creation of institutions that bound specific groups within the empire to the shāh, using these to balance one another's interests while allowing the shāh to retain control over appointments and the fiscal-military apparatus. We should remember, of course, that three of Shāpūr II's immediate successors had been assassinated at the end of the fourth century: the use of the catholicoi as spies and diplomats; diplomatic recognition by the Roman bishops; Kayanid ideology; bureaucratic reform and the institutional reform of the Magi were all experiments aimed at creating long-term legitimacy for the shāhs and engendering loyalty and an ability to intervene in different localities.

This centralization was important for Christians because it promised great power to those who were willing to cooperate with the shāh and successfully act on his behalf, but it also threatened tension, both with other competitors for the shāh's favour and with other Christians, who stood to lose out in various ways from the relationship between shāh and catholicos. The relationships between the catholicos and the shāh and the catholicos and his bishops were closely connected to the relationships between Persians and Romans and between the shāh and the Magi. And it is with this nexus of patronage in mind that we should analyze the persecutions of the reigns of Yazdegird and Bahrām and the controversy about loyalty that was associated with these events.

THE MARTYRS OF YAZDEGIRD AND BAHRĀM

The Roman ecclesiastical historian Theodoret of Cyrrhus reports (*c.* 440) that one 'Abdas, 'adorned with virtue and stirred by undue zeal to destroy paganism' tore down a fire temple in Khuzistan. He reports that Yazdegird made moderate requests to 'Abdas to restore the temple, but that these were refused and that Yazdegird responded by having him killed and the churches destroyed. He goes on to describe the death or imprisonment of other martyrs under Yazdegird: Hormisdas 'an Achaemenid and the son of a prefect', Suenes 'master of a thousand slaves'[27] and Benjamin, a deacon who refused to renounce proselytism. He adds that 'just as Diocletian destroyed churches in the Roman Empire on the day of our saviour's Passion', he, like Yazdegird, 'perished in iniquity'.

Theodoret's report suggests that Yazdegird's chief concern was the conversion of high-ranking Persians and Christian proselytism, and that churches presented a suitable target to threaten Christians into greater obedience. Theodoret was clearly anxious about the wisdom of 'Abdas' actions: he notes that 'not even [Paul] destroyed the altars of the Athenians', though he agrees that it is 'honourable to seek a martyr's crown and to refuse to rebuild a temple of paganism'.[28] This account inspired Neusner's analysis that Christian expectations of imminent conversion generated tension with the Magi that led to

---

[27] This may reflect the Sasanian title '*hazārbandag*', also ascribed to Mehr-Narseh (Ṭabarī, *Ta'rīkh*, i, 868).

[28] Theodoret of Cyrrhus, *Ecclesiastical History,* V. 38, ed. G. Hansen, Berlin 1998, GCS 19 NF 5.

persecution.[29] Van Rompay has noted in turn that this ignores the emphasis on loyalty and obedience in many of the contemporary Syriac hagiographies, especially those produced by the monk Abgar, from a monastery close to Ctesiphon.[30] I suggest here that, instead of looking for a single Christian pattern of behaviour, the Syriac martyrologies must be read alongside the *Synodicon* to reveal the contradictory tensions within the Church in the East and the range of objections to its recent institutional framework.

One of these martyrologies, that has not been incorporated into this discussion, is a fragmentary account of the same 'Abda of Hormizd-Ardashir that Theodoret mentions. The text is dated to the twenty-second year of Yazdegird. It begins by telling how the magi went to the king, warning him that 'in the lands of your dominion, these Nasarenes, who are called bishops, priests, deacons and *bnay qyama*, transgress your command and disobey your kingship: they disgrace your gods and mock fire and water and overturn the fire temples, the buildings where we worship, and greatly disobey our laws.' Next the king 'gathered all the nobles of his dominion and asked them whether the things he heard were true. Then the nobles and the magi oppressed our people and prevailed [in argument] and from this time a harsh order went down from the king that the churches should be uprooted in all the lands of his dominion.'[31]

'Abda and his companions[32] are brought before the king, where he asks them 'why [they] did not lower [themselves] to the teaching which we received from our fathers [and] follow a wandering path according to the will of your own hearts?' Here Christians reply that it is senseless to worship created things, such as the water, fire and the sun, instead of the creator, who is God.

Next Yazdegird proceeds to criticize 'Abda's style of government, implying that it is a kind of democracy: 'Since you are the leader and governor of these men, why do you neglect them so much that you disobey our kingship and neglect our command and govern according to their will?' His specific objection, it transpires, is to 'Abda's destruction of a fire temple: 'For we have received places of worship and fire temples that have been glorified from the time of our fathers' fathers, but you have overturned them and uprooted them!' 'Abda's defence is simply that this is a false accusation: the Magi have lied against the Christians at court, though the king denies this strenuously.[33]

The issues of 'Abda's debate with Yazdegird, of church 'democracy' and the accusation of the destruction of a fire temple, remain the focus of the debate when 'Abda's deacon Hosea (Hashuʿ) enters the debate:

---

[29] J. Neusner, *A History of the Jews in Babyonia*, v, Leiden 1970, 8.

[30] L. Van Rompay, 'Impetuous martyrs? The situation of the Persian Christians in the last years of Yazdegard I (419–20)' in M. Lamberigts and P. Van Deun (eds.), *Martyrium in a Multi-Disciplinary Perspective. Memorial Louis Reekmans*, Louvain 1972, 363–75 at 372–73.

[31] *Acts of 'Abda*, ed. P. Bedjan, *Acta Martyrorum et Sanctorum*, Paris 1890–7, iv, 251. Now see the discussion by F. Jullien, 'La passion syriaque de Mār 'Abdā. Quelques relations entre chrétiens et mazdéens, in R. Gyselen, C. Jullien and F. Jullien (eds.), *Rabban l'Olmyn. Florilège offert à Phillippe Gignoux pour son 80e anniversaire* (Leuven, 2011), 195–205.

[32] There are seven companions, including two priests, a deacon and 'Abda's brother Papa.

[33] *Acts of 'Abda*, 252.

> Then Hosea the priest took up the power of God and said 'We did not attack the building of God and we did not go against a holy altar. Then the king said 'I did not speak to you but to your leader and is he who must give me a reply.' Then the blessed Hosea said 'Our teaching commands thus: that great and small should not be ashamed of the word of God when speaking before the king. Also the saviour told us that 'I have brought you speech and wisdom that your persecutors will not be able to withstand. And because of this our words are true whether they come from great or small'. Then the king said 'What is your teaching O bold one? That you should speak instead of your leader and that you should be clothed in zealotry on behalf of your people?' Then the holy man said 'I am a Christian, a servant of the living God and I cannot blame my own hand and say 'what are you doing?'. Then the king said 'An honest man indicated to me that you attacked the fire and quenched it and transgressed our command'. Then the holy Hosea said 'I did attack a building and quench a fire because it is not a house of God and fire is not the daughter of God, but it is a servant, which serves both kings and paupers, both the rich, the poor and the beggars, and is generated from dry wood. [34]

The text, then, presents an environment where the Magians have challenged Christians at court for their role in religious vandalism. Other hagiographies set in the reign of Shāpūr II often include a *topos* of false accusation by Zoroastrians and Jews against Christians, but here the denunciation is specific and is only denied in part: Hosea admits to destroying the temple, but not that it is a 'holy thing'.[35] The hagiographer intends the *Acts* to seem provocative, to remind audiences accustomed to hagiography that the Magi will denounce them, but also that it is Christian norms, rather than Zoroastrian ones, that are true criteria for judgement. Moreover, by emphasising this distinction he shows that the shāh is controlled by the Magi: Christians are only bound by a higher law. Yazdegird's objection that he can rely on his trustworthy advisors may well reflect the self-presentation of the court, especially given Yazdegird's conscious promotion of Christians and Jews and the notables' complaints of interference in local governance, and this may have involved statements that all were equal before the law and that all might seek his ear at court. But 'Abda refuses to participate in this invitation: following another *topos* of the martyria, the inversion of social norms, he denies the testimony of the magi, because it involves a category error (i.e. that they do not understand what is really holy), rather than because they did not really destroy the fire.[36]

Similarly, the *Acts* reflects a second aspect of Yazdegird's self-presentation in his appeal to Zoroastrianism as an ancestral religion, the religion of 'our fathers'. This presentation shows the ethnic language that had been employed by earlier shāhs that connected *Ērān* with the religion of the 'Mazda-worshipping shāhs', an image that Yazdegird and his successors would extend with their propagation of an ancient Kayanid history for their dynasty.[37] Importantly, Yazdegird appeals to 'Abda to respect this ancestral religion: since

---

[34] *Acts of 'Abda*, 253. The manuscript breaks off shortly afterwards.

[35] E.g. *Acts of Tarba*, ed. AMS II, 254; *Acts of Simeon*, ed. and tr. M. Kmosko, *Patrologia Syriaca* II, 240.

[36] E.g. Gushtazad's audience with Shāpūr II in *Acts of Symeon A*, (756).

[37] T. Darayee, 'History, epic and numismatics. On the title of Yazdegird I', *American Journal of Numismatics* 16, 2004, 89–92 on the use of the Kayanid term '*rām shahr*'. Also see idem, 'Kingship in early Sasanian Iran' in V. Curtis and S. Stewart (eds.), *The Sasanian Era: The Idea of Iran vol. III*, London 2008, 60–66.

the confrontation takes place in Khuzistan, 'Abda's position as a convert from Zoroastrianism may have been more obvious than in Iraq, where it and Christianity were surrounded by a variety of other forms of polytheism.

Thus the *Acts of 'Abda* rejects Yazdegird's attempts to include Christians in a political framework or to get them to respect the bonds of common ancestry. Instead Hosea repeats the most popular defense of Christianity against Zoroastrianism that is copied from defenses against idolatry in older martyr literature: it is better to worship the creator than created things. Indeed, by following the *topoi* of Magian accusation, subversion of earthly justice and the attack on Zoroastrianism as idolatry, the *Acts*' protagonists *act out* the hagiography of earlier martyrs to show that Christians of all kinds, laymen as well as priests, owe no allegiance to the false justice of a government that remains inclined towards idolatry.

This resistance is most strikingly seen in the shāh's criticisms of church government. Yazdegird asks 'Abda why, as 'leader of the men', he 'neglects them so much that you disobey our kingship and neglect our command and govern according to their will (i.e. the will of the mob)'. Yazdegird envisions a tripartite model of authority, where 'Abda's role is to serve as conduit for royal authority, being obedient to it himself and encouraging obedience in others. Instead, 'Abda is behaving at the behest of the mob. This issue is pursued in Hosea's reply, which is phrased in terms of *parrhēsia*, the bold speech of a martyr before his accuser, modeled on that of Christ before Pilate.[38]

Hosea presents his ability to speak before the king as a sign of his God-given reason, his freedom to act outside the confines of ceremony, while to Yazdegird his act of 'boldness' is a subversion of the proper chain of authority: Hosea speaks instead of his leader and has taken on the 'zealotry' of the crowd. Hosea's reply returns to the *topos* of justice in the earlier martyria – his act of vandalism was caused by God and it illustrates the flaw in Yazdegird's model of authority. Where the shāh imagined that authority ought to flow through the bishop 'Abda to his men, and that 'Abda and Hosea had subverted this by taking on the behaviour of the mob, Hosea emphasizes instead that authority flows from God to all Christians, and that he is as capable of speaking before the shāh as any bishop. Finally, Hosea includes fire itself into this matrix: whereas as it a false object of worship for the Zoroastrians, he calls it 'a servant of kings and paupers'. Ultimately, Hosea draws a parallel between the shāh's false chain of authority, leading to himself, and the Zoroastrian elevation of fire into an object of worship, which also underlines the Zoroastrian nature of government, even by a shāh who had made efforts to include Christians in governance.

This text is only a fragment, but, given its opposition to the powers that be, it seems that scribes and patrons would have had many incentives *not* to copy such a text during the rapprochements between the shāh and the Church of the East at the end of the sixth century. Therefore its survival, coupled with Theodoret's account of Persian converts and controversial proselytism, suggests that the *Acts of 'Abda* represents the tip of an iceberg, of a hagiographical literature that opposed the inclusion of some high-ranking Christians into government patronage.

---

[38] G. Bartelink, 'PARRHESIA', *Greacitas et Latinitas Christianorum*, supp. 3, Nijmegen 1970, 5–57, esp. 12–4 and 35–44 summarise the models of 'positive *parrhēsia*', based on Christ's relationship with God, and 'negative *parrhēsia*', based on Christ before Pilate.

REMEMBERING THE MARTYRDOMS: THE TESTIMONY OF THE CHRONICLE OF SEERT

The text's geographical location in Khuzistan becomes significant when we read it alongside the *Synodicon* and the East Syrian ecclesiastical histories. As we have seen, Hormizd-Ardashir was a centre of resistance to the catholicos throughout the period 410–24 where we have synodal evidence. In addition, another eastern see that rebelled against Dadisho, Belashparr, was the site of a later hagiography, the *Lives of Pethion, Ādur-Hormizd and Anāhīd*, composed in the 440s, that celebrated conversion from Zoroastrianism, even imagining the conversion of a famous magus and his daughter.[39] *The Acts of 'Abda* evoke a contrast between the behaviour of the saintly heroes and the catholicoi who were patronized by the shāh. They encourage a continued conversion from Zoroastrianism, in an environment where there were fewer 'neutral' avenues for expansion, as existed among the Jews or pagans of Iraq.

This conflict of interests within the church, and the disappointment of the shāh's wish to employ the catholicoi, is visible after the 420 synod in the brief reigns of the catholicoi Maʿna and Pharabokht. Maʿna is supposed to have authored a number of translations from Syriac into Persian[40] before being recommended for the catholicosate by 'the head of the army', Mehr-Shabur, who would later play a role in the persecutions, as 'a Persian man who could serve you well'. However, after the destruction of fire-shrines by Hosea the shāh demanded that he be accorded the same rights as Caesar within his own territory. The tenth-century *Chronicle of Seert* (an Arabic compilation of earlier Syriac histories) reports that a priest, Narsai, replied on Maʿna's behalf saying that the shāh could indeed demand that Christians pay tax or fight the shāh's enemies, but not deny their religion. The shāh responded by attempting to force Narsai's conversion, before ultimately ordering his execution, and by banishing Maʿna to Fars, where he died.[41] After this, Yazdegird was killed by a demon that had long been suppressed by the ministrations of the Christians and was succeeded by Bahrām, under whom the *Chronicle* places a general persecution of the church.[42] Pharabokht, his successor, is only given a brief note in Mari, but appears as a very short-lived appointee of the same 'head of the army'.[43]

The tradition of the medieval compilations is garbled: the close succession of shāhs and patriarchs means the historians have placed the persecution of Christians at different points, possibly influenced by a later impression of Yazdegird as a protector of the Christians.[44] But their narrative produces three features that accord with the material in

[39] *Life of Pethion, Ādur-Hormizd and Anāhīd.* This text was popular enough to be transmitted in Sogdian, so its tale of missionary success in western Iran may have been seen as a model in missionary fields further east (e.g. N. Sims-Williams, *Sogdian Manuscript C2*, Berlin 1985). The text is also highly sensitive to Iranian language and Zoroastrian ideas.

[40] This description may stem from a confusion of the catholicos with the later translator Maʿna of Rev-Ardashīr. S. Gero, Barsauma *of Nisibis and Persian Christianity in the 5th Century*, Louvain 1981, 21 and 43, n. 96.

[41] *Chronicle of Seert*, ed. A. Scher, *Patrologia Orientalis* V, LXII (328–9); Mari, *HE*, 29/33.

[42] *Chronicle of Seert*, LXXIV, 331–32.

[43] Mari, *Historia Ecclesiastica*, 31/ 36.

[44] On the later image of Yazdegird see S. McDonough, 'A second Constantine? The Sasanian king

the *Synodicon* and the saints' lives. Firstly, the shāh selected two catholicoi from Fars, emphasising the importance of relations with Christians in this, the home province of the Sasanians. Secondly, these figures benefited from court contacts: other notables than just the shāh were involved in the patronage of Christians. And thirdly, two figures, Hosea and Narsai, are identified as troublemakers, even though the tradition has smoothed over their departure from the diplomatic policies of catholicoi. Hosea is named a 'priest of 'Abda of Ahwaz' during the reign of Iaballaha. He vandalises a fire temple after a persecution of Christians by the shāh's general 'Shāpūr', and this prompts a wider persecution by the shāh until Ishaq, bishop of Armenia, intercedes on behalf of the Christians. Narsai appears as a religious vandal in his Syriac saint's life, but this is not mentioned in the *Chronicle of Seert*. Instead we see him speaking out against the shāh: when Yazdegird claims 'the rights of Caesar within his own domain', Narsai speaks up instead of the catholicos Maʿna and tells the shāh that Caesar 'never tried to force his subjects to change their religion'.[45]

Some of the details of the accounts of Hosea and Narsai are probably later inventions, such as the image of Hosea's vandalism as a *response* to earlier persecution, of which there is no indication in the *Acts of 'Abda*. But it is interesting that Narsai's interruption of Maʿna seems to imitate that of 'Abda by Hosea in the *Acts*, which may suggest that the two tales of religious vandalism exchanged material before becoming embedded in the patriarchal history. In addition, this story, changes several of the features of a narrative that had challenged the authority of the catholicoi. Iaballaha is made to pray for his own death before persecution resumes after Ishaq's intervention, which is probably an invention to preserve the reputation of a famous catholicos and absolves him of any blame. Moreover, by placing a persecution of Christians *before* Hosea's vandalism, the saint's extreme actions, which produced mixed responses in both Iraq and the Roman world, were rendered more palatable. In the same vein, Narsai is relocated from Rayy to Ctesiphon and his own vandalism is replaced by a more reasonable appeal for the equal treatment of religions.

Thus the *Chronicle of Seert* reflects a later re-writing of these events, in which the volatile actions of two famous holy men were made to accord with the political positions of later catholicoi. Popular hagiographies were co-opted into a history on Ctesiphon. But the career of Maʿna, together with the rebellious factions in the synod of Dadisho and the *Acts of 'Abda*, point towards the existence of groups of Christians east of Iraq who refused to accept the authority of the shāh or to renounce proselytism. Perhaps like the Donatists of late Roman Africa they used the language of earlier martyrdoms to continue to accentuate the differences between themselves and the 'secular' society, and this analogy might also extend to their opposition to the catholicos, implied in the *Acts of 'Abda* with its 'democratic' language and explicit in the rebel faction of 424. The shāh's attempt to use men like Maʿna to control this movement failed, perhaps because of the involvement of court figures such as Mehr-Shabur in selecting unsuitable proxies who were rejected by the rest of the church, as happened more obviously in the case of Pharabokht.

Yazdegird I in Christian history and historiography', *Journal of Late Antiquity* 1 (2008), 127–40 at 133–4. 'Amr, *Historia Ecclesiastica*, 27 shifts the persecution to the reign of Iaballaha, Mari, *Historia Ecclesiastica*, 29/ 33 places the persecution under Maʿna.

[45] *Chronicle of Seert*, LXXI–II, 327–29.

Yazdegird's attempts to co-opt the leadership of the church failed, in part because they in turn proved unable to control more radical members of the lower clergy, such as Hosea and Narsai, who behaved according to an older paradigm of martyrdom, resistance and active proselytism. Yazdegird's public support for an institution that was implicated in this religious strife, and the lack of power this implied, may have been an important cause of the coup that replaced him with his son Bahrām. The persecutions unleashed in this era suppressed effective central leadership within the Church of the East: there were no central synods between the years of 424 and 485. However, the restoration of an effective catholicosate under Acacius in 485 rested on the earlier reforms of Ishaq, not least in the very idea of an eastern catholicos. The restored catholicosate of the sixth century and beyond would remember a sanitized version of its own history, in which Narsai was re-invented as an ally of the catholicos and expunge many of the political complexities of the relationship between the shāh and the Christians, re-writing history to suit a later era of compromise and cooperation.

6

The Khurasan Corpus of Arabic Documents

Geoffrey Khan

The vast majority of extant original documents from the early Islamic period have been found in Egypt. These date from the very beginning of the Arab settlement in Egypt in the first century AH/seventh century CE and continue to be attested through the following centuries. In the first three Islamic centuries the documents are written on papyrus, the ancient writing material of Egypt. From the fourth century onwards papyrus was replaced as the common writing material in Egypt by paper, which had been originally introduced into the Islamic world in the eastern provinces. Although thousands of Arabic papyrus documents have been preserved from the first three centuries AH, they are not evenly distributed across this period. By far the largest proportion of the extant papyri from Egypt are datable to the third century AH/ninth century CE.

A small number of Arabic documents on papyrus have been discovered at sites outside of Egypt in the Levant and Iraq. These include papyri from Damascus,[1] Nessana (ʿAwjāʾ al-Ḥafīr) near Beʾersheva,[2] Khirbet al-Mird in the Judaean desert,[3] and Samarra.[4] Some papyrus documents that have been discovered at sites in Egypt may, indeed, have originally been written elsewhere. This is the case, for example, with P.Khalili 6, which is an account of expenditure of a Christian monastic community in Northern Syria or Iraq.

Until recently, very little early Arabic documentary material had been discovered in the eastern Islamic world. The only document available was an Arabic letter from Central Asia written in 100 AH/718–719 CE. This caused great excitement when it was discovered in 1933 in the ruins of a fortress on Mount Mūgh situated in the valley of Zarafshān in Tajikistan (ancient Sogdiana). The document, which was published by I. Y. Krachkovski and V. A. Krachkovskaya is a letter written to the Arab governor of the region, al-Jarrāḥ

---

[1] N. Abbot, 'Arabic papyri of the reign of Ǧaʿfar al-Mutawakkil ʿalā-allāh (AH 232–47/AD 847–61)', *Zeitschrift der Deutschen Morgenländischen Gesellschaft* 92, 1938, 88–135.

[2] C. J. Kraemer, 'The Colt papyri from Palestine', *Actes du Ve Congrès International de Papyrologie*, Brussels 1938, 238–44; idem, *Excavations from Nessana*, iii, *Non-literary Papyri*, Princeton 1958.

[3] A. Grohmann, *Arabic Papyri from Ḫirbet el-Mird*, Louvain 1963.

[4] E. Herzfeld, *Erster vorläufiger Bericht über die Ausgrabungen von Samarra*, Berlin 1912, pl. xxxvib.

ibn ʿAbdallāh.[5] A few fragments of Arabic documents from the eastern provinces datable to the third century AH/ninth century CE have recently come to light amongst a collection of Pahlavi documents at Berkeley.[6] These are likely to have originated in Iran, as is the case with the Pahlavi documents. One notable feature of these documents is that they are written on paper, whereas documents from the same period written in Egypt are on papyrus, indicating that paper was in use as a writing material for documents in the eastern provinces earlier than in Egypt. This is in conformity with the statement of Jāḥiẓ, writing in the third century AH/ninth century CE, that 'the papyri of Egypt are for the West what the papers of Samarqand are for the East'.[7]

By far the most important discovery of eastern documentary material that has been made in recent years is a collection of Arabic documents from a private archive of a family resident in Khurasan in the early Abbasid period. They consist of 32 legal and administrative documents datable from 138 AH/755 CE to 160 AH/777 CE and one letter datable to the same period.[8] Like the document from Mount Mūgh, these newly discovered documents are on parchment. With one exception, they were all written during the reign of the Abbasid caliph Manṣūr (r. 136–158 AH/754–775 CE). The majority (23 documents) are official quittances for the receipt of taxes. The others include a document relating to a cadastral survey, documents relating to the manumission of slaves, and documents recording the renunciation of debts. The letter relates to a private business matter.

These Arabic documents appear to have the same provenance as a collection of Bactrian documents that has been published by Sims-Williams.[9] The latest documents of the Bactrian corpus are datable to the first two centuries of Islam and mention many of the personal and place names that appear in the Arabic documents. Both collections, therefore, are of immeasurable historical importance in that they provide first hand evidence of everyday life in early Islamic Khurasan.

There are no records of the place of discovery of the two corpora of documents, yet it is clear from internal evidence that they originate from north-eastern Khurasan, in an area lying between Balkh and Bamiyan. This was the region of ancient Bactria. Balkh is, indeed, the Arabic form of the name of the ancient province's chief city (Greek Βακτρα, Avestan *Bāχδī*). As is demonstrated by the newly discovered documents, the local Iranian

[5] I. Y. Krachkovski, and V. A. Krachkovskaya, 'Le plus ancien document arabe de l'Asie Centrale', *Sogdiĭskĭ Sbornik*, Leningrad 1934, 52–90. Reprinted in I. Y. Krachkovski, *Izbrannye Socineniya* I, Moscow-Leningrad 1955, 182–212.

[6] G. Khan, 'The Arabic paper fragments from Berkeley', *Bulletin of the Asia Institute* 17, 2007, 31–34.

[7] Quoted by Thaʿālabī, *Laṭāʾif al-Maʿārif*, ed. P. de Jong, Leiden 1867, 97, and Suyūṭī, *Kitāb Ḥusn al-Muḥāḍara fī Akhbār Miṣr w-al-Qāhira*, Bulaq 1881, ii, 28.

[8] The documents are now in the private collection of David Khalili. The legal and administrative documents are published in G. Khan, *Arabic Documents from Early Islamic Khurasan*, London 2007. The document numbers referred to in this paper with the prefix P.Khurasan are the edition numbers of this volume.

[9] N. Sims-Williams, *Bactrian Documents from Northern Afghanistan I: Legal and Economic Documents*, Oxford 2000, and idem, *Bactrian Documents from Northern Afghanistan II: Letters and Buddhist Texts*, London 2007.

language of this region, Bactrian, continued to be used down to the second century of Islam.

In the pre-Islamic period Bactria had been overrun by numerous invaders. Before being conquered by the Sasanians in the first half of the third century CE, its rulers were the Kushans, who themselves had invaded the country from the north at an earlier period. Sasanian control of the area never seems to have been well established. When first coming to power, the Sasanians ruled through Kushan viceroys known as *Kushān-shāhs*. In the middle of the fourth century CE, Bactria was invaded from the north by an ethnic group known as the Chionites, who are identified with the Huns. These came to an agreement that allowed the Sasanians to retain some measure of authority. Shortly afterwards control of Bactria passed from the Sasanians to a people known as the Kidarites, who were also Huns and may have been identical ethnically to the Chionites. Around the year 400 CE, another people, known as the Hephthalites, invaded Bactria from the north. These are called in Indian Sanskrit sources *Sveta Hūṇas* 'White Huns'. They were a confederation of peoples, which was probably Indo-European in leadership but which may well have contained ethnically Turkish elements.[10] The Hephthalites drove the Kidarites south of the Hindu Kush. In the middle of sixth century CE the Hephthalites in turn were driven out of the region by an alliance between the Sasanians and the Turks, who had recently established their empire north of the Oxus river.[11] The Hephthalites remained largely unsubdued in the territory adjoining eastern Khurasan in the early Arab period.

The personal names attested in the Arabic documents in the Khurasan corpus reflect a variety of different ethnic layers in the local population, which is a legacy of the region's earlier history. In addition to Arabic names, one finds names of Iranian and Turkish origin.[12] The Iranian onomastic elements do not all have the form they would be expected to have in the local Bactrian dialect. Some are clearly of Middle Persian origin, as is the case with the name of one of the local governors Abū Ghālib ibn al-Iṣbahbadh (P.Khurasan 5–8). The word al-Iṣbahbadh is an Arabicized form of New Persian *Ispahbad*, which is derived from Middle Persian *spāhbed* 'army-commander'. This differs from the local Bactrian form *spālbid* (σπαλοβιδο).[13] Likewise the suffixed element meaning 'given' or 'created' in Iranian theophoric names sometimes appears in its Bactrian form *-lād*, e.g. Žulād (<ı Žūn-lād 'given by Žūn', P.Khurasan 30), and other times in the Middle Persian form *-dād*, e.g. Žundād (P.Khurasan 24 and 32).

---

[10] Cf. R. Ghirshman (*Les Chionites-Hephtalites*, Cairo 1948) who argues that the Hephtalites were only one element of the Chionite federation, perhaps the ruling house.

[11] N. Sims-Williams, *New Light on Ancient Afghanistan: The Decipherment of Bactrian* [Inaugural Lecture Delivered on 1 February, 1996], London 1997, 4–6.

[12] An awareness of the ethnic diversity of the population is reflected in the Bactrian document Sims-Williams, *Bactrian Documents I*, W (757 AD/139–140 AH). In this document a warranty is offered against anybody who disputes the sale of the property in question, the generic term 'anybody' then being specified by listing the various elements of the population: 'whether men of Rob, or men of Bamiyan, or Turks, or Arabs, or locals (presumably men of Gandara, since the document was drawn up in the town of Gandara).'

[13] N. Sims-Williams, 'Four Bactrian economic documents', *Bulletin of the Asia Institute*, new series, 11, 2000, 5.

The Bactrian documents from the early Abbasid period reflect a local community using their ancestral Iranian language, adhering to local religious practices and under the jurisdiction of a local ruler. This form of devolved local government is identical to what appears to have existed in the Umayyad period and indeed before the arrival of the Arabs. The Bactrian documents generally refer to the local ruler as the *khar*, which is an Iranian dialectal form derived from Old Iranian **xšāθriya-* 'ruler'. A variant dialectal form with the same etymology is *shēr*, which is mentioned by several Muslim writers, spelt either شير or شار,[14] as the title of the rulers of Bamiyan, Gharchistan and other places in the area of ancient Bactria.[15]

The Bactrian documents also refer to a leader with the title of *ser* (σηρο). Since the Bactrian script has a symbol to represent the /š/ sound, it is unlikely that this is to be identified with the *shēr* of the Arabic sources and, unlike the titles *khar* and *shēr*, is not a derivative from Old Iranian **xšāθriya-*. The title *ser* is found on several extant 'Hunnish' coins from the region.[16] It is associated with Turkish leaders in the Bactrian corpus. In one document[17] he is described as '*ser* of the Turks' (σηροτορκο) and in another[18] he has the Turkish title *qaghan*. Document 25 of the Arabic corpus refers to a local ruler with the title السير with no diacritical dots written over the first letter. In principle, this could be read as الشير as in the Arabic historical sources mentioned above. Since, however, this document concerns a man, who in the Bactrian documents is said to be under the jurisdiction of the *ser* rather than the *khar*, it is likely that the Arabic term should be read as السير (*al-sēr*) rather than الشير (*al-shēr*).

The *khar* who appears in the Bactrian corpus had his court at the town of Rob, which can be identified as modern Ru'i, lying fifty miles south of Samangan. He can be identified with Ruʾb-khān, the ruler of Ruʾb and Samangan, who helped Qutayba ibn Muslim defeat the Hephthalite rebel Nēzak Ṭarkhān in the year 91 AH/710 CE.[19]

As remarked above, a large proportion of the Arabic corpus of documents are tax receipts. These were issued by tax officials under the authority of a local governor (*amīr*). The men to whom the receipts were issued came from a local non-Arab family who had not converted to Islam. The documents indicate that the central government had taken direct charge of the collection of government taxes. This differs from the Umayyad period, in which the local *marzbāns* were responsible also for collecting taxes. Some of the *amīrs*

[14] Both the *yā'* and the *alif* of these orthographies were no doubt intended to represent a long /ē/ vowel.

[15] Ibn Khurradādhbih, *Kitāb al-Masālik wa-l-Mamālik*, ed. M. J. de Geoje, Leiden 1889, 39; Iṣṭakhrī, *Masālik al-Mamālik*, ed. M. J. de Goeje, Leiden 1870, 280; *Ḥudūd al-ʿĀlam, 'The Regions of the World'. A Persian Geography 372 AH–982 AD Translated and Explained by V. Minorsky*, second edition ed. C. E. Bosworth, London 1970, 109, 327, 332, 335, 341, 344, 359; J. Marquart, *Ērānšahr nach der Geographie des Ps. Moses Xorenacʻi*, Berlin 1901, 79; R. Göbl, *Dokumente zur Geschichte der Iranischen Hunnen in Baktrien und Indien,* Wiesbaden 1967, i, 165–66. Yaʿqūbī (*Kitāb al-Buldān*, ed. M. J. de Goeje, Leiden 1892, 289) mistakenly identifies the title as the Persian word for lion.

[16] Göbl, *Dokumente zur Geschichte der Iranischen Hunnen*, i, 165–66.

[17] Sims-Williams, *Bactrian Documents I*, S.

[18] Sims-Williams, *Bactrian Documents I*, Y.

[19] Ṭabarī, *Taʾrīkh al-rusul wa'l-mulūk*, ed. M. J. de Goeje and others, Leiden 1879–1901, ii, 1219. Cf. Sims-Williams, *New Light on Ancient Afghanistan*, 15.

and tax officials have Iranian elements in their names, for example Abū Ghālib ibn al-Iṣbahbadh (P.Khurasan 5, 6, 7, 8), al-Ḥasan ibn Warazān (P.Khurasan 1, 2), Amr ibn Marzūq (P.Khurasan 12, 13, 15), Jarīr ibn Māhān (P.Khurasan 13), al-Ḥasan ibn Farrukh (P.Khurasan 17). The Middle Persian title Iṣbahbadh suggests that this man came from an Iranian aristocratic family of administrators, the *spāhbed* being the term used to designate a military governor of a province in Sasanian administrative terminology.[20] It would appear that members of Iranian administrative families were incorporated into the Abbasid administration. Under the Sasanians the same families remained in state service over several generations and many of these seem to have continued in administrative positions well into the Abbasid period.

The Arabic tax receipts from Khurasan are remarkably similar in formulaic structure to equivalent documents from the same period that have been preserved among the Arabic papyri in Egypt. This reflects a highly centralized administration during the reign of Manṣūr, which was operating in rural areas outside the main towns. The Bactrian corpus shows, nevertheless, that the reach of the Abbasid administration did not extend much beyond tax collection. The *amīr* had military and fiscal responsibilities but not judicial. The regulation of law in so far as they affected the non-Muslim population was largely in the jurisdiction of the local ruler. Most affairs connected with the daily lives of a non-Muslim rural community were still under the jurisdiction of the local ruler. Several of the men who are issued tax receipts by the Abbasid officials appear in the Bactrian documents and are described as 'the servants of the *khar* of Rob'. The Bactrian documents, moreover, were written in traditional formulaic structures that had remained unchanged since Late Antiquity. These differed from the formulaic structures of the Arabic documents, which were brought to Khurasan by the Arabs.

We shall now take a closer look at the formulaic structure of the tax receipts of the Khurasan corpus. All of the documents are presented as a quittance (*barāʾa*) that releases the recipient from an obligation to pay as a consequence of the receipt of tax payments. The formula of the documents consists of the following components:

1. *Opening*

After the *basmala* the documents exhibit the following types of opening formula:
The issuer of the document, who is identified after the preposition *min* 'from' in the formulae above, is the financial administrator(s) (*ʿāmil*) of the governor.

(i) هذه / هذا براة من فلان ... لفلان 'This is a quittance from so-and-so ... for so-and-so'

(ii) هذا كتاب من فلان ... براة لفلان 'This is a document from so-and-so ... a quittance for so-and-so'

(iii) هذا كتاب براة من فلان ... لفلان 'This is a document of quittance from so-and-so ... for so-and-so'

[20] The term originally designated the supreme military commander in the Sasanian empire, but in the sixth century AD Khusraw I divided the office and appointed four *spāhbeds* for each of the quarters of the realm, cf. C. E. Bosworth (tr.), *The History of al-Ṭabarī (Taʾrīkh al-rusul waʾl-mulūk)*, v, *The Sāsānids, the Byzantines, the Lakhmids, and Yemen*, Albany 2000, 91. According to Masʿūdī, the *spāhbed* belonged to the second rank of courtiers immediately after the high nobility (*Murūj al-Dhahab wa-Maʿādin al-Jawāhir*, ed. and trans. C. Barbier de Meynard and Pavet de Courteille, *Les prairies d'Or*, Paris, 1861–1877, ii, 153). According to Yaʿqūbī (*Taʾrīkh*, ed. M. Th. Houtsma, Leiden 1883, 479) the term al-ʾIṣbahbadh was still used as the title of the king of Ṭabaristān in the time of al-Mahdī.

2. Operative Clauses

The operative clauses are presented in subjective style in that the issuer of the document is referred to in the first person and the taxpayer referred to in the second person. There are two operative clauses, the first confirming that the payment has been made to the financial administrators and the second declaring that the taxpayer has consequently been released from his obligation.

3. Payment

There are two variant formulae for the clause confirming the performance of the payment.

(i) انى قبضت منك / انا قبضنا منك 'I / we have received from you'
(ii) انك اديت الـىّ / انك اديت الينا 'You have delivered to me / us'

In formula (i) the focus is put on the act of receipt whereas in formula (ii) it is on the delivery by the taxpayer.

The occurrence of the operative clause referring to delivery (انك اديت الـىّ / الينا) has a chronological correlation. It first appears in a document dated 150 AH/767 CE (8) and becomes the regular formula in documents written after this date. Documents written before 150 AH/767 CE do not mention delivery but only receipt, in that the corresponding operative section has the form انى قبضت منك / انا قبضنا منك .

4. Liability

The liability clause indicates what the payment is for. In most documents this is introduced by the phrase مما صار عليك من ... 'what you owe with regard to ...' The tax that was owed is then specified. This is in most cases the land tax (*kharāj*) of a particular year, e.g. مما صار عليك من خراج سنة ست واربعين ومية 'what you owe with regard to the land tax of the year one hundred and forty-six' (P.Khurasan 5). Although it is not explicitly stated, it should be assumed that this is the solar tax year (*sana kharājiyya*), which followed the agricultural seasons. In most cases this is two or three years earlier than the year indicated in the closing date formula of the document, which would be the civil lunar year (*sana hijriyya*). In some cases the land tax was combined with supplementary taxes referred to as *qisam* 'shares' (sing. *qisma*).

5. Amount of payment

The amount of tax that has been paid is now mentioned. This is in the silver coinage of *dirhams* with fractions being expressed in *dānaqs*.

6. Release from obligation

In all documents this clause has the formula قبضت/ قبضنا ذلك منك وبرئت الـىّ/ الينا منه/ منها 'I/we have received that from you and you have become released from [the obligation to pay] it/them (i.e. the amount of money specified) to me/us'.

7. Closure

The document closes by indicating the date on which it was written according to the civil *hijri* calendar, specifying the month and year.

8. Seal

Most documents contain a clay bulla that is attached to the bottom of the document. These contain authorizations in the form of seal impressions that bear the names of the financial administrator(s) who issued the document or their emblems.

Many of the formulaic elements that occur in the tax receipts from Khurasan can be found also in documents that have been preserved among the Arabic papyri from Egypt.

Official documents from Egypt datable to the second century AH/eighth century CE that relate to tax and are issued by the financial administrators (*ʿummāl*) of a governor (*amīr*) generally open with the phrase ... هذا كتاب من 'This is a document from ...' and have the operative clauses in subjective style. This is regularly the case, for example, in agricultural leases, which are extant from the early Abbasid period.[21] In these documents the government official refers to himself in the first person and the lessee is referred to in the second person.

A similar format is found in official documents extant from the second century, some from the late Umayyad period, that grant permission to travel for the purpose of finding work and paying tax in a different region.[22] These open ... هذا كتاب من ... and the financial administrator who issues the document refers to himself in the first person in the operative clauses. Since the document was intended to be a permit that was to be read by a third party, the recipient of the document is in the third person, e.g. انی اذنت له ان یعمل باسفل اشمون 'I have permitted him to work in lower Ushmūn' (P.Cair.Arab. 175).

A considerable number of tax receipts from Egypt datable to the second century AH/ eighth century CE are extant in Arabic papyrus collections. Many of these, however, are not issued by the financial administrators of the governor but rather are what Frantz-Murphy classifies as unofficial tax receipts.[23] Unlike the official receipts issued by executives of the governor with a defined fiscal jurisdiction, the unofficial receipts are issued by a lower ranking tax collector without any specification of fiscal jurisdiction. In some cases the unofficial receipts make no reference at all to the issuing agency.

If we focus our attention on the extant official tax receipts that were issued by financial administrators of an Egyptian governor in the second century AH/eighth century CE, we see that the opening formula of these exhibits parallels with the Khurasan tax receipts. One type of opening that is found in the Egyptian official receipts is: هذا كتاب براة من فلان 'This is a document of quittance from so-and-so', in which the personal name is that of

[21] Frantz-Murphy, *Arabic Agricultural Leases*, 22–23.

[22] P.Cair.Arab. 174–75, Y. Rāġib, 'Sauf-conduits d'Égypte Omeyyade et Abbasside', *Annales Islamologiques* 31, 1997, 143–68.

[23] G. Frantz-Murphy, *Arabic Agricultural Leases and Tax Receipts from Egypt 148–427/756–1035*, Corpus Papyrorum Raineri XVII, Vienna 2001, 64–65.

the administrator of the governor.[24] Such an opening corresponds to opening formula (iii) in the Khurasan corpus. Another type of opening that is attested in the Egyptian official receipts is براة من فلان 'A quittance from so-and-so' (e.g. P.Cair.Arab. 197 [148 AH/765 CE]). This corresponds to opening formula (i) in the Khurasan corpus (هذه براة من فلان) with the omission of the initial demonstrative pronoun. The unofficial Egyptian tax receipts that are datable to the second century AH/eighth century CE generally open براة لفلان 'A quittance for so-and-so' and the issuing agency is mentioned later in the document or is sometimes left unspecified.[25] It is a general characteristic of the official receipts that the issuing agency is announced at the beginning of the document. In terms of the opening formula, therefore, it can be seen that the Khurasani receipts closely correspond to those of the official tax receipts from early Abbasid Egypt.

The operative clauses in the extant Egyptian tax receipts from the second century have been classified by Frantz-Murphy into official and unofficial formulae.[26] The official formula is found in Grohmann 'Probleme', 18 [196 AH],[27] which is a receipt for *kharāj* issued by a financial administrator of an *amīr*. The operative clause in this document is انی قبضت منك 'I have received from you', which is in subjective style.

In the third century AH/ninth century CE various changes take place in the structure of tax receipts from Egypt.[28] The key term in operative clauses of most receipts becomes the verb *addā* 'to deliver', referring to the delivery of the tax by the taxpayer, whereas the term *qabaḍa* 'to receive', referring to the receipt of the tax, is rarely used, a typical formula being: ادی فلان ... الی فلان 'So-and-so (the taxpayer) has delivered to so-and-so (the issuing agency)'. The focus is, therefore, put on the delivery rather than on the receipt. Furthermore, the issuing agency, even in official receipts, is placed after the mention of the taxpayer. The use of the verb *addā* in this type of formula is first attested in Egypt in a document dated 216 AH/831 CE.[29] By the third century it had become the technical term for paying taxes, the noun *al-mu'addā* being used to refer to the place where taxes were delivered.[30]

It is significant that the use of the verb *addā* in this technical sense is attested in the Khurasan tax receipts in the middle of the second century, antedating the first attestation in the Egyptian documents by about seven decades. Within the corpus of Khurasan documents, the verb is used regularly in documents datable to 150 AH/767 CE and later but is not found in documents written before that date (P.Khurasan 1–7).

---

[24] E.g. W. Diem, 'Einige frühe amtliche Urkunden aus der Sammlung Papyrus Erzherzog Rainer (Wien)', *Le Muséon* 97, 1984, 6 [180 AH]; A. Grohmann, 'Probleme der arabischen Papyrusforschung II', *Archiv Orientální* 6, 1934, 18 [196 AH]).

[25] Frantz-Murphy, *Arabic Agricultural Leases,* 64–65.

[26] Frantz-Murphy, *Arabic Agricultural Leases,* 66.

[27] Grohmann, 'Probleme der arabischen Papyrusforschung II', 18 [196 AH].

[28] Frantz-Murphy, *Arabic Agricultural Leases,* 70ff.

[29] Grohmann, 'Probleme der arabischen Papyrusforschung II', 12.

[30] R. Dozy, *Supplément aux Dictionnaires Arabes*, second printing, Leiden-Paris 1927, 15; cf. Balādhurī, *Futūḥ al-Buldān*, ed. S. Munajjid, Cairo 1957, 68 (glossary 11); J. von Karabacek, *Das arabische Papier*, Mittheilungen aus der Sammlung der Papyrus Erzherzog Rainer II–III, Vienna 1887, 163; and Frantz-Murphy, *Arabic Agricultural Leases,* 100. The older structure of receipts opening with phrases such as براة فلان or براة لفلان continued to be used in the third century AH in Egypt for other types of payments, e.g. the payment of the rent of buildings.

The technical use of the verb *addā* to denote the payment of taxes is likely to have been introduced by the central Abbasid administration in Iraq. It is possible that the motivation for this was its phonetic similarity to the Aramaic term for tax *maddattā*.[31] In some Syriac sources this term is used specifically for land tax.[32] In the second century AH/eighth century CE several Aramaic technical terms were introduced into Arabic by the legal scholars of Iraq by assigning their meaning to similar sounding Arabic words.[33] Another motivating factor may have been that this term is used in the Qurʾān with a similar meaning. Most of the innovations in technical terminology do not appear in the formularies of Arabic documents from Egypt before the third century AH/ninth century CE. We may interpret the appearance of the technical term *addā* in the Khurasan documents as evidence that such terms came into usage in Khurasan, and presumably the eastern provinces in general, earlier than in Egypt. Another case is the appearance of the technical legal term *adraka* 'to make a claim against' in document 25 of the Khurasan corpus, which is dated 145 AH/762 CE. This seems to be an imitative calque of the Aramaic term *adrekh*, which had the technical legal sense of 'to authorize [a creditor] to step [on the property pledged to him as surety by a debtor]'. The term was introduced in the second century AH/eighth century CE by Iraqi jurists in their legal formularies (*shurūṭ*) but is not attested in the Egyptian documents before the third century.[34]

The practice of attaching a bulla stamped with a seal, which is a feature of the Khurasan tax receipts, is found also in the Egyptian documents. Most of the seal impressions that have been preserved on the papyri contain the names of the issuers of the documents or pious phrases, which no doubt functioned as the motto of the issuers.[35] A five-pointed star symbol similar to the one that is found on the seal of some of the Khurasan documents is found in some seals preserved on Arabic papyri from Egypt.[36] Of particular interest is the occurrence of similar star-like scribal marks that are written by pen at the bottom of several extant Arabic papyri from Egypt, which are mostly of an administrative nature, e.g. P.Berl.Arab. 8 (an order of payment) P.Khalili 11 (a receipt) (see Figs 1 and 2).[37]

[31] Cf. R. Payne Smith, *Thesaurus Syriacus*, Oxford 1879–1901, 2011.

[32] Cf. M. Kmosko *et al.*, *Patrologia Syriaca*, Pars prima, tomus secundus, Paris 1907, 791, where Shemʿōn bar Sabbāʿe, a bishop of Ctesiphon in the fourth century AD, is said to have been required to collect a double poll tax (*ksaph rēša*) and land tax (*maddattā*). The same distinction is made in Syriac sources relating to the early Islamic period, e.g. J. B. Chabot, *Synodicon Orientale, ou Recueil de Synodes Nestoriens*, Paris 1902, 225.

[33] Cf. G. Khan, 'The pre-Islamic background of Muslim legal formularies', *ARAM* 6, 1994, 193–224.

[34] Khan, 'The pre-Islamic background', 214ff. Similar arabicizations of native Egyptian technical terms are found in the Arabic papyri from Egypt, e.g. *nawāʾib* 'extraordinary dues', which appears to be a continuation of the Demotic Egyptian term *nb*, via the Greek ναυβιον; cf. Frantz-Murphy, *Arabic Agricultural Leases*, 155–56.

[35] Frantz-Murphy, *Arabic Agricultural Leases*, 79; Rāġib, 'Sauf-conduits d'Égypte Omeyyade et Abbasside', nos VI, VIII.

[36] A. Grohmann, *Allgemeine Einführung in die Arabischen Papyri, nebst Grundzügen der Arabischen Diplomatik*, Corpus Papyrorum Raineri Archiducis Austriae, III, Series Arabica, Tomus I, Pars I., Wien 1924, 80.

[37] See also the references cited by Grohmann (*Allgemeine Einführung* 20, 87, 88) and P.Cair. Arab. I, 81.

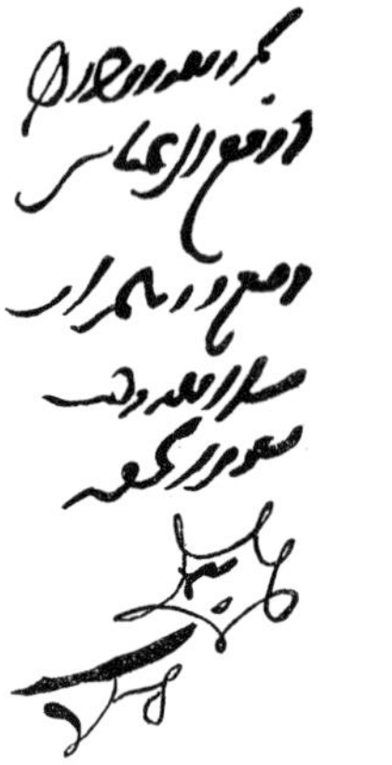

Fig. 1 (top) Astral seal, P. Khurasan 1. The Nasser D. Khalili Collection DOC 29 [AR 9]. © The Nour Foundation. Courtesy of the Khalili Family Trust.

Fig. 2 (bottom) Astral mark made by pen, P. Berl.Arab. 8.

It is reasonably clear that the term *kharāj* in the Khurasan documents refers to land tax rather than poll tax. The reference in several documents to 'the *kharāj* that you owe in the citadel of (the river of) Yaskin and Ghandar' may be interpreted as meaning that the tax was due on lands owned in those places.

Numerous extant papyri from early Islamic Egypt relate to taxation. The earliest of these are datable to the Umayyad period and include Greek, Arabic and bilingual Arabic-Greek documents.

Greek papyri from early Umayyad Egypt indicate that land and poll tax were collected together with a supplementary tax called δαπάνη ('maintenance'), which was levied to fund provisions and transport expenses for governors and officials, Arab troops and corvée workmen on government building projects. From the accounts preserved in the Greek papyri it is clear that many people who paid land tax did not pay poll tax. It seems that tax on cultivators was basically a land tax and that a poll tax was additionally levied only when there was sufficient ability to pay more. The Khurasan corpus of documents may reflect a similar situation or possibly may reflect the payment of land and poll taxes as a combined assessment.[38]

The tax assessment procedures that were authorized by ʿAmr ibn al-ʿĀṣ in Egypt at the beginning of the Umayyad period are described by Ibn ʿAbd al-Ḥakam.[39] His description agrees with what is attested in the papyri. First of all, the register called κατάγραφον for each village (χωρίον), which formed the smallest unit as a tax district, was prepared. The amount of poll tax payable by each man was assessed as well as his holdings in vineyards and arable land. Then tax demand notes (ἐντάγια) were sent to the villages. Separate demand notes were sent for the supplementary taxes.[40]

Arabic and bilingual papyri from the first century AH/seventh century CE (e.g. P.Cair. Arab. 60–163, P.Heid. III, 5, 6, a–l.) refer to *jizya*, which was a money tax, and *ḍarībat al-ṭaʿām*, which was a corn tax. The term in the Greek version of the bilinguals corresponding to *jizya* is δημόσια meaning 'public taxes'. This included both land and poll taxes. Supplementary taxes in Arabic documents from this period are referred to as *abwāb*. Already in papyri from the first century AH/seventh century CE there is evidence of individual rather than communal liability for payment of tax and this became the norm in the following centuries.[41]

---

[38] It has been proposed by some scholars that the agricultural population of Iraq in the early Islamic period paid both taxes as a combined assessment; cf. M. G. Morony, *Iraq after the Muslim Conquest*, Princeton 1984, 109.

[39] Ibn ʿAbd al-Ḥakam, *Futūḥ Miṣr wa-ʾAkhbāruhā*, ed. C. C. Torrey, New Haven 1922, 152–53; cf. Maqrīzī, *Kitāb al-Mawāʿiẓ w-al-ʾIʿtibār bi-Dhikr al-Khiṭaṭ w-al-ʾĀthār*, Būlāq 1270/1853, i, 77.

[40] K. Morimoto, *The Fiscal Administration of Egypt in the Early Islamic Period*, Kyoto 1981, 81–94.

[41] Frantz-Murphy, *Arabic Agricultural Leases*, 105ff.

In the second half of the Umayyad period in Egypt, after 100 AH/718 CE, poll tax is referred to in the Arabic papyri as *jizyat raʾs* and land tax as *jizyat al-arḍ*. The expression *jizyat al-arḍ* for land tax seems to be unique to Egyptian sources from the late Umayyad period.[42]

The *kharāj* tax is not mentioned in the Arabic papyri from Egypt until the Abbasid period. The earliest reference to this tax in the Egyptian papyri that I am aware of is found in the unpublished papyrus A 241 from the collection of the Oriental Institute, St. Petersburg, which alludes to the *kharāj* of the year 150 AH/767 CE.[43] The earliest reference to *kharāj* in a published Arabic papyrus from Egypt is in David-Weill 'Papyrus arabes du Louvre II', no. 16,[44] which is dated Shawwāl 156 AH/773 CE. The term originated in the adminstrative nomenclature of the eastern provinces and was introduced into Egypt by Abbasid officials. In fact, documents 1–6 from the Khurasan corpus, which refer to *kharāj*, predate 150 AH/767 CE and so these are now the earliest documentary records of *kharāj*. The first references to the term in the Egypt papyri fall within the reign of the caliph Manṣūr, who attempted to consolidate Abbasid control of the provinces by a policy of fiscal unification.[45]

The term *kharāj* came into Arabic from the substrate languages of the eastern provinces. Close parallels are found in Aramaic and Middle Persian from the first half of the first millennium CE, e.g. Pahlavi *harg*, Manichaean Middle Persian *harāg*[46] and Babylonian Talmudic Aramaic *krāgā*.[47] These are all derived from the earlier Aramaic form *halākh*, which is attested in Biblical Aramaic (Ezra 4:13, 20, 7:24). This, in turn, is related to the Akkadian term *ilku*, which denoted a kind of state service or tax paid in lieu (< *alāku* 'to go'). The /*l*/ of the Aramaic form shifted to /*r*/ when the word entered Old Iranian, which did not have /*l*/ in its sound system. The initial /*h*/ of the Middle Persian forms was strengthened to a /*kh*/ by a regular process,[48] which resulted in the Aramaic form *krāgā* and the Arabic form *kharāj*. The Babylonian Talmudic Aramaic form *krāgā* denoted 'poll tax' rather than 'land tax', which suggests that the Arabic term came directly from Middle Persian rather than through Aramaic.[49]

Another example of the introduction of Abbasid administrative nomenclature into Egypt is the term *jāliya* (pl. *jawālī*) for 'poll tax'. This appears in Arabic papyri from the third

---

[42] Morimoto, *Fiscal Administration*, 136.

[43] A plate of this papyrus is published in O. F. Akimushkine et al., *De Bagdad à Ispahan: Manuscrits Islamiques de la Filiale de Saint-Pétersbourg de l'Institut d'Études Orientales, Académie des Sciences de Russie*, Paris 1994, Fondation ARCH [Catalogue of an exhibition held at la Musée due Petit Palais, 14 October 1994 – 8 January 1995], 93.

[44] J. David-Weill, 'Papyrus arabes du Louvre II', *Journal of the Economic and Social History of the Orient* 14, 1971, no. 16.

[45] Morimoto, *The Fiscal Administration*, 150–51.

[46] D. N. MacKenzie, *A Concise Pahlavi Dictionary*, Oxford 1971, 43,

[47] M. Sokoloff, *A Dictionary of Jewish Babylonian Aramaic of the Talmudic and Geonic periods*, Ramat-Gan 2002, 599.

[48] W. Henning, 'Arabisch ḫarāǧ', *Orientalia* 4, 1935, 291–93

[49] This was suggested already by Th. Nöldeke, *Geschichte der Perser und Araber zur Zeit der Sassaniden aus der Arabischen Chronik des Ṭabarī*, Leiden 1879, 241, n.1. An alternative etymology has been proposed that derives Arabic *kharāj* from Greek χορηγία '(military) supplies' via Aramaic (A. K. S. Lambton, 'kharādj', *EI*^{2},).

century AH/ninth CE onwards and replaces the late Umayyad term *jizyat al-raʾs*. According to the Ḥanafite jurist Abū Yūsuf (d. AH 182/798 CE), in late second century under the caliph Rashīd, the term *jāliya* had become the administrative term for poll tax in Iraq.[50] The term *jizya*, however, continued to be used in Islamic law.[51] The introduction of the term *jāliya* postdates the corpus of documents from Khurasan. Although the Arabic documents from Khurasan do not mention *jizya*, it can be identified in the words γαζιτο and βαριτο that occur in the parallel corpus of Bactrian documents (Sims-Williams 2000 W, 7) and refer to taxes paid to the Muslim authorities. The term γαζιτο, which seems to represent the pronunciation *gazit*, is related to New Persian *gazīt* and Pahlavi *gazīdag*.[52] These Persian forms and the Arabic term *jizya* appear to be derived ulimately from an Aramaic term *gzīṯā*.[53] The term βαριτο, most likely pronounced *barit*, appears to represent Arabic *barāʾa*. If γαζιτο refers to poll tax, then βαριτο would be expected to be referring to the payment of land tax. The acquisition of the certificate of quittance (*barāʾa*) from the obligation to pay the tax seems here to be used metonymically to denote the tax itself. The two terms in the Bactrian document occur together in a collocation: 'A large *gazit* and *barit* have been assessed to be given by me'.[54] This may reflect the payment of both taxes as a combined assessment, which could explain why there is no mention of *jizya* in our Arabic documents.

If both the terms *kharāj* and *jizya* came into Arabic from an Iranian or Aramaic substrate, it is curious that the term *jizya* appears in the papyri from Egypt in the Umayyad period but *kharāj* appears only in the Abbasid period. Both terms, in fact, occur in the Qurʾān, as well as the variant form *kharj* (cf. Pahlavi *harg*). It seems that the terms had entered Arabic before the Islamic conquests. The immediate cause for the appearance of the term *kharāj* in the Abbasid period in the Egyptian papyri was, therefore, the adoption of the term into official administrative usage at this period rather than its adoption into the Arabic language. In the Umayyad period *jizya* was the official term used for both poll tax and land tax. Another early term for specifically land tax was *ṭasq*, a loan from Aramaic *ṭasqā*, which in turn was ultimately derived from Greek τάξις.[55] The Aramaic term *ṭasqā* is found in the Babylonian Talmud, which would be a reflection of Sasanian administrative terminology.[56] The term was adopted into Arabic in the early Islamic period, but by the Abbasid period *kharāj* had become the official term for land tax. The term *ṭasq* is still found in legal and

50 Abū Yūsuf, *Kitāb al-Kharāj*. ed. Cairo 1352/1933., E. Fagnan (tr.), *Le Livre de l'Impôt Foncier*, Paris 1921, iv , 49.

51 Morimoto, *Fiscal Administration*, 176.

52 MacKenzie, *A Concise Pahlavi Dictionary*, 36.

53 Nöldeke, *Geschichte der Perser und Araber*, 241; A. Jeffery, *The Foreign Vocabulary of the Qurʾān*, Baroda 1938, 101–102; C. E. Bosworth, "Abū ʿAbdallāh al-Khwārazmī on the technical terms of the secretary's art. A contribution to the administrative history of medieval Islam', *Journal of the Economic and Social History of the Orient* 12, 1969, 132; A. Asbaghi, *Persische Lehnwörter im Arabischen*, Wiesbaden 1988, 87.

54 Sims-Williams, *Bactrian Documents I*, W.

55 F. Løkkegaard, *Islamic Taxation in the Classic Period, with Special Reference to the Circumstances in Iraq*, Copenhagen 1950, 125–26.

56 A. Ben Shemesh, *Taxation in Islam. I. Yaḥyā ben Ādam's Kitāb al-Kharāj*, Leiden 1958, 115.

literary sources after its replacement by the term *kharāj* in official administrative usage.[57] This may be compared with the fate of the term *jizya*, which, as described above, was replaced by the term *jāliya* in official Abbasid usage at the end of the second century AH/eighth century CE, but continued to be used in legal and literary sources.

The predominance of the term *kharāj* in the east and in Egypt in the Abbasid period was also associated with developments in the legal status of this tax. According to early Islamic legal theory, *kharāj* was a tax paid by non-Muslims on land that was conquered 'by treaty' (*ṣulḥan*).[58] By the Abbasid period, however, all landholders, including Muslims, became liable to pay the *kharāj*. The payment of *kharāj* by Muslims came to be justified by the argument that the land belonged to 'God' (i.e. the caliph and the state) and that all, whether Muslims or not, who enjoyed its usufruct were obliged to pay it.[59] In the papyri from Egypt the term *kharāj* came to be used with a more generic sense, in that it denoted all taxes that were assessed in money, including poll tax.[60]

The introduction into Egypt of Abbasid administrative practice that had been developed in the eastern provinces coincided with the advent of an increasing number of high level Persian administrators. Several Persian directors of *kharāj* in Egypt held relatively long tenure. Members of some Persian administrative families served for many generations in Egypt. In the third century AH/ninth century CE Persians were increasingly appointed as district and higher level governors in Egypt, offices that previously been given generally to members of the caliph's family. In 242 AH/857 CE, in fact, a policy was introduced to exclude Arabs systematically from governorships.[61] The presence of these Persian officials was one of the factors that fomented endemic tax revolts in the local population in the Abbasid period.[62]

In addition to adoption of Abbasid terms for taxes, such as *kharāj* and *jāliya*, the Persianized administration brought with it an Iranian term for a tax collection official, viz. *jahbadh* 'assayer, cashier'. This term, which is first attested in 249 AH/863 CE (PAP 14) in the Fayyūm, replaced the Arabicized Greek term *qusṭāl*.[63]

We have seen that a shift occurs in the formulaic structure and terminology of documents written in Egypt between the second and third centuries AH. In the case of legal and administrative documents the Khurasan corpus now shows us that many of the innovations began in the eastern provinces and were transferred subsequently to Egypt. Concomitant with the shift in formulae in the third century in Egypt there was a shift in the style of script used in all types of documents. In the third century most documents begin to be written in a hand that is far more cursive than that of the first two centuries AH. The radical nature of this shift makes it unlikely that it developed in Egypt by natural evolution, but rather was introduced from outside. Evidence for this is now provided by the Khurasan

---

57 Løkkegaard, *Islamic Taxation*, 126; Bosworth, "Abū ʿAbdallāh al-Khwārazm', 133.

58 Cf. Qudāma ibn Jaʿfar, *Kitāb al-Kharāj*, in Ben Shemesh, *Taxation in Islam*, 28.

59 For the complicated issue of the legal status of *kharāj* and its historical development see Løkkegaard, *Islamic Taxation*, 72ff., and A. K. S. Lambton, 'kharādj,' *EI*².

60 Frantz-Murphy, *Arabic Agricultural Leases*, 141–42.

61 Al-Kindī, *Kitāb al-Wulāt wa-Kitāb al-Quḍāt*, ed. R. Guest, Leiden 1912, 202.

62 Frantz-Murphy, *Arabic Agricultural Leases*, 81–83.

63 Frantz-Murphy, *Arabic Agricultural Leases*, 81.

document corpus from the second century. Many of the documents in this corpus, especially those of an administrative nature, exhibit a script that is more cursive than the script of Arabic papyri from Egypt datable to the same period (see Fig. 3). It corresponds more closely to the cursive type of script that is characteristic of the papyri from the third century AH/ninth century onwards. It is probable, therefore, that the appearance of a more cursive script style in the papyri from the third century AH/ninth century was another aspect of eastern administrative practice that was introduced into Egypt by officials trained in the eastern provinces. This, therefore, would explain the shift in documentary script type in the Arabic papyri.

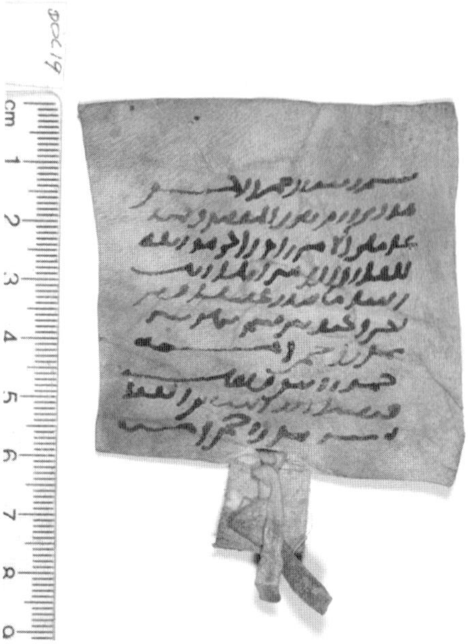

Fig. 3. P.Khurasan 22, Tax receipt, 158 AH/774 CE. The Nasser D. Khalili Collection DOC 19 [AR 1]. © The Nour Foundation. Courtesy of the Khalili Family Trust.

As we have seen, many of the officials who drew up the administrative documents in the Khurasan corpus were of Iranian background. Terms used in the nomenclature of these officials such as *al-Iṣbahbadh* (< Sasanian *spāhbed*) suggest that some of these were members of Iranian administrative families who could have been in state service over several generations. What may be of crucial significance is that some Iranian administrators in the early Abbasid period were still writing administrative documents in Pahlavi. We read in sources such as Jahshiyārī's *Kitāb al-Wuzarāʾ wa-l-Kuttāb* that Arabic was substituted for Persian in the administration of the eastern territories under Ḥajjāj in 78 AH/697 CE. Recently, however, various Pahlavi administrative documents have been discovered that are datable to as late as the second century AH/eighth century CE,[64] suggesting that Pahlavi survived in administrative documents after 78 AH/697 CE. The most conspicuous feature of the script of the Pahlavi administrative documents is its advanced degree of cursiveness, which resulted in many of the Pahlavi letter shapes becoming similar in appearance. Angles are transformed into curves and curves into straight strokes.[65] For an example of a Pahlavi

[64] P. Gignoux, 'Une nouvelle collection de documents en pehlevi cursif du début de septième siècle de notre ère', in *Comptes Rendus de l'Académie des Inscriptions et Belles-Lettres*, 1991, 783–800; idem, 'Six documents Pehlevis sur cuir du California Museum of Ancient Art', *Bulletin of the Asia Institute* 10, 1996, 63–72; G. Azarpay, 'Rare Pahlavi texts now at Bancroft', *Bancroftiana, Newsletter of the Friends of the Bancroft Library* 123, 2003.

[65] O. Hansen, *Die mittelpersischen Papyri der Papyrussammlung der Staatlichen Museen zu Berlin*, Berlin 1938; J. de Menasce, 'Recherches de papyrologie pehlevie', *Journal Asiatique* 241, 1953, 185–96; idem, *Ostraca and Papyri.* Corpus Inscriptionum Iranicarum Part III. Pahlavi Inscriptions. Volume IV-V. Ostraca and Papyri, London 1957; D. Weber, 'Einige Beobachtungen an Pahlavi Papyri', *Acta Orientalia* 35, 1973, 83–88; idem, 'Die Pehlevifragmente der Papyrussammlung der Österreichischen

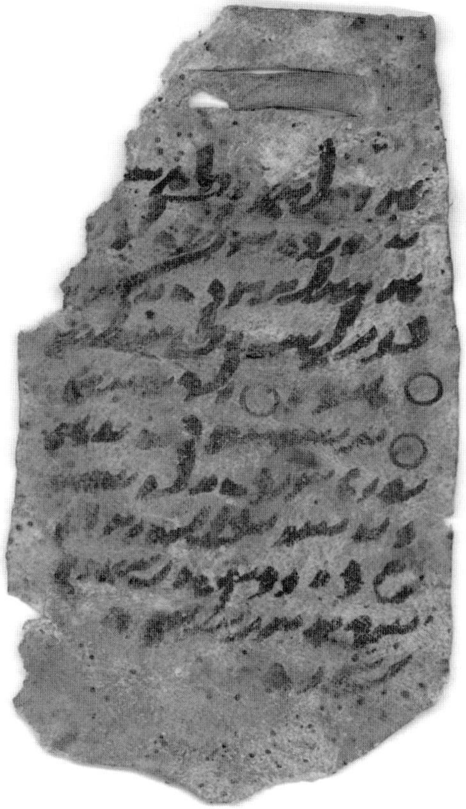

Fig. 4. Pahlavi document from the Islamic period. The Nasser D. Khalili collection DOC 129. © The Nour Foundation. Courtesy of the Khalili Family Trust.

document discovered in Afghanistan (see Fig. 4). One possible explanation for the development of similar cursive tendencies in the Arabic documentary script of the eastern Islamic empire, therefore, could be that they were introduced through the influence of a Pahlavi 'substrate' by administrators who were trained in the Pahlavi administrative tradition. It should be noted that Pahlavi was not the local Iranian language of Khurasan in the early Abbasid period. The extant corpus of Bactrian documents indicate that the local population had a tradition of writing documents in the local Bactrian language. Administrators trained in Pahlavi are likely, therefore, to have come from Iran, nearer the Abbasid, and formerly Sasanian, administrative centre. This is, indeed, indicated by the form of some of the Iranian elements in the names of the administrators in the Arabic documents from Khurasan. As remarked above, the term *al-Iṣbahbadh*, for example, is derived from Middle Persian *spāhbed* 'army-commander' and differs from the local Bactrian form *spālbid*.[66] The seals with astral imagery used by these administrators in the Arabic documents are also not a local Bactrian tradition but rather are characteristic of iconography originating in the Sasanian heartlands.[67]

We see, therefore, that a philological comparison of the Arabic documents of the newly discovered Khurasan corpus with the extant early Arabic documentary material from Egypt shows that many features of documentary practice were introduced into Egypt in the

Nationalbibliothek in Wien', *Papyrus Erzherzog Rainer* (P. Rainer Cent.). *Festschrift zum 100-jährigen Bestehen der Papyrussammlung der österreichischen Nationalbibliothek*, Wien 1983, 215–28; idem,'Pahlavi, Papyri und Ostraca: Stand der Forschung', *Middle Iranian Studies, Proceedings of the International Symposium organized by the Katholieke Universiteit Leuven 1982*, Leuven 1984, 25–43; idem, *Ostraca, Papyri und Pergamente*. Corpus Inscriptionum Iranicarum. Part III. Pahlavi Inscriptions. Volume IV–V. Ostraca and Papyri, London 1992; Gignoux, 'Six documents Pehlevis'.

[66] Sims-Williams, *New Light on Ancient Afghanistan*, 5.

[67] For the seals with astral images in the documents see G. Khan, *Arabic Documents from Early Islamic Khurasan*, London 2007, 86–88. I am grateful to Judith Lerner for drawing my attention to the background of these seals.

Abbasid period from the East. It is not clear how far West these features spread, due to a lack of comparable documentary material from the Islamic West datable to this period. It is worth noting, however, that the 'eastern' innovation in Arabic script which had a radical impact on the documentary hand in Egypt did not have such a thorough-going influence on the Arabic script used in the Maghrib, which retained many of the features of the early script down to modern times. Furthermore, a number of archaic Arabic legal formulae can be found in medieval Arabic documents from Andalus long after they had been replaced by innovations made by the eastern jurists in documents written in Egypt.[68]

Abbreviations

EI^2	*Encylopaedia of Islam*, second edition.
P.Berl.Arab.	*Ägyptische Urkunden aus den Königlichen Museen zu Berlin*, Arabische Urkunden, ed. L. Abel, Berlin, 1896–1900.
P.Cair.Arab.	Grohmann, A., *Arabic Papyri from the Egyptian Library*, 6 vols., Cairo, 1934–1974.
P.Heid III	C. H. Becker, *Veröffentlichungen aus der Heidelberger Papyrus-Sammlung III, Papyri Schott-Reinhardt I*. Heidelberg, 1906.
P.Khalili	Khan, G., Arabic Papyri, Selected Material from the Khalili Collection, Oxford, 1992.

[68] G. Khan, *Arabic Legal and Administrative Documents in the Cambridge Genizah Collections*, Cambridge 1993, 43–44.

7

The Late Sasanian Army

James Howard-Johnston

I. SASANIAN IRAN AND ITS NEIGHBOURS

Sasanian Iran was a continental power (Fig. 1). Eurasia stretched east, west, north and south-east far beyond the horizons of diplomatic vision. The new empire created by Ardashīr (224–239/40) in a few decades of dynamic growth at the beginning of the third century was a massive, resource-rich political entity. The highlands of Iran, a natural nursery of fighting men, were clamped together with the fertile lowlands of Mesopotamia and Khuzistan. The taxes of the one funded the martial efforts of the other, as long as the ruling dynasty maintained good order on earth and secured the favour of Ohrmazd and the Holy Immortals. But this re-creation, within the remembered past, of something akin to the Iran which had championed the cause of good on earth against the forces of evil, with extraordinary fluctuations of fortune, in a remote legendary past, was as vulnerable to attack as its mythic precursor. Fear as much as ambition or emulation of past achievements drove Ardashīr's successors into wars of expansion both west and east in the third, fourth and fifth centuries. Sasanian Iran, unlike its real, historical predecessor, the empire of the Achaemenids, was aware of its exposed, central position in a potentially hostile world.[1]

In the far south-east, where the Zagros mountains subside and spread out in the desiccated, wind-scarred landscape of Makran and Sakastan, in what are now the most refractory of all *terres d'insolence*, in north-west Pakistan and south-west Afghanistan, the tribesmen, then as now, were hard, if not impossible, to manage, save by drawing them into armed activity elsewhere on behalf of a higher, imperial power. It was a region of perennial instability, in contrast to the relatively urbanised worlds of Bactria and Sogdiana to the north. The latter rose at the expense of the former in Late Antiquity, its cities growing in size and the whole region beyond the Oxus developing into the economic motor of the continent. Here the threat to Iran was more insidious than in the south-east. The

[1] K. Schippmann, *Grunzüge der Geschichte des sasanidischen Reiches*, Darmstadt 1990; M. Boyce, *Zoroastrians: Their Religious Beliefs and Practices*, London 2001, 17–144; E. Yarshater, 'Iranian National History', *Cambridge History of Iran*, iii.1, Cambridge 1983, 359–477.

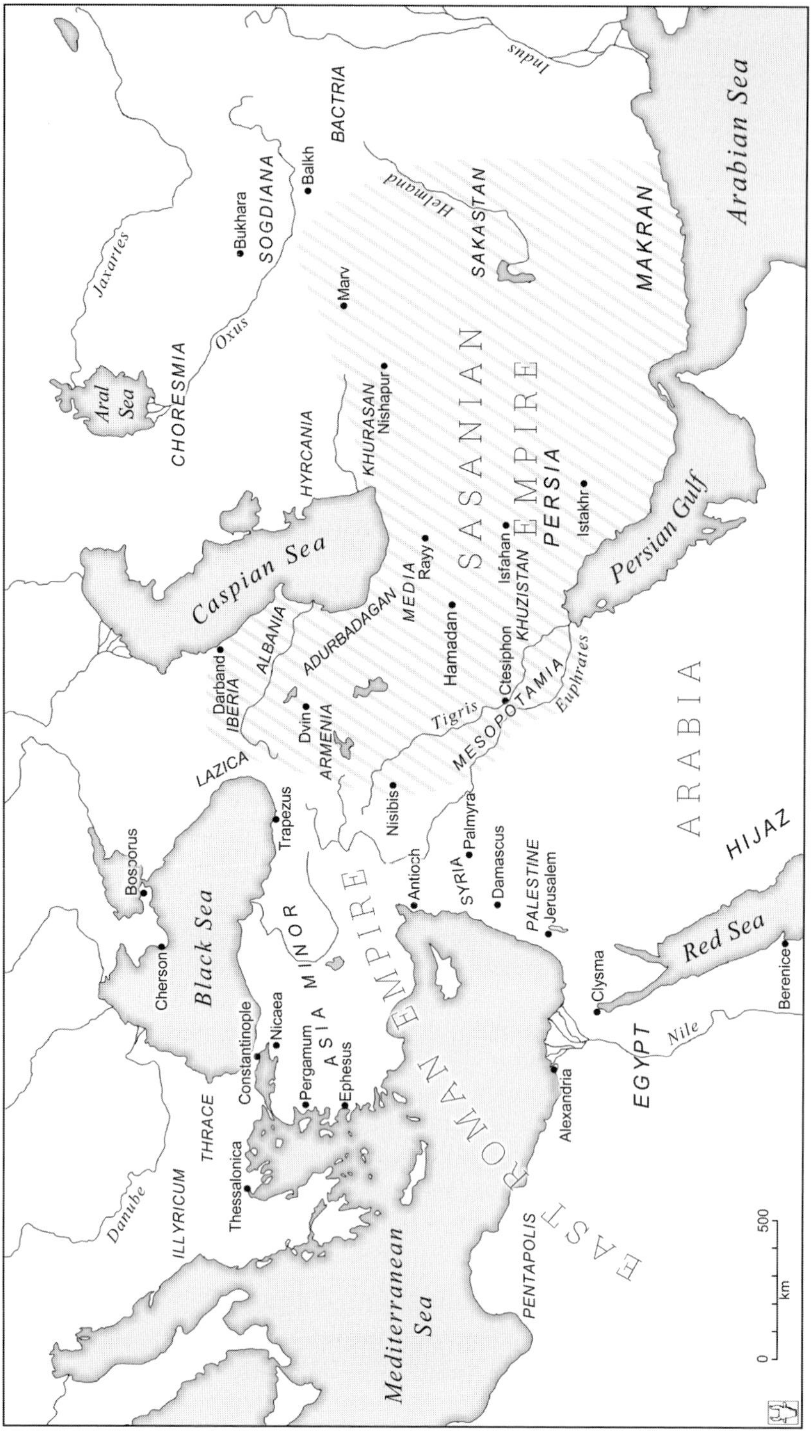

Fig. 1. The Sasanian Empire and its Neighbour

late Boris Marshak, who spent much of his life at work in Sogdiana, was inclined to look down on Sasanian Iran as a mere military enterprise, geared to holding and exploiting Mesopotamia, whereas the cities of Sogdiana (equally Iranian in culture) and its colonial territories to the east generated their own wealth, both by investing in large-scale irrigation schemes within their own territories and by engaging in highly profitable long-distance transcontinental trade. In aggregate, their agrarian resources more than matched those of highland Iran.[2] Compared to their governing elites, highly cultivated, at once aristocratic landowners and mercantile entrepreneurs, the provincial landowners of Sasanian Iran who made up the mass of middle-ranking *āzādān* were backwoodsmen, leading lives dominated by country pursuits, feasts, heroic stories retailed by minstrels and service in the armed forces.[3]

The steppes which enveloped the urbanised plains of Sogdiana and lapped against the formidable mountain ranges fronting the Tibetan plateau to the east generated far greater dangers. A watershed was crossed, both literally and figuratively, in the middle years of the fourth century, when the Huns/Xiongnu/Chionitae were driven west after occupying northern China for some 40 years. They were the first East Asian, Turkic nomads to cross the Hindu Kush-Altai-Tien Shan divide and to venture into the more hospitable west Eurasian steppes. They brought with them a governmental capability and statecraft considerably more advanced than that of the Indo-European nomadic peoples who had hitherto dominated the outer world around Iran. For they had to build up political institutions (the layered organisation of an imperial confederacy) which could generate (and manage) armed forces on the same scale as those fielded by successive great powers in China. Equally they had to match China diplomatically, devising (and implementing) policies appropriate for periods both of nomadic and of Chinese ascendancy (inner and outer frontier strategies). On the ideological plane too, they had emancipated themselves, developing an imperial ideology of their own, striving to create on earth a limitless realm reflecting that of the supreme god, Tängri, in heaven.[4]

It was no wonder then that Shāpūr II (309–79) broke off from his western, Roman war and concentrated on containing the Chionitae when they first entered the Sasanian field of diplomatic vision in the 350s, or that Bahrām V (421–439) made his name as a great champion of Iran campaigning in the north-east. The steppes had been transformed into an outer world as menacing as the legendary Turan which confronted Iran in the heroic

---

[2] E. de la Vaissière, *Sogdian Traders: A History*, Leiden 2005, 97–117, 159–84.

[3] The world of provincial landowners is hidden from us, but something of their ethos – conservative, prizing order very highly, devoted to the crown – and tastes – for hunting, feasting and minstrel lays – may be retrieved from such Sasanian texts as have survived (above all *The Letter of Tansar*, tr. M. Boyce [Rome, 1968]) or have contributed material to later Arab works. Cf. A. Christensen, *L'Iran sous les Sassanides*, Copenhagen 1944, 57–59, 62–69.

[4] De la Vaissière, *Sogdian Traders*, 43–46, 97–103; T. J. Barfield, *The Perilous Frontier: Nomadic Empires and China*, Oxford 1989, 1–103; X. de Planhol, *Les fondements géographiques de l'histoire de l'Islam*, Paris 1968, 14–33; J. Howard-Johnston, 'Huns in the North', *Norwegian Archaeological Review* 40, 2007, 199–202.

tales of the Iranian national epic.[5] The danger was amplified by the alliance which first Huns, then Hephthalites, finally Turks struck with the cities of Sogdiana. It was mutually beneficial. Confident of security, Sogdian elites could invest in large capital projects. The irrigation schemes which were introduced and which greatly increased agricultural production were, in effect, developed under nomad sponsorship. The same was true in the commercial sphere, where the ramified connections of nomads and their military muscle both extended and secured trade-routes for Sogdian merchants. The nomad world reached an apogee of power and wealth at the end of antiquity, when Turks and Sogdians engaged in what soon became a joint imperial venture and were able to play off the great powers against each other at both ends of Eurasia.[6]

The Huns did not halt on the Inner Asian frontier of Iran, but, over the following two–three generations, moved westward, until, by the 420s, their political centre came to rest in the Carpathian basin.[7] At all stages of their apparently ordered migration, they were able to project their power to great distances. So they were able to reach round the Köpet Dagh, the mountain range which shields the Iranian plateau on the north-east, and around the Caspian Sea, so as to bring the north Caucasus steppes under their control. This meant that Iran could be attacked by a powerful nomadic adversary at its vulnerable spots in the north: (1) the steppes of Hyrcania (modern Gurgan) to the east of the southern Caspian coastlands, (2) the easy passage around the east end of the Caucasus, known as the Caspian Gates, and (3) the Dariel Pass over the high Caucasus. It was a threat which did not diminish with the demise of the Hun Empire in eastern Europe and Ukraine. For the Huns and their subordinated nomad peoples did not dissolve into thin air. All manner of Turkic/Hunnic peoples continued to dominate sub-regions of the former Hun Empire – Bulgars in the Carpathian region, Sabirs in the north Caucasus, Kidarites east of the Caspian. In due course they were incorporated into later, higher-level nomad states, led by Hephthalites, Avars and Turks. Thus to the age-old problems generated by the Caucasus, nursery of a multitude of highland peoples, virtually impossible to pacify, many of whom have survived into the twenty-first century, was added the ever-present danger of swift nomadic thrusts into the Sasanian north-west and the Caspian lowlands.[8]

The most formidable of all Iran's foreign adversaries in terms of resources and ideological drive were the Romans in the west. The Roman Empire had, of course, been the pre-eminent power in western Eurasia for at least two and a half centuries before the rise of the Sasanians. The Parthians who had taken a great swathe of sedentary Eurasia from the

---

[5] Chionitae: Ammianus Marcellinus, ed. C. U. Clark, tr. J. C. Rolfe, 3 vols., Cambridge, Mass. 1935–9, xiv.3.1, xvi.9.3–4. Bahrām V: C. E. Bosworth (tr.), *The History of al-Ṭabarī, V. The Sasanids, the Byzantines, the Lakhmids and Yemen*, Albany 1999, 94–99; J. Mohl (tr.), *Le livre des rois par Abou'lkasim Firdousi*, v, Paris 1977, 539–551.

[6] De la Vaissière, *Sogdian Traders*, 107–12, 199–215, 227–49; Barfield, *Perilous Frontier*, 131–38; M. Whitby, *The Emperor Maurice and His Historian: Theophylact Simocatta on Persian and Balkan Warfare*, Oxford 1988, 218; R. C. Blockley (ed. and tr.), *The History of Menander the Guardsman*, Liverpool 1985, fr.10, 13.5.

[7] P. Heather, *The Fall of the Roman Empire: A New History*, London 2005, 146–54, 202–205.

[8] P. B. Golden, *An Introduction to the History of the Turkic Peoples: Ethnogenesis and State Formation in Medieval and Early Modern Eurasia and the Middle East*, Turcologica 9, Wiesbaden 1992, 79–154.

Seleucids, laid no claim to parity of status. While they may have given occasional shocks – the worst being victory over Crassus's army at Carrhae – the Parthians were generally no match for the Romans in the field. Roman expeditionary forces were able to penetrate at will into the heartlands of Mesopotamia. Roman emperors exercised virtually unchallenged suzerainty over much of Transcaucasia. So it was hard for Romans to reconcile themselves to the existence of an equipollent eastern neighbour, once loose Parthian rule was replaced by a more managerial Sasanian regime. It took a century and a half of conflict before they recognised, in a treaty signed probably in 387, that the Persians were partners in the direction of human affairs, that there were, in effect, two centres to the *oikoumene*, the civilised world, one around the Mediterranean, the other in Mesopotamia and Iran.[9]

Achievement of parity with the Romans was an extraordinary Sasanian feat, given the superior resources upon which the Romans could draw, their centralised and tiered system of provincial administration, and, above all, a military tradition going back many centuries. The Mediterranean lands taken on their own almost certainly matched the whole Sasanian Empire in terms of agricultural output. With the diffusion of new technologies – particularly in mining, building and irrigation, but also in industrial processes – non-agricultural production had risen and urbanisation had advanced further than ever before. Manufacturing and commerce may well have contributed a larger proportion of Roman GDP than is commonly supposed, especially if allowance is made for a bias against trade in the reporting of Roman sources. If so, it is not simply the agricultural output of the northern hinterlands of the Mediterranean provinces, in the Balkans and the west, which increased Roman resources well above those of Iran, but also the aggregate industrial output of the Near Eastern provinces (from Egypt to northern Syria) and the rest of the empire.[10]

Government as well as commercial exchange was facilitated by the presence at the heart of the empire of a relatively benign sea. Its fiscal system was efficient at hoovering up resources from the localities and exercised reasonably effective oversight over spending. The efficacy of government is perhaps best illustrated, in the reign of Justinian (527–565), by the building of the cathedral of St. Sophia in Constantinople, a mere five and a half years elapsing between initial design and completion of the project.[11] Of the Roman military tradition, little need be said. It was Roman legions which had conquered the Mediterranean *oikoumene*. The smaller units, infantry and cavalry, which had succeeded the legions,

---

[9] E. W. Gray, 'The Roman Eastern *Limes* from Constantine to Justinian – Perspectives and Problems', *Proceedings of the African Classical Associations* 12, 1973, 24–40; Whitby, *Emperor Maurice*, 202–205; R. C. Blockley, *East Roman Foreign Policy: Formation and Conduct from Diocletian to Anastasius*, Leeds 1992, 5–52; M. P. Canepa, *The Two Eyes of the Earth: Art and Ritual of Kingship Between Rome and Sasanian Iran*, Transformation of Classical Heritage 45, Berkeley 2009.

[10] J. Howard-Johnston, 'The Two Great Powers in Late Antiquity: A Comparison', in A. Cameron, ed., *The Byzantine and Early Islamic Near East*, III *States, Resources and Armies*, Princeton 1995, 157–226, repr. in J. Howard-Johnston, *East Rome, Sasanian Persia and the End of Antiquity*, Aldershot 2006, i; A. I. Wilson, 'Machines in Greek and Roman Technology', 'Large-Scale Manufacturing, Standardization and Trade', in J. P. Oleson, ed., *Oxford Handbook of Engineering and Technology in the Classical World*, Oxford 2008, 337–66, 393–417.

[11] R. J. Mainstone, *Hagia Sophia: Architecture, Structure and Liturgy of Justinian's Great Church*, London 1988.

supplemented by highlanders recruited from within the empire and foreign troops, chiefly German, recruited from without or from authorised settlements within, amounted to 500,000 men or so in the fourth century, falling to 300–350,000 in the sixth. The armies fielded were formidable fighting forces, trained to exploit to the full the paved roads and systems of deep forward defence which, in aggregate, formed prepared arenas of combat for engaging the enemy. The Sasanians had to be ready to confront forces 25–30,000 men strong in normal circumstances, which might on occasion rise considerably higher, as in 363 when Julian (361–363) launched his offensive on the Mesopotamian front with some 80,000 men and in 504 when five armies, perhaps as many as 100,000 men in total, conducted coordinated operations in and around the upper Tigris basin.[12]

Finally, in the south-west, Arabia abutted on to Mesopotamia. Historians should always beware of presumptions induced by hindsight. The unification of the tribes, nomadic and sedentary, of the peninsula and their subsequent outrush into the fertile lands arching over the desert in the seventh century, could not have been foreseen. For the ultimate cause was quite unpredictable, as all new ideas are. The whole dramatic sequence of events originated in the sudden intrusion of a new notion – in this case, of a single, all-knowing, all-powerful, interventionist deity who governed the affairs of man and nature and before whom, at the end of time, *which was imminent*, every individual human being would be brought, alone and quailing, for judgement. Nor should much be made of the large nomadic element among the Bedouin. For the nomads of the hot southern deserts were not organised into large, cohesive tribes on the pattern of those of the northern steppes, nor, outside Yemen, had they developed notions of rule beyond that of the *shaykh*, whose authority was personal and contestable. Nonetheless, Arabia stretched away to the south, a large region of competing kin-based groups, outside the control of the two great northern sedentary powers but susceptible to assertions of authority by the kingdom of Himyar in Yemen. It was yet another *terre d'insolence*, though of very different character to the Caucasus and the far south-east. There was a perennial danger of Arab predation, given the tempting proximity of the rich, highly urbanised lands of Mesopotamia. There had also been a glint of a yet greater threat, in the 260s and 270s, when a regional, north Arabian union led by Palmyra had been able to mobilise substantial military resources and inflict defeats on both Persians and Romans.[13]

[12] H. Elton, 'Military Forces' and P. Rance, 'Battle', in P. Sabin *et al.* (eds.), *Cambridge History of Greek and Roman Warfare*, II *Rome from the Late Republic to the Late Empire* Cambridge 2007, 270–309, 342–78; R. Tomlin, 'A.H.M. Jones and the Army of the Fourth Century', in D. Gwynn, ed., *A.H.M. Jones and the Later Roman Empire*, Leiden 2008, 143–65; J. Haldon, *Warfare and Society in the Byzantine World, 565–1204*, London 1999, 99–101; Howard-Johnston, 'Two Great Powers', 165–69.

[13] De Planhol, *Fondements géographiques*, 11-33; R. Hoyland, *Arabia and the Arabs from the Bronze Age to the Coming of Islam*, London 2001; F. Millar, *The Roman Near East 31 BC–AD 337*, Cambridge, Mass. 1993, 167–73; M. Rodinson, *Mohammed*, Harmondsworth 1971; F. M. Donner, *The Early Islamic Conquests*, Princeton 1981.

II. PRINCIPAL COMPONENTS OF THE SASANIAN EMPIRE

The Sasanian Empire enjoyed the advantages and suffered from the disadvantages of a central position. Troops could be shifted relatively swiftly over secure land routes between frontiers. Diplomats too could take advantage of interior lines to stir up trouble or to cultivate allies at times and in regions of their own choosing. In this respect, it was the precursor of several great powers which made the most of their central positions – the Carolingian empire, Byzantium in the age of revival (ninth–eleventh centuries), the Moghuls in the Ganges plain, France in the seventeenth and eighteenth centuries, Germany after unification, and, in the twentieth century, the Soviet Union. But centrality entailed encirclement. There were opportunities for expansion and the projection of power on all sides, but equally danger might materialise from any quarter. So beneath the imperialism of central powers there might well lurk a deep anxiety. In the case of Iran, the fearfulness was openly expressed in tales of the legendary past which took their penultimate form in the Sasanian period. In what became the national epic, Iran was beset from without. Good was unceasingly beleaguered by evil. Iran only survived through the actions of a few great national heroes. Sasanian claims to a divinely sanctioned, dominating role in earthly affairs can be viewed, at least in part, as diplomatic bluster, which masked an enduring insecurity. Indeed insecurity, perhaps even outright paranoia, was (and is), along with wishful thinking, rising at times to grandiose ambition, one of the prime movers in international relations.[14]

The prime tasks of government were to ensure good order at home and to uphold Iran's position abroad as the leading power of the further Near East. Very large capital investments were made in military infrastructure, and the largest single item of recurring expenditure was undoubtedly army pay and equipment, as it was for the Romans. The security of the core territories of the empire had to be guaranteed, and, if possible, Sasanian influence was to be projected far afield. The defensive installations varied according to circumstance, terrain, climatic conditions and the character of the potential adversary on different frontiers. Concentration of force was the guiding principle in some sectors, dispersal in block houses or small forts in others, linear extension along a defensive wall in yet others. In all cases, though, there was a marked forward orientation to the defensive systems, giving them an offensive cast. Frontier bases were potential spring-boards for attack, and, by their presence and monumental scale, acted as permanent advertisements of the daunting power of a great empire.

What then were the constituent parts of the empire built up by Ardashīr in the early third century? What were the core territories which had to be secured and, ideally, enlarged, if a *shāhānshāh* was to retain the *khwarrah* (glory) vital to a king as a mark of continuing divine favour?[15] Two great mountain ranges, the Elburz in the north and the Zagros in the

---

[14] Yarshater, 'Iranian National History'.

[15] A. Soudavar, *The Aura of Kings: Legitimacy and Divine Sanction in Iranian Kingship*, Costa Mesa 2003; A. Panaino, 'Astral Characters of Kingship in the Sasanian and Byzantine Worlds', in *La Persia e Bisanzio*, Atti dei convegni lincei 201, Rome 2004, 555–59. Cf. V. S. Curtis, 'Royal and Religious Symbols on Early Sasanian Coins', in D. Kennet and P. Luft (eds.), *Current Research in Sasanian Archaeology, Art and History*, Oxford 2008, 137–47.

south frame the huge interior plateau of Iran proper. The Elburz runs from the Köpet Dagh, a natural bulwark facing the open steppes in the east, to Transcaucasia in the west, the Zagros from the wild country of the far south-east to the rugged mountains of Kurdistan by Lake Van. Four principal resource-bases may be identified within Iran:

1) Media in the west, which is endowed with plenty of agricultural land, dispersed over the rolling country around Ecbatana (modern Hamadan) and along the edges of the plateau, and which could offer virtually limitless grazing in the north-west, in open country presided over by the huge mausoleum of Öljeytü at Sultaniyya;
2) Persia proper in the nearer south-east, where the ridges of the Zagros open out into fertile valleys and plains, the region from which the Sasanians, like their distant and largely forgotten Achaemenid precursors, set out on their imperial venture;
3) Khurasan, a swathe of open land which is comparatively well-watered, running north-west from Tus between the two main ridges of the Köpet Dagh; and
4) Adurbadagan (classical Atropatene) in the north-west, a region of fertile plains, many with volcanic alluvium, centred on Lake Urmia.

These were the natural power-centres within Iran, with the greatest concentrations of population and wealth, from which the authorities sought to cast their control over neighbouring highlands and thus to tap them for additional fighting manpower.[16]

But it was the lands to the south-west of Iran which generated most of the wealth of the Sasanian Empire. With the development of agriculture and irrigation in the fourth millennium BC, Mesopotamia engendered early city-based states capable of controlling large areas and of asserting themselves militarily far afield. Investment over the centuries in increasingly elaborate and extensive irrigation systems transformed the alluvial plain of lower Mesopotamia and the adjoining region of Khuzistan into highly productive agricultural lands. There was no need for similar interventions by man in the fertile, undulating, rain- and river-fed lands on the left (north) bank of the upper Tigris. The size and density of settlements in all three regions grew, peaking in the late Sasanian and early Islamic periods. With canals and rivers providing easy routes for the transport of commodities in bulk, the metropolitan area around Ctesiphon and Veh Ardashīr could be provisioned from its hinterlands (the upper Tigris basin to the north-west and the Diyala plains to the north, the development of which climaxed in a gigantic sixth-century irrigation scheme centering on the Cut of Khusraw).[17] It is hard to gauge the extent of commercial and manufacturing activity in the fertile, urbanised lands of Mesopotamia and Khuzistan, because of the paucity of useful source material. But there is evidence that the Sasanian Empire was a major player in Indian Ocean trade in Late Antiquity and was ready to defend

[16] W. B. Fisher, 'Physical Geography', *Cambridge History of Iran*, i, Cambridge 1968, 3–110.

[17] R. McC. Adams, *Land Behind Baghdad: A History of Settlement on the Diyala Plains*, Chicago 1965; R. McC. Adams and H. J. Nissen, *The Uruk Countryside: The Natural Setting of Urban Societies*, Chicago 1972; McG. Gibson, *The City and Area of Kish*, Miami 1972; R. McC. Adams, *Heartland of Cities: Surveys of Ancient Settlement and Land Use on the Central Floodplain of the Euphrates*, Chicago 1981; R.J. Wenke, 'Imperial Investments and Agricultural Developments in Parthian and Sasanian Khuzestan: 150 BC to AD 640', *Mesopotamia*, 10–11, 1975–76, 31–221.

its commercial interests from rival Roman and Turkish challenges. We should perhaps be ready to envisage a mercantile class growing up in the cities of Mesopotamia and reaching out to tap the resources of the Indian subcontinent. A network of contacts would help to explain the early spread of the Nestorian brand of Christianity to south India.[18]

These core territories, in the Iranian uplands and Mesopotamian lowlands, constituted the Iran of Late Antiquity, which, in early Sasanian propaganda, was marked off from *an-Ērān* , a collection of peripheral regions beholden to Iran, regarded as integral components of a wider Iranian sphere of influence (their near abroad).[19] *An-Ērān*, which looked or was expected to look exclusively towards Iran, comprised most of Transcaucasia (the eastern lowlands of Albania [ex-Soviet Azerbaijan], Iberia [Georgia], Siunia [roughly equivalent to Nagorno Karabakh] and the four fifths of Armenia which belonged to Persarmenia), the Gulf coast of Arabia which was conquered in the third century, and large buffer territories in the east and south-east, stretching, at the empire's apogee, as far as the Oxus, eastern Bactria and the Indus plain.

One region, potentially an economic resource of great importance, has not been mentioned so far. We are remarkably ill-informed about the Caspian and its southern coastlands in classical times and especially in Late Antiquity. Not much weight can be attached to a passing reference to commercial activity on the Caspian in Ammianus Marcellinus' long geographical digression on the Sasanian Empire, since he simply pieced it together out of antiquarian materials culled from ancient texts.[20] For other Roman historians, the Caspian lay outside their field of vision, largely restricted as it was to arenas of warfare. The east Syrian writers, who included secular material in their histories of the Nestorian church (semi-established within the Sasanian Empire), did not lift their gaze over the mountains which bound Mesopotamia on the north and west. Even the Armenian histories which provide near-contemporary evidence about the geo-political convulsions of the seventh century and take a broad view of the world around Armenia have nothing to say about the lowlands between the Caspian and the foothills of the Elburz. They first come into view in the early middle ages, under Muslim rule, when their agriculture (rice being the principal crop) and industry were well developed and the elites of the great cities played an important part in the wider cultural life of the Abbasid caliphate.[21] The question which gnaws at the mind of the historian of Late Antiquity, especially after travelling along the southern coast of the Caspian, is whether or not the Sasanian regime (and its Parthian predecessor) invested as much effort in developing them as it did in Mesopotamia. There is no physical evidence of water management schemes, nor of urban

---

18 D. Whitehouse and A. Williamson, 'Sasanian Maritime Trade', *Iran* 11, 1973, 29–49; G. Gropp, 'Christian Maritime Trade of Sasanian Age in the Persian Gulf', in K. Schippmann *et al.* (eds,), *Golf-Archäologie: Mesopotamien, Iran, Bahrain, Vereinigte Arabische Emirate und Oman*, Internationale Archäologie 6, Buch am Erlbach 1991, 83–88; de la Vaissière, *Sogdian Traders*, 227–32.

19 G. Gnoli, *The Idea of Iran: An Essay on its Origin*, Rome 1989.

20 Ammianus, xxxiii.6.51.

21 V. Minorsky (tr.), *'The Regions of the World': A Persian Geography, 372 AH–982 AD*, London 1970, 134–135; Ibn Ḥawqal, *Configuration de la terre (Kitāb ṣūrat al-arḍ)*, tr. J. H. Kramers and G. Wiet, Paris 1964, ii, 370–72, 379; al-Muqaddasi, *The Best Divisions for Knowledge of the Regions*, tr. B. A. Collins and M. H. al-Tai, Reading 1994, 313, 316–17.

structures, because of the destructive effect of the subtropical climate on all manmade structures. But why would the Sasanian (and Parthian) authorities who showed themselves adept at devising and implementing large infrastructure development schemes elsewhere have refrained from doing so in the Caspian lowlands? It is not as if promotion of agricultural production and urban life was not encouraged in the north. For evidence has now been found of extensive irrigation works before and during the Sasanian era in the southern Gurgan plain immediately to the east of the Caspian lowlands.[22]

So the Caspian lowlands on the northern flank of the Elburz should probably be bracketed with Khuzistan, lower Mesopotamia and the basin of the upper Tigris on the southern flank of the Zagros and Armenian Taurus as a fourth massive agricultural resource, thus narrowing the gap between Iranian and Roman economic output and between the amounts of fiscal revenue which each could allocate to their army. In terms of military manpower, the Sasanians were certainly not at a disadvantage, since both great mountain ranges were nurseries of fighting men, foremost among them being the Daylamites of the western Elburz and the Kurds at the northern extremity of the Zagros. There were also the tribal lands of the far south-east, from which other elite forces were raised.[23] The key role of the main agrarian regions within the plateau, Persia proper, Khurasan, Media and Azerbaijan, and their principal urban centres was to bind highlands and lowlands together, to maintain the commitment of the heterogeneous peoples of the empire to the Sasanian imperial enterprise, and to sustain the Zoroastrian rites which would keep the empire free from contamination and maintain the favour of the gods.

III. DEFENSES, NATURAL AND MANMADE

In the south and west, the Sasanians were well endowed with natural defenses (Fig. 2). The Euphrates shielded Mesopotamia from attack from the desert, while the two Zabs provided convenient defensive lines against a regular army advancing down through the fertile lands on the left bank of the Tigris. Rivers which had carved out deep channels were harder to

---

[22] J. Nokandeh, E. Sauer and H. O. Rekavandi, 'Linear Barriers of Northern Iran: The Great Wall of Gorgan and the Wall of Tammishe', *Iran* 44, 2006, 121–73, at 138–48; H. O. Rekavandi *et al.*, 'An Imperial Frontier of the Sasanian Empire: Further Fieldwork at the Great Wall of Gorgan', *Iran* 45, 2007, 95–136, at 95–98; H. O. Rekavandi *et al.*, 'Sasanian Walls, Hinterland Fortresses and Abandoned Ancient Irrigated Landscapes: The 2007 Season on the Great Wall of Gorgan and the Wall of Tammishe', *Iran* 46, 2008, 151–78, at 151–61.

[23] Daylamites: Procopius, *Wars*, ed. J. Haury, tr. H. B. Dewing, 5 vols., Cambridge, Mass. 1914–28, viii.14.5–10, 12, 41–42; Agathias, *Histories*, ed. R. Keydell, CFHB 2, Berlin 1967, tr. J. D. C. Frendo, Berlin 1975, iii.17.6–8, 18.1–11, 22.5–8, 26.1–8, 28.6–7; Bosworth (tr.), *History of al-Ṭabarī*, v, 160. Kurds: Łazar P'arpets'i, *Patmut'iwn Hayots' (History of Armenia)*, ed. G. Ter-Mkrtch'ean and Y S. Malkhasean, Tiflis 1904, repr. Delmar, NY. 1985, tr. R. W. Thomson, *The History of Łazar P'arpec'i*, Atlanta 1991, 121, 124–25, 129 (Katišk'); F. R. Trombley and J. W. Watt (tr.), *The Chronicle of Pseudo-Joshua the Stylite*, TTH 32, Liverpool 2000, cc.22, 24, 57 (Qadushaye); Procopius, *Wars*, i.14.38–39 (Cadiseni). Tribesmen from far south-east: Ammianus, xix.2.3 (Segestani, described as the most zealous fighters among the troops arrayed against Amida in 359).

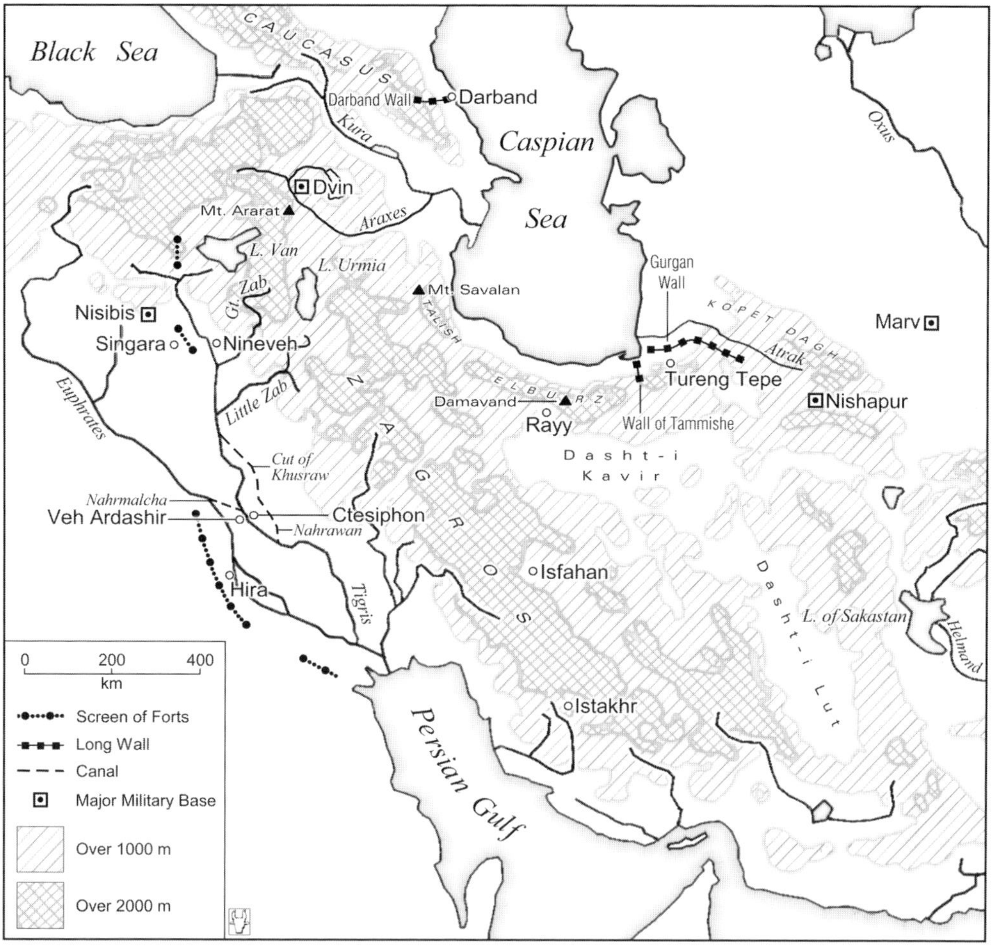

Fig. 2. Sasanian Defenses

cross than all but the highest and most broken of mountain ranges. Aware, like the Romans, of the potential danger posed by Arabs, the Sasanians took care to reinforce the works of nature. They created a defensive line on the margin of a belt of fertile land west of the Euphrates, stretching from Hīt in the north to Basra in the south. There were small, hard-point forts commanding key points in the communications network – the remains of three have been found (Ruda, north of the Karbala lake, Dab‘, near Ukhaydir, and Qusayr South, south-west of Nasiriyah), measuring between 35 × 35 m and 42 × 46 m and defended, in at least two cases, by eight semi-circular towers. They probably acted as outliers for larger fortresses (one, Qasr Yeng, measuring 150 × 150 m, has been identified west of the Karbala lake) and fortified towns analogous to those which grew up in Late Antiquity in the Roman *bādiya* (again one, Qusayr North, 7 km north-west of Ukhaydir has been identified). These manmade fortifications were, according to later Islamic sources, fronted by a canal, built under Shāpūr II, running south from Hīt, supposedly as far as the sea.[24]

Well to the north, close to the Roman frontier, where the Euphrates encloses a large sweep of desert on its left bank, a network of fortified settlements (five have been provisionally identified) and guard posts secured the routes which Arab raiders might use to attack the fertile land between Nisibis and the Tigris, the one sector of Nisibis' hinterland to have been subjected to systematic survey.[25] Similar systems of local defense may be postulated for other relatively exposed areas on the right bank of the Tigris to the south as far as the Nahrmalch canal which ran along the northern edge of the central alluvial plain. Forward defense was provided by a fortress at Singara, on a low range of hills which rise from the desert due west of Nineveh and provide plentiful winter grazing. Singara commanded the approaches to these local defensive systems.[26] A yet more important deterrent took the form of the Sasanians' principal Arab client, the Nasrid dynasty of the Lakhm, who were given plenipotentiary, i.e. royal, power to manage the tribes of north-east Arabia from their capital at Hira. This they seem to have done successfully for over three centuries, remaining resolutely loyal to the Sasanian dynasty. By the sixth century, they had brought about a clear shift in the balance of power in northern Arabia in favour of the Sasanians. Their court at Hira was also recognised as the pre-eminent political and cultural centre of the whole of Arabia. It was at Hira probably that the heroic poetry of the pagan age which was collected and studied under the early Abbasids was composed and that the economical and elegant script used for classical Arabic was developed.[27]

Traces of a similar system of area defense which is probably attributable to the Sasanian period – a string of two-storey block-houses, varying in size but built to the same specification – were glimpsed by Aurel Stein in the area of Zarang, close to the modern Afghan-Iranian frontier, nearly a century ago. They were guarding what was probably a fertile swathe of irrigated land between the great lake of Sakastan and the Helmand river.[28]

As for the greater conventional military threat posed by Turkic nomads from Central Asia (against whom the block-houses would have been utterly ineffectual), the Sasanian high command relied on a very different defensive strategy, one of maximum concentration of force in large, heavily fortified strongholds. Marv, a massive hard-point base, strategically placed to command the approaches to Khurasan from beyond the Oxus, was the outer bulwark of Sasanian power. In times of confidence, as in the reign of Bahrām V, Marv was

---

[24] B. Finster and J. Schmidt, *Sasanidische und frühislamische Ruinen im Iraq*, Baghdader Mitteilungen 8, Berlin 1976, 13, 27–39, 44–46, 47–48, 49–54.

[25] T. J. Wilkinson and D. J. Tucker, *Settlement Development in the North Jazira, Iraq: A Study of the Archaeological Landscape*, Warminster 1995, 70–1, 188–189 (figs 46–47).

[26] St. J. Simpson, 'From Tekrit to the Jaghjagh: Sasanian Sites, Settlement Patterns and Material Culture in Northern Mesopotamia', in K. Bartl and S. R. Hauser (eds.), *Continuity and Change in Northern Mesopotamia from the Hellenistic to the Early Islamic Period*, Berlin 1996, 87–126, at 90–92.

[27] G. Fisher, *Between Empires: Arabs, Romans and Sasanians in Late Antiquity*, Oxford 2011; Hoyland, *Arabia and the Arabs*, 236-243; M. C. A. Macdonald, 'Reflections on the Linguistic Map of Pre-Islamic Arabia', *Arabian Archaeology and Epigraphy* 11, 2000, 28–79, at 57–60, repr. in M. C. A. Macdonald, *Literacy and Identity in Pre-Islamic Arabia*, Aldershot 2009, iii.

[28] A. Stein, *Innermost Asia*, Oxford 1928, ii, 972–79.

the forward base where expeditionary forces gathered before campaigning in the steppes or pushing south-east towards the Indus. At other times, when the Sasanians were on the defensive, the presence of a large field army in what was an impregnable position, might well be enough to deter an invading force from pressing on, lest it be caught in a pincer attack or so harassed as to be unable to replenish its provisions by foraging.[29] Marv was backed by Nishapur, another powerful stronghold, lurking just behind the south-eastern tip of the range backing the Köpet Dagh (the Kuh-i Binalud).[30] From there it commanded the relatively narrow passage between the mountains and the interior desert to the south. Control of this natural pinch-point on the only feasible route for the invasion of Iran proper carried with it a plain threat of entrapment for any enemy foolhardy enough to venture further west.[31]

A similar strategy was adopted by the Persians on their western, Roman frontier. South of the Taurus, the key forward base was Nisibis, once it had been forcibly disgorged by the Romans after the disastrous failure of Julian's expedition in 363. The presence of large numbers of military personnel at times of international tension does not appear to have dampened intellectual or commercial life in the city, but it certainly deterred even the greatest of Roman generals in 541, when he was confident of the superiority of his own army, from advancing past it and leaving so great a potential threat to his rear.[32] In the north, a similar role seems to have been played by Dvin, capital of Persarmenia. It was well-placed, on the largest of the plains in the Araxes valley, to block the difficult route down the river as well as the pass which runs first east from the plain of Bagrewand and then north over the great western shoulder of Mount Ararat. Its garrison could either bar access to the plain or, preferably, trap an invasion force once it had come in.[33] It remains unclear, for lack of a Persian or Armenian source to match Procopius' *Buildings*, to what extent the Persians developed a zone of deep defense in their western frontier provinces. If it is safe to extrapolate from what is recorded by Theophylact Simocatta about Arzanene, the province immediately to the south of the Bitlis pass over the Armenian Taurus, where the fighting was concentrated in the 580s, the Persians, like the Romans, integrated fortified towns and specialised military forts into regional defensive systems. In the case of Arzanene, there was an additional element – underground refuges for the civilian population of rural areas.[34]

---

29 G. Herrmann, V. M. Masson, K. Kurbansakhatov *et al.*, 'The International Merv Project: Preliminary Report on the First Season (1992)', *Iran* 31, 1993, 39-62, at 40–50; G. Herrmann, K. Kurbansakhatov *et al.*, 'The International Merv Project: Preliminary Report on the Second Season (1993)', *Iran* 32, 1994, 53–75, at 53–61.

30 R. W. Bulliet, *The Patricians of Nishapur: A Study in Medieval Islamic Social History*, Cambridge, Mass. 1972, 3–10.

31 The only alternative route would involve a long detour south to Zahedan and then west to Bam over difficult, largely arid country, before reaching the eastern edge of the northern outliers of the Zagros.

32 Procopius, *Wars*, ii.18.1–19.25.

33 Procopius, *Wars*, ii.25.

34 L. M. Whitby, 'Arzanene in the Late Sixth century', in S. Mitchell (ed.), *Armies and Frontiers in Roman and Byzantine Anatolia*, Oxford 1983, 205–18. Underground refuges: Theophylact Simocatta, *History*, ii.7.1–5.

The forward defenses were backed, as has been seen, by a series of reserve lines of defense on the left-bank tributaries of the Tigris (there were few bridges to seize and hold). The narrow valley of the Euphrates, where it cuts its way through the desert well to the south, was effectively barred to an invader by a series of well-fortified island towns. The innermost line of defense was formed by the Nahrmalcha, 'royal canal', running from the Euphrates, on the north side of the low ridge on which Fallujah now stands, to join the Tigris above the capital. It was secured by troops stationed at Pirisabora, in the southern angle between the Euphrates and the canal, and by Veh-Ardashir, in a similar position at its eastern confluence with the Tigris.[35] A gigantic sixth-century project, which greatly extended the irrigation system in the Diyala plains, involved the construction of a canal, well over 200 kilometres long, on the left bank of the Tigris, from an off-take between Dura and Karkha (above modern Samarra), to a point well downstream of the capital. Besides acting as a major distributor of water and providing a waterway for the transport of bulk cargoes, this canal, known in its northern section as the 'Cut of Khusraw' and in the southern as the Nahrawan, provided Ctesiphon, hitherto exposed to attack, with virtually impregnable defenses.[36]

Finally, we turn to the north, to the defenses built, in the imagination of Christians, to hold off the threat of Gog and Magog. Long walls were constructed across the two inviting avenues of invasion which led south on either side of the Caspian. The Caspian Gates on the coastal strip at the eastern end of the Caucasus, where it narrows to 3.5 km, were blocked by two parallel walls running inland from a heavily fortified town and port at Darband. They were impressive, some 4 m thick, faced with limestone slabs and 18–20 m high, with 73 massive round and rectangular towers facing north, some 70 m apart, and 27 round towers at intervals of 170–200 m facing south. A single wall, guarded by at least 40 forts, continued for some 40 km into the mountains. This Darband wall was the main component of the Caspian Gates defenses, which included four other defensive lines, one to the north and three to the south.[37] Two features, the towers facing south on the double Darband wall and the three southern linear defenses, are rather puzzling if the function of the defenses was simply to keep out attackers, nomad or other, from the north. It looks as if the Sasanian authorities had laid out an artificial arena, its periphery defined by mountains to the west, sea to the east and manmade defenses to north and south, within which to lure, trap and engage intruders.

The creation of a strong line of defense to the east of the Caspian was a much more difficult task. For the distance between sea and mountains, in this case the north-western extremity of the Köpet Dagh (the Arab Dagh which ends in the Pishkamar Rocks), was over 180 km. The Gurgan River which flows west across the southern section of the plain had nothing like the defensive capability of great rivers like the Euphrates, Tigris or left-bank

---

[35] J. Matthews, *The Roman Empire of Ammianus*, London 1989, 145–55.

[36] Adams, *Land Behind Baghdad*, 76-80.

[37] K. V. Trever, *Ocherki po istorii i kul'ture kavkazkoj Albanii IV v. do N.E. - VII v. N.E.*, Moscow-Leningrad 1959, 267–87; S. Khan Magomedov, *Derbent*, Moscow 1979, 69–127, 207–27; E. Kettenhofen, 'Darband', *Encyclopedia Iranica*, VII, Costa Mesa 1996, 13–19, at 15–16; R. H. Hewsen, *Armenia: A Historical Atlas*, Chicago 2001, 89–91.

tributaries of the Tigris. Nor were there natural features to exploit in the plain itself except for the river. The plain forms a natural salient offering easy access to the Caspian lowlands and the two principal passes over the eastern Elburz. Long-established settlements on either bank of the Gurgan River and the irrigation system on which they relied were utterly exposed to attack. Only a few isolated protuberances rose from the surface of the plain, of which the most notable were two tepes (manmade, occupation mounds), Qizlar Qaleh, 16.5 m high, on the north bank of the river, and, some 15 km to the south, Tureng Tepe, rising to a height of 35 metres and crowned by a dilapidated fortress dating back to prehistoric times.[38]

It seems to have been experience of the fighting capability of the Turkic nomads from eastern Eurasia, from the 350s to the early fifth century, which decided the Sasanian government to embark on the massive programme of investment in military infrastructure needed to protect the southern Gurgan plain and thereby to plug what was a serious hole in the defenses of Iran as a whole. For the long wall which was built is securely dated to the fifth or early sixth century.[39] Its course can still be traced as it snakes across the plain as a broad, low swelling, suffused for much of its length with a dark red colouring from the billions of brick fragments embedded in the soil. Its construction was an extraordinary feat of engineering and logistics. The wall, which climbed up the Pishkamar Rocks and carried on for some 15 km into the Arab Dagh at the eastern end, was guarded by approximately 36 forts and fronted by a wide ditch in the plain. The water which filled the ditch was drawn by a series of off-takes from the Gurgan River a short distance to the south. Two small forts on the Pishkamar Rocks extended the defenders' field of vision at the eastern end. In the west Qizlar Qaleh was incorporated as a forward lookout post. The wall curved to the south as it approached the Caspian, where it may have ended, like the Darband wall, in a fortified harbour, now submerged beneath the Caspian, or, conceivably, may have continued to join up with the northern end of the Wall of Tammishe (for which see below).[40]

There were other elements in this grand regional fortification system beside the main wall with its ditch, forts and observations posts. The Wall of Tammishe, which ran for some 11 km inland from the south-east corner of the Caspian into the foothills of the Elburz, was probably built by the same units as the westernmost section of the main wall, to judge by the dimensions of the bricks used. Intriguingly, it faced west, since that was the side protected by a ditch. It was designed, it seems, to prevent hostile forces – Elburz highlanders? sea-raiders? – from entering the protected southern segment of the Gurgan plain.[41] Of greater significance, probably, are the vestiges of eight mud-brick compounds in the immediate hinterland of the wall. Four of these are of strikingly similar design – large, square fortresses, averaging 40 ha in area. They have been characterised plausibly as

---

[38] Nokandeh, Sauer and Rekavandi, 'Linear Barriers', 148–51; R. Boucharlat and O. Lecomte, *Fouilles de Tureng Tepe*, I *Les périodes sassanides et islamiques*, Paris 1987, 7.

[39] Nokandeh, Sauer and Rekavandi, 'Linear Barriers', 158–63 for OSL (optically stimulated luminescence) and radiocarbon dating.

[40] Nokandeh, Sauer, and Rekavandi, 'Linear Barriers', 121–51; Rekavandi *et al.*, 'Imperial Frontier', 95–107, 112–13; Rekavandi *et al.*, 'Sasanian Walls', 166–69.

[41] Nokandeh, Sauer and Rekavandi, 'Linear Barriers', 151–58; Rekavandi *et al.*, 'Imperial Frontier', 112–13.

ready-made encampments for temporary occupation by field armies, with large cavalry components. This is suggested by relatively shallow deposits of detritus and by the internal lay-out of the one fortress which has been examined in detail, Qaleh Kharabeh, with broad avenues between double rows of tent enclosures for the tethering of mounts. One or two of the other four compounds which have been detected may well have served the same purpose. So it seems that a large offensive capability was incorporated into the Gurgan defensive system.[42]

Finally, there is Tureng Tepe to consider. It commands the western half of the Gurgan Wall from the edge of the alluvial plain to the south of the river. It is a large site, some 35 ha in extent, elevated well above the plain. It has several distinct elements: the main tepe, 35 m high, was well defended and served as the citadel; a narrow ridge runs north-east from the tepe, forming a useful outer line of defense on the north-west side of the site. What may be construed as a large outer enclosure incorporated two smaller mounds which lie to the south and west of the tepe and a broad platform, rising some 5–6 m from the plain, which extends east and south from the large and small tepes; a depression which transects the platform is blocked by a dam at its north-west end, where it passes between the two small tepes, so as to create a small lake – if a reservoir of this sort existed in antiquity, it would have solved the problem of water supply for the site.[43] Given its strategic position, it is tempting to identify the complex as a regional military command centre, responsible for organising logistics and for co-ordinating operations along and behind the wall.[44] This must remain in the realm of speculation, since only the main tepe, which served as the citadel, has been subjected to systematic investigation. It is telling, though, that the third building phase, during which the fortifications of the citadel were refurbished and improved, was roughly contemporary with construction of the Gurgan Wall.[45] Tureng Tepe would undoubtedly have made an impressive headquarters base, worthy of a senior general, with the citadel rising above the rest of the base and presenting a daunting face to all those approaching from the north – five closely-spaced round towers rising from a glacis, with a row of tall arrow-slits above a decorative band.[46]

The main Gurgan Wall and its forts were completed in a single building phase. Work began at the western end and moved east. Bricks were manufactured in hundreds, if not thousands, of kilns placed at regular intervals along the line of the wall. The fronting ditch and its feeder canals served several useful purposes during the period of construction – providing excavated material for the platforms of the forts, clay and water for the manufacture of bricks, and access for barges bringing in other materials.[47] The processes of design, procurement of materials, assembly and deployment of labour, and so forth,

---

[42] Rekavandi *et al.*, 'Sasanian Walls', 161–66, supplemented by further information from Eberhard Sauer.

[43] Boucherlat and Lecomte, *Fouilles de Tureng Tepe*, 7.

[44] *Contra* Boucherlat and Lecomte, *Fouilles de Tureng Tepe*, 49, 195–96.

[45] Without secure, scientific evidence, the excavators can only place it in the later Sasanian era, preferring to credit it to Khusraw I rather than Pērōz, on the grounds that Khusraw is known as a great builder (Boucherlat and Lecomte, *Fouilles de Tureng Tepe*, 192–95).

[46] Boucherlat and Lecomte, *Fouilles de Tureng Tepe*, 25–49.

required managerial skills of a high order. It was a gigantic project, the largest single investment in military infrastructure made by Iran in classical antiquity or the middle ages, only surpassed in the civil sphere by the Cut of Khusraw/Nahrawan project. It demonstrated that the Sasanian state was capable of organising projects almost on the scale of Chinese imperial regimes in Late Antiquity.[48] Its construction should probably be credited to Pērōz (459–84). For it was he who embarked on a policy of head-on military confrontation with the most powerful neighbouring nomads of the time, the Hephthalites, in an apparent attempt to break the power of Turan for several generations. A vital preliminary act would have been to strengthen Iran's defenses and to establish a secure forward area for the mobilisation of expeditionary forces. Circumstances also were relatively propitious for undertaking so large a project, after the successes achieved in the steppes earlier in the century by Bahrām V. Later, after the disastrous end of Pērōz's final expedition, which is reported to have been launched from Hyrcania (Gurgan), such a project would have been out of the question.[49] The cost would have been prohibitive, at a time when large sums of tribute were being paid out to the Hephthalites, and it is inconceivable that the Hephthalites would have authorised it in what remained in effect a protectorate of theirs up to the early sixth century .[49a]

Two functions of the Gurgan Wall and associated installations have already been picked out. In the first place, it greatly improved security. The weakest sector in the perimeter defenses of Iran was transformed into one of the strongest. All but the largest forces could be opposed at the wall itself. The very appearance of the wall and its protective forts was likely to deter attack, by impressing the majesty and power of the Sasanian Empire on northern peoples. The wall clearly demarcated the territory of Iran, as bastion of civilisation and prime earthly agent of the good, from the outer world of Turan. Cross-border traffic could be policed thenceforth with ease, and custom duties raised from goods in transit. In the second place, the Gurgan Wall provided the Sasanian high command with a secure setting for the gathering, training and provisioning of expeditionary forces. This was probably its prime intended function at the time of construction. The Romans had developed a similar sort of secure forward assembly area, in the early third century, when they became aware of the offensive striking power of Iran under its new dynasty. But theirs was withdrawn well back from the frontier – in the Arabissus plain, nestling in the Anti-Taurus – and they relied primarily on God-given defenses, in the form of mountain ridges which splayed out north and south of the interior basin.[50] The Sasanians' fifth-century assembly area was much more aggressively positioned.

A third function may also be suggested. On those occasions when an enemy attacked

---

[47] Nokandeh, Sauer and Rekavandi, 'Linear Barriers', 130–35, 147–48; Rekavandi *et al.*, 'Imperial Frontier', 108–12.

[48] A. Waldron, *The Great Wall of China: From History to Myth*, Cambridge 1990, 42–47.

[49] Łazar P'arpec'i, 155–56.

[49a] This rules out the second half of the period defined by carbon-14 dating (fifth–early sixth century).

[50] J. Howard-Johnston, 'Military Infrastructure in the Roman Provinces North and South of the Armenian Taurus in Late Antiquity', in A. Sarantis, L. Lavan and N. Christie, ed., *Warfare in Late Antiquity: New Perspectives*, Late Antique Archaeology 8, Leiden forthcoming.

in massive force, when it was judged imprudent to try to hold the line of the wall at all costs, the whole southern section of the Gurgan plain could be treated as a large prepared arena of combat. As in the case of the Caspian Gates, the arena of combat was defined by manmade structures and natural barriers – the Gurgan Wall itself with its forts, a well-defended redoubt south of the river (Tureng Tepe), the Caspian together with the wall of Tammishe (admittedly facing the other way but still a significant obstacle) to the west, the Arab Dagh to the east, and the Elburz to the south. Within these fixed boundaries, with which the defenders would be so much more familiar than the attackers, Sasanian commanders would be able to devise various scenarios for trapping, engaging and defeating enemy forces. The combination of a mobile field army and well-garrisoned fixed defenses would always pose great danger to an intruder, the danger of being manoeuvred into a position where he could be attacked from two or more sides at once, or of being exposed to harassing attacks as he withdrew and had successively to cross river, wall and ditch.

IV. MILITARY CONSTRUCTION PROJECTS: CHRONOLOGY

With the completion of the Gurgan Wall, the Sasanian Empire had been rendered as secure as was humanly possible. Different strategies were programmed in by the configuration of physical defenses, both manmade and natural. Where great powers were faced, nomadic in the east, sedentary in the west, resort was had to massive, hard-point bases, where maximum concentration of force could be achieved, as at Marv, Dvin and Nisibis. Where the distances were not too great and the cost consequently not prohibitive, extended linear defenses were developed:

(1) along the Euphrates, strengthened in the south by a long fronting canal,
(2) along the Caucasus with an artificial extension (the Darband wall) to the sea, and
(3) to the east of the Caspian, the Gurgan Wall defending the north-western flank of the Köpet Dagh, Iran's great natural redoubt facing the steppes.

Of course, military forces had to be spread thin to hold these lines, but fixed defenses more than made good the dispersal of force. In most circumstances, the garrison troops, supported by a mobile reserve, would be able to halt and repel invasion forces, thus guaranteeing the security of Sasanian territory in their hinterlands and justifying the capital invested in military infrastructure. On all frontiers, efforts were made to deepen the military zone behind the frontier, whether (1) by construction of a single large backing stronghold (for example Nishapur, far to the rear of Marv), or (2) by creation of a network of smaller forts to discourage enemy dispersal and thus to limit the damage which might be caused (as in the canal zone fronting the lower Euphrates, or in the hinterland of Nisibis, or in the lowest section of the Helmand valley), or (3) by development of reserve lines of defense, to contain forces which might have breached the forward defenses (as behind the Darband and Gurgan walls).

The development of the eastern frontier defenses of the Roman Empire can be broken down into distinct phases, above all because of the chronological precision imparted by a rich epigraphic record and the comparative wealth of written source material. So it is possible to define (1) the initial development, under the Flavians (in the 70s and 80s AD), of forward defenses on the Euphrates, between Trebizond and Samosata, with support roads reaching back into the heart of Asia Minor, followed (2), in the early second century, after the annexation of the Nabataean kingdom, by the extension of the forward defensive line south to the Red Sea at Aila. Several further phases can also be picked out: (3) improvements to the strategic road network carried out over two generations around 200 CE, followed (4) by a general upgrading of defenses along the whole length of the frontier, begun by Diocletian (284–305) and extending into the second half of the fourth century; finally (5), after a long intermission during the many decades of peaceful co-existence (*c.* 387–502), a crash programme of fortification, involving new and improved projects, carried through to completion in a little over twenty years between 505 and 527 and described in detail by Procopius.[51]

We would dearly like to know how the Sasanians responded to Roman building activity from the late third century onward, especially to the massive investment in military infrastructure in Armenia and north Mesopotamia made by Anastasius (491–518) after the rude breaking of the peace by Kavād (488–96, 499–531) in autumn 502. It would be no less interesting, not least from the point of view of Sasanian state finances, to be able to date specific infrastructure projects, including those with military functions. However, given that there are very few dating indications, we have no choice but to resort to educated guesses for the most part. We may conjecture that great cities like Marv, Nishapur, Dvin and Nisibis, which were given key strategic roles, both defensive and offensive, had their existing defenses upgraded on annexation. In the case of Nisibis, the work can be placed in the period immediately following the ignominious retreat of the Roman army in 363, when there was virtually no chance of disruption to building work.[52] As for Marv, all we can say is that, if the Seleucid fortifications of the lower city (Gyaur-Kala, 340 ha) and the 20 m high walls of the adjoining polygonal Achaemenid fortress (Erk-Kala, 20 ha), both mud-brick, needed improving, the work was probably carried out before, perhaps well before, the phase of Sasanian aggression in Central Asia, which is associated with Bahrām V.[53] Nothing beyond basic maintenance and repair work was probably done at Dvin, after the abolition of the Arsacid client-kingdom, given that the peace treaties in force (from *c.* 387 CE) are likely to have included a clause banning fortification work on or close to the Roman frontier.[54]

The ground becomes somewhat firmer in the fifth century. The Romans acknowledged that they had an interest in the defense of the Caucasus and agreed to contribute to the cost of the Caspian Gates, possibly as early as 387.[55] Development of its multi-layered

---

[51] Procopius, *Buildings*, ed. J. Haury, tr. H. B. Dewing, Cambridge, Mass. 1940, ii–iii. Cf. Howard-Johnston, 'Military Infrastructure'.

[52] M. H. Dodgeon and S. N. C. Lieu, *The Roman Eastern Frontier and the Persian Wars AD 226–363: A Documentary History*, London 1991, 231–74.

[53] Herrmann *et al.*, 'Merv Project, First Season', 40–41.

[54] Howard-Johnston, 'Military Infrastructure'. Cf. Blockley, *East Roman Foreign Policy*, 42–45.

[55] Blockley, *East Roman Foreign Policy*, 50–51.

system of defense may therefore be placed early in the fifth century, when the Persians, like the Romans, were all too aware of the continuing threat posed by the Huns and the Roman subsidy was to hand. Later, in the middle of the century, attention shifted to the eastern shore of the Caspian. The ambitious Gurgan plain fortification scheme may be dated, with reasonable confidence, taking account of general historical considerations as well as the results of scientific analysis, to the reign of Pērōz. Completion of that massive project was then followed by a hiatus after Pērōz's last, disastrous expedition, when Iran was reduced to tributary status *vis à vis* the Hephthalites and was subject to serious social and religious stress.

The time of troubles ended with Kavād's Roman war, extraordinarily successful in 502 but ending in a forced withdrawal from the main prize, Amida, in 505. An uneasy peace followed, during which an arms race, taking the form of rival fortification programmes, almost certainly gathered pace.[56] Kavād, it may be conjectured, sponsored upgrading work in the two main theatres of war, north and south of the Armenian Taurus, and, in addition, may have encouraged, even funded, the construction of new forts to add to the security of highland districts in Persarmenia.[57] The upgrading of the principal line of defense in the Caspian Gates, involving the reconstruction *in stone* of the Darband wall, was probably a contemporary project, prompted by an enhanced threat from the north Caucasus Huns, first evident in 503–4 (Kavād was forced to divert troops from the upper Tigris basin, allowing the Romans to seize the strategic initiative). Since a date, given in the form of a regnal year (ending with the digit 7, or just possibly 3) of an unnamed king (taken to be either Kavād or Khusraw I [531–79]), is included on one of the official inscriptions on the wall, completion of the project may be placed most plausibly in Kavād's twenty-seventh year (514–15) or Khusraw's third (533–4).[58]

A much larger infrastructure project, explicitly associated with Khusraw in medieval sources, was the Cut of Khusraw-Nahrawan scheme in the districts adjoining the Diyala's junction with the Tigris. It was probably initiated at the very start of Khusraw's reign, once he was flush with cash under the terms of the treaty for a Peace without End which Justinian had been forced to sign in 532. While it was primarily a civilian project, increasing massively the irrigated proportion of the hinterland of capital, it brought with it an important strategic gain. For the new trunk canal on the left bank of the Tigris formed an inner, virtually impregnable line of defense around the metropolitan area. This significant improvement in security was achieved without in any way infringing the 532 treaty with the Romans.[59]

Such is the provisional chronology of major Sasanian military construction projects which may be pieced together from the scanty available evidence. What cannot be in doubt

---

[56] G. Greatrex, *Rome and Persia at War, 502–532*, Leeds 1998, 73–122; Howard-Johnston, 'Military Infrastructure'.

[57] It would help explain the early appearance of castles in private hands in Armenia, if the structures were built by the Sasanians and then taken over by local princes with the receding of Sasanian authority in the seventh century.

[58] Kettenhofen,'Darband', 16.

[59] Greatrex, *Rome and Persia at War*, 213–18; Adams, *Land Behind Baghdad*, 76–80.

is the strength of Iran's outer defenses in the middle of the sixth century, when bubonic plague struck the Sasanian state a devastating demographic and fiscal blow. The marked slow-down in building activity in the 540s attested by Procopius for the Roman Empire, was assuredly paralleled further east.[60] Minor work may have taken place subsequently, as the revenue base began to recover – for example, to provide accommodation for a large influx of Turkish troops, who, we know, were resettled in several different areas, away from their point of entry at the Caspian Gates.[61] Khusraw's great project in the metropolitan area must have absorbed almost all of whatever capital was available for investment.

The peripheral bases, lines of fortification and systems of area defense developed under earlier kings proved their worth towards the end of Khusraw's reign, around 570, when Turks and Romans formed an unholy alliance and Iran was threatened from all quarters. Of course, resources of many sorts were drawn on as Khusraw clawed his way out of trouble – Sasanian statecraft, a versatile and resilient military, carefully modulated propaganda and brilliant strategic planning. But military and diplomatic action required solid bases to be effective, if it was:

(1) to dissipate potential danger from the south (as was achieved by the 571 Yemen expedition),
(2) to contain the trouble fomented by the Romans in Transcaucasia and gradually to re-impose Persian authority (a process completed by Khusraw himself in 576),
(3) to prevent the Turks breaching the defenses of Iran in the east and north (they held in the critical opening year of full-scale warfare, 573, in contrast to 627 when the Darband wall was attacked in overwhelming force), and
(4) to launch a devastating counter-offensive in the west in 573 (which resulted in the capture of Dara).

All component parts of the peripheral defensive system contributed to the successful outcome from these years of crisis, both by securing Sasanian authority on the ground and acting as platforms of counterstrikes.[62] Within 30 years the same set of installations was to prove its worth in very different circumstances, when, in 603, Khusraw II launched

---

[60] P. Sarris, 'The Justinianic Plague: Origins and Effects', *Continuity and Change* 17, 2002, 169–82; L. M. Whitby, 'Justinian's Bridge over the Sangarius and the Date of Procopius' *De Aedificiis*', *Journal of Hellenic Studies* 105, 1985, 129–48 at 146.

[61] Z. Rubin, 'The Reforms of Khusraw Anūshirwān', in Cameron, *Byzantine and Early Islamic Near East*, iii, 227–297, at 279–284.

[62] Principal sources: Theophylact Simocatta, iii.9.1–15.7; *History of Menander*, fr.10, 13, 16, 18; Photius, *Bibliotheca, cod.* 64 (Theophanes of Byzantium), ed. and tr. R. Henry, 8 vols., Paris, 1959–1977, i, 76–79; Bosworth (tr.), *History of al-Ṭabarī*, v, 160, 237–52, 264 (occupation of Yemen), 298–301 (gravity of crisis [mistakenly transposed to the later 580s]). With the attention of Romans, Armenians and Syrians focused on events closer at hand, nothing is reported about events on the north-eastern frontier. This silence assuredly implies that disaster was avoided. Cf. Whitby, *Emperor Maurice*, 250-268 and Rubin, 'Reforms of Khusraw', 284–86.

a war of aggression against the Romans in the west and, with a single exception in the east in 615–16, maintained security on all other frontiers.[63]

Iran certainly had the physical endowment, in natural defences and military installations, to take on and beat its foreign enemies. Khusraw's achievement in 571–6 may even cap that of the Dutch Republic in its *annus nefastus*, 1672, when it came under attack simultaneously by land and sea from all its neighbours, and had to break the dikes to secure its core territory. What, though, of the fighting men who defended long walls, river and canal banks, who garrisoned forts, fortresses and fortified cities, and who were ready to venture forth from defended forward positions to take on the enemies of Iran? How many of them were there? Whence were they recruited and on what terms? How were they equipped? How well were they trained? What can be learned of their deployment in peace and war, and of the command structure? How was strategic cohesion achieved, when troops were distributed over so large a territory? These and many other questions cry out for answers.

V. TROOP NUMBERS, RECRUITMENT, CAPABILITIES

What then was the strength of the late Sasanian army? Figures are to be found in well-informed Roman sources for Sasanian forces engaged in major operations on the western front. They range from 20,000, the number of troops whom Kavād put into winter quarters at Singara after the fall of Amida in January 503, to the 40,000 who advanced to the plain south of Dara in 530 and, after being reinforced with another 10,000 from Nisibis, made ready to destroy Belisarius' army in front of Dara.[64] But such figures tell one little about the Sasanians' full military establishment. For the size of a field army was limited in the pre-modern age, both by logistical constraints (the larger the army, the wider the range of foraging and grazing needed to keep men and horses fed) and by its manageability on the march and on manoeuvre. A general could not exercise effective command over a force larger than 25–30,000 men, nor could it move fast enough, if too much time were lost at the beginning and end of each day on the march, in forming up and falling out to camp.[65] Rather more useful are those rare occasions when massive Roman armies were successfully opposed – say the 60,000-strong army commanded by the emperor Philip the Arab (244–9) which was defeated at Barbalissus in 250, or the main invasion force of 65,000 men[66] which

[63] R. W. Thomson and J. Howard-Johnston, *The Armenian History Attributed to Sebeos*, TTH 31, Liverpool 1999, xxii–xxv, 183–89, 193–228. Note that the dating by regnal years of Khusraw II should be corrected (brought forward one year), to take account of the re-dating of his accession to 590–591 by S. Tyler-Smith, 'Calendars and Coronations: The Literary and Numismatic Evidence for the Accession of Khusrau II', *Byzantine and Modern Greek Studies* 28, 2004, 33–65.

[64] *Chronicle of Pseudo-Joshua*, c.55; Procopius, *Wars*, i.13.23, 14.1.

[65] Cf. Haldon, *Warfare, State and Society*, 139-176; M. Whitby, 'Recruitment in Roman Armies from Justinian to Heraclius (*c.* 565–615)', in Cameron, *Byzantine and Early Islamic Near East*, iii, 61–124, at 100–102.

[66] P. Huyse, *Die dreisprachige Inschrift Šabuhrs I. an der Ka'ba-i Zardušt (ŠKZ)*, Corpus Inscriptionum Iranicarum III.1, London 1999, i, 28 and ii, 55–56; Eunapius' figure is transmitted by Zosimus, *Historia nova*, iii.13.1, ed. and tr. F. Paschoud, *Zosime, Histoire nouvelle*, II.1, Paris 1979, 27.

Julian led to its doom in 363 – or when the Sasanians deployed substantial forces in separate theatres – as in 528, when a pre-emptive strike by one army broke up a planned Roman offensive from Lazica and a second army, 30,000 strong, won a victory in north Mesopotamia, or 530 when, in addition to the 50,000 troops facing Belisarius, a 30,000-strong army advanced west against Satala in the north.[67]

But what percentage of the standing army could be mobilised for operations on two connected sectors of a single front? Clearly troops were needed outside the active theatre or theatres of war – above all for internal security. In an era before the development of specialist civilian police, the authorities relied ultimately on the military to enforce their will and to preserve the good order expected on earth. So troops were assuredly dispersed across the length and breadth of the empire, spread thin perhaps in the plains but more in evidence in and around the great mountain ranges. There were, of course, other demands on the military – guard duties in the palace, defense of the binary capital and its outer perimeter along the Cut of Khusraw-Nahrawan canal, and defense of all sectors of the frontier away from that which was the primary focus of action. If it seems reasonable to put the ratio of large field army to full military establishment at 1:4 (it seems to work for the rump east Roman state of the dark age), then we may envisage a total of some 320,000 troops of all sorts in the Sasanian army – a figure somewhat below that suggested for the fourth century Roman Empire (500,000) but roughly equal to that customarily given to the eastern empire in the sixth century.[68]

It is possible, however, to estimate the military strength of the Sasanian Empire independently of the written evidence. For a detailed survey has been carried out at one of the larger forts on the Gurgan Wall, fort 4 (5.5 ha), which was defended by 32 towers. Eight barrack blocks have been identified, with accommodation for 1000 men (at 4 soldiers per room) or 2000 (at 8 per room). Given that the total area enclosed by the 36 or so forts on the wall comes to some 90 ha, a rough total of 30,000 may be suggested for the permanent garrison.[69] From this point on, extrapolation becomes more hazardous: we may assign roughly equivalent forces (say, of 20,000 men) to the six other main frontiers of the empire: the east Caucasus where the Caspian Gates defenses needed to be manned in strength, with other units assigned to patrol the mountains to the west; Persarmenia where capable garrisons were required to secure the regional capital Dvin, other fortified towns and the forts which may be conjectured to have been built to give depth to the defenses; the northern approaches to the metropolitan region in Mesopotamia, which were already heavily fortified in the fourth century; the defensive installations fronting the lower Euphrates, and to be found on the Gulf coast of Arabia; the far south-east where there was much policing work to be done in addition to protection of settlements in the lower Helmand basin; and finally, the open frontier facing the steppes of Central Asia, where substantial forces had to be stationed at all times to uphold Sasanian prestige and daunt potential aggressors. We thus obtain a figure of some 150,000 soldiers engaged in guard

---

[67] Malalas, xviii.4 and 26; Procopius, *Wars*, i.13.23,14.1, 15.11.

[68] See n.12 above

[69] Rekavandi *et al.*, 'Imperial Frontier', 113–31. Eberhard Sauer now identifies eight shorter rather than four longer barrack blocks in fort 4 (pers. comm.).

duties on Sasanian frontiers, to which should be added perhaps another 30,000 involved in policing the interior provinces. This would put the Sasanian analogues to the late Roman *limitanei* at approximately 180,000.

Rather more important, in terms of striking power, were the mobile forces which could be deployed in offensive or defensive operations in the field, analogous to the late Roman *comitatenses*. Here again there is some solid material evidence from which to extrapolate – the internal lay-out of one quadrant of one of the four similar square mud-brick fortresses situated behind the Gurgan Wall, Qaleh Kharabeh (41 ha). Tent enclosures, each capable of accommodating 8–10 men, were arranged in 14 rows of 20 (or, possibly, 21), each pair of rows being fronted by 17 m wide avenues where mounts could be tethered. This puts the capacity of one quarter of the fortress at between 2240 and 2800 men. If, as seems likely, at least one other quadrant accommodated infantry, with more tent enclosures packed in, the total capacity of Qaleh Kharabeh would have been at least 10,000 men.[70] If similar totals may be attributed to the three strikingly similar fortresses which have been identified and to one or two of the other four compounds, we may envisage their total capacity as 50–60,000 men.[71] They were designed, it appears, as permanent camps or campaign bases for the secure accommodation of expeditionary forces of 50–60,000 men, on the edge of the open steppes into which they would be venturing before long. We can then make the more hazardous leap from the capacity of the Gurgan plain fortresses to the total offensive capability of the empire – putting it perhaps at three times the size of the lower figure for the Gurgan compounds' capacity which tallies with the largest recorded force operating in a single theatre of war (50,000), or twice the maximum number of troops ever recorded in action on a single front (80,000 in the west, in Persarmenia and northern Mesopotamia, in 530). This gives us a figure of 150,000–160,000 field troops, or a grand total of 300,000 or 310,000 men serving in the Sasanian forces – a number which does not include the guards-regiments stationed in Ctesiphon and its vicinity, responsible for the personal protection of the *shāhānshāh* and for security in the inner zone of the metropolitan region on both banks of the Tigris within the shielding canals to north and east.

Both these lines of argument, inevitably conjectural, point to a total of over 300,000 men serving in the Sasanian army in time of war. The peacetime establishment was probably rather lower, with a reduction in the strength of mobile field forces. As in the case of the late Roman army, the extra manpower required when there was the prospect of serious fighting on one or more fronts was probably generated in the Iranian core of the empire by concerted recruiting drives, initiated from the centre and conducted in the localities by generals with high reputations.[72] In the periphery, the task of mobilising a given number of troops was delegated, we know, to client-rulers. How, though, was the standing army replenished normally? What were the terms on which soldiers, whether cavalry or infantry, were recruited? Such scraps of evidence as there are suggest that soldiers serving in the field armies were paid in cash, before as well as after the reform programme initiated by

---

70 Rekavandi *et al.*, 'Imperial Frontier', 130-131; Rekavandi *et al.*, 'Sasanian Walls', 161–66.

71 Gabri Qaleh, Qaleh Daland and Qaleh Gug A. Information on the other four compounds from Eberhard Sauer.

72 Cf. Whitby, 'Recruitment in Roman Armies', 63–68, 83–85, 116–19.

Khusraw I in the 530s. Hence the regular output of silver drachms, of a single authorised design, to the same high standard, from mints distributed across the empire throughout the Sasanian period.[73] Equipment seems to have been issued by the state: hence the regime of rigorous inspection which was the principal military reform introduced by Khusraw I and a legal requirement to return equipment at the death of a soldier.[74] We may also conjecture that military families benefited from certain fiscal concessions.

It is hard to say whether or not regular soldiers were allotted land in return for military service, whether or not there was a special category of military estates, the holders of which were hereditarily obliged to join the army, on the pattern of the system developed in the Byzantine rump of the east Roman Empire in the course of the dark age. The only evidence is indirect: reference is made in the *Book of a Thousand Judgements* to the sealing (formal registration) of a son by his father into the *asabar nipik*, 'List of Horsemen'. The circumstances envisaged are far from clear: the sealing may or may not have been a voluntary act of the father, in return for which he received a benefit from the state, say exemption or partial exemption from tax; if it was obligatory, it may have fallen on the family or may have been attached to the land, in which case the father merely retained the right to choose which of his sons would take the duty over from him.[75] The only firmly attested grants of land to individual subjects of the king in return for military service were made to senior commanders in recognition of past achievements.[76] Foreign forces, however, might be offered land (with the vital addition of water) for resettlement within the empire, as an inducement to come over and fight for Iran. This happened in the case of the Turks (53,000 all told) who sought asylum and were, after some hesitation, admitted through the Caspian Gates in 568–9. It was a time of gathering crisis when the Qaghan of the Turks was initiating talks to forge a Roman-Turkish alliance against the Sasanians. Any boost to Persian military strength, as was on offer from these Turks, in reality probably dissident subjects of the Turks who probably included Hephthalites and Sabir Huns, was eagerly grasped. For reasons of security, the incomers were reorganised into seven subdivisions and dispersed to the Marv region, Adurbadagan and, at least, one other area, where local military commanders could watch over them and make sure that they and their families were provisioned and accommodated. Those selected by the Sasanian authorities to take

[73] M. Alram and R. Gyselen, *Sylloge Nummorum Sasanidarum: Paris-Berlin-Wien*, I *Ardashir I.-Shapur I.*, Vienna 2003; N. Schindel, *Sylloge Nummorum Sasanidarum: Paris-Berlin-Wien*, iii.1–2 *Shapur II.-Kawad I./2. Regierung*, Vienna 2004.

[74] Bosworth (tr.), *History of al-Ṭabarī*, v, 262–63. Cf. Christensen, *L'Iran sous les Sassanides*, 367–70; Rubin, 'Reforms of Khusraw Anūshirwān', 289–91. A. Perikhanian, *The Book of a Thousand Judgements*, Costa Mesa 1997, 189.

[75] M. Macuch, *Das sasanidische Rechtsbuch "Matakdan i Hazar Datistan" (Teil II)*, Abhandlungen für die Kunde des Morgenlandes 45.1, Wiesbaden 1981, 163, 165, 173–74. Cf. M. Zakeri, *Sasanid Soldiers in Early Muslim Society: The Origins of 'Ayyaran and Futuwwa*, Wiesbaden, 1995, 53–55.

[76] Thus Juansher, commander (*sparapet*) of the Albanian army, was rewarded for his gallantry at Qadisiyya with villages as well as military and court insignia - Movses Daskhurants'i (or Kałankatuats'i), ed. V. Arak'eljan, *Movses Kałankatuats'i: Patmut'iwn Ałuanits'*, Erevan 1983, 175.13–14, tr. C. J. F. Dowsett, *Moses Dasxuranc'i's History of the Caucasian Albanians*, London 1961, 112.

command were offered the additional inducement of individual landholdings, their companions (perhaps their leading retainers) that of 'stately attire'.[77]

There can be no doubt about the fighting capability of the Sasanian army in the early centuries (third–fifth), given the sequence of victories won over the Romans between 230 and 260, the successful defensive operations against the Huns in the east in the 350s, and the expeditions of Bahrām V into the steppes.[78] Roman generals never lost their respect for their Persian adversaries. Both Belisarius (in 530) and Heraclius (in 622) had to contend with a widespread sense of inferiority among their men.[79] From the first the Sasanians had developed the logistics to keep large forces in the field. Persian soldiers, like their Roman counterparts, were adept at all types of warfare: new roads could be pushed through difficult, wooded terrain, to improve mobility; rivers could be bridged on campaign, with pontoons brought up on wagons; a full array of siege machines could be deployed, both to attack enemy strongholds and to fend off enemy besiegers.[80] Man for man, the Persian soldier was a match for his Roman counterpart. Belisarius' denigration of the infantry should be taken for what it was, a morale-boosting speech on the eve of battle in 530, a rhetorical counterblast to the defeats inflicted on Roman forces in Lazica and north Mesopotamia in 528.[81] The advantage enjoyed by the Persians in heavy cavalry and heavy infantry in the fourth century, which was noted by Ammianus Marcellinus, had apparently been lost by the sixth century. The Roman army had developed its own heavy fighting arms, both for defense (the key role being played by close-knit formations of heavy infantry) and offense (a new penetrative power being achieved by heavy cavalry charging in close formation). It was rather Persian light infantry from Daylam, capable of operating in rugged terrain, their light cavalry adept at fighting and manoeuvering away from flat, open ground, and their swift rate of arrow fire, which impressed Roman commanders in the sixth century.[82]

---

[77] Rubin, 'Reforms of Khusraw Anūshirwān', 279–284.

[78] Dodgeon and Lieu, *Roman Eastern Frontier*, 9–67; Ammianus, xiv.3.1, xvi.9.3–4; Bosworth (tr.), *History of al-Ṭabarī*, v, 94–99; Mohl, *Firdousi*, v, 539–51.

[79] Procopius, *Wars*, i.14.21; George of Pisidia, *Expeditio Persica*, iii.281–304, ed. A. Pertusi, *Giorgio di Pisidia, Poemi, I. Panegirici epici*, Studia Patristica et Byzantina 7, Ettal 1960, 128–9.

[80] Road-building: Procopius, *Wars*, ii.15.31–34, 17.1. Pontoons: Agathias, iii.20.1. Examples of siege warfare: Ammianus, xix.5.1– Amida in 359; Procopius, *Wars*, ii.26–7 – Edessa in 544; Procopius, *Wars*, viii.14.3–13 – Archaeopolis in 551.

[81] Procopius, *Wars*, i.14.25–7.

[82] Ammianus, xxiv.6.8, xxv.1.11–13 (heavy cavalry and infantry); Procopius, *Wars*, viii.14.6–9 (Daylamites); Mauricius, *Strategicon*, ed. G. T. Dennis, CFHB XVII, Vienna 1981, xi.1, lines 29–32, 54–70, tr. G. T. Dennis, *Maurice's Strategikon: Handbook of Byzantine Military Strategy*, Philadelphia 1984, 114–15 (light cavalry); Procopius, *Wars*, i.18.31–34 (rapid rate of fire). Rance, 'Battle', 352–355 for the late Roman army. D. Nicolle, *Sassanian Armies: The Iranian Empire Early 3rd to Mid-7th Centuries AD*, Stockport 1996 for line drawings of weaponry (bow, lance and lasso) used in combat and out hunting (as pictured in monumental reliefs and on silver vessels), and for rare illustrations of heavy cavalry lancers and infantry archers (from Penjikent). Additional evidence, documenting *inter alia* central Asian influence (splint armour and conical helmets), is gathered by St. J. Simpson in his review of Nicolle in *Antiquity* 71, 1997, 242–46.

By 620, two years before Heraclius began the difficult process of trying to re-invigorate his demoralised forces (through intensive training in combat together with speeches presenting the war as a holy war against an impious enemy), the Sasanian army had succeeded in conquering virtually the whole of the Near East and was poised to overrun Asia Minor and to take out Constantinople. Khusraw II (590–628) could take justifiable pride in the achievements of his great generals, Shahrvaraz, Shahen and K'rtakaren, whom he threatened to let loose against the Turks if they dared to give help to Heraclius.[83] They were the men who had, in effect, mastered the world. The mere mention of their names together with the reputation of Persian arms would, he hoped, give the Turks pause. In the event, the Turks, who plainly had good intelligence, were able to take advantage of Persian overstretch and to break through the Caspian Gates, soon after the first serious reverse suffered by the Persians when they and their Avar allies failed to take Constantinople in 626. This was the beginning of the end for Khusraw. But it was only the fortuitous conjunction of Turkish intervention in force in Transcaucasia at the critical time and the strategic ingenuity of Heraclius (a unique mix of boldness and guile) which brought about a palace coup against Khusraw.[84]

The army's morale was sapped over the following few years. For troubles multiplied. A period of political turbulence, with rival claimants striving and fighting for power, followed Khusraw's execution on 28 February 628. His scheme of world conquest was not merely frustrated. Within two years, all his territorial gains had to be disgorged under the terms of the peace eventually agreed with the Romans. But the army proved remarkably resilient and showed itself to be a capable fighting force in the later 630s, when it put up stiff resistance to the Arabs. A brilliant counteroffensive drove them out of the irrigated alluvium of lower Mesopotamia and imperilled the whole Islamic venture at the outset. Even after the climactic battle of Qadisiyya, on January the sixth 638, when a large Persian field army was decisively defeated in open, orthodox combat, resistance continued, engagements were fought and the pace of Arab advance was slowed. It took them sixteen years to impose their authority to some degree on the whole territory of the empire and to drive the last *shāhānshāh* off into the steppes and to his death.[85]

VI. ARMY ORGANIZATION

The late Sasanian army was a formidable fighting force, large, resilient, skilled in all branches of warfare, with a remarkable record on all fronts, until the rise of Islam. The efficient marshalling of its component units and their effective deployment in designated theatres of war bespeak an organisational capability of a high order (Fig. 3). This can be seen best at the very end of the Sasanian era. A collection of texts about the history of the Caucasian Albanians (Ałuank') in the seventh century, put together between 682 and 685,

---

[83] Movses Daskhurants'i, 134.6–13, tr. Dowsett, *Moses Dasxuranc'i's History,* 82.

[84] J. Howard-Johnston, 'Heraclius' Persian Campaigns and the Revival of the Eastern Roman Empire, 622–630', *War in History* 6, 1999, 1–44, repr. in Howard-Johnston, *East Rome*, VIII.

[85] Thomson and Howard-Johnston, *Armenian History*, 221–26, 243–46, 251–53, 264–66.

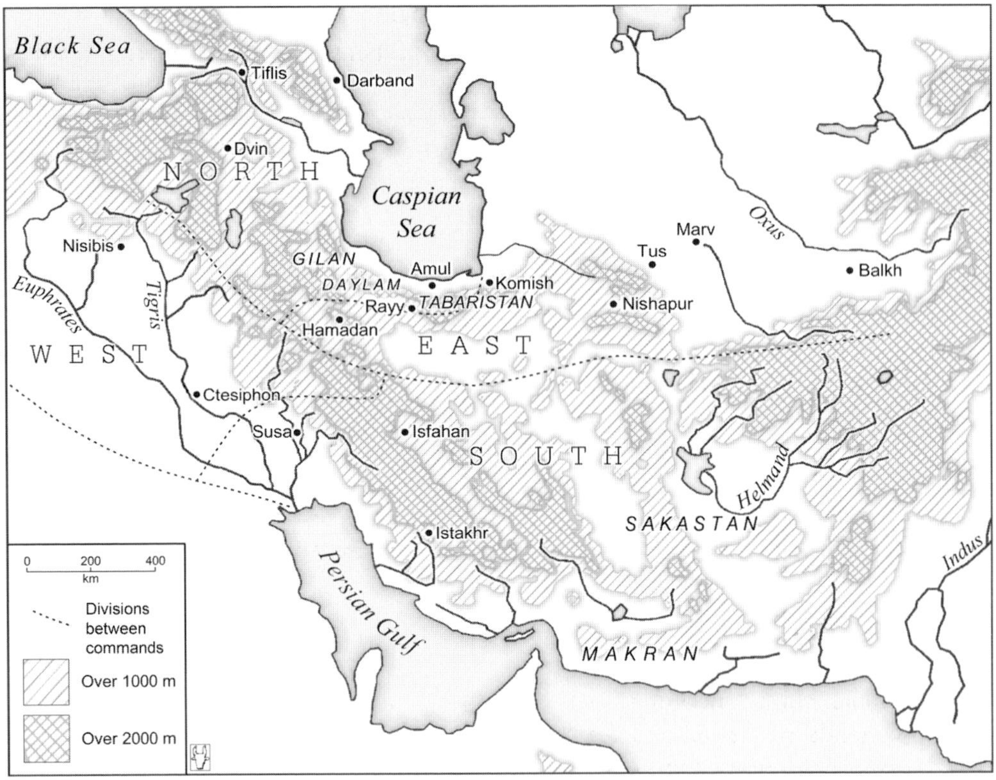

Fig. 3. The Four spāhbed *Commands*

which has been preserved in a later universal history, includes an account of the call to arms issued in Transcaucasia after the initial Arab successes in lower Mesopotamia in 636. Troops were mobilised by 'generals and princes, lords and indigenous nobles of the various regions subject to the kingdom of Persia'. The prince of the Albanians sent a contingent under the command of his son Juansher to the designated assembly place, where they joined the forces commanded by the prince of Siwnik' and the *sparapet* of Armenia. The Transcaucasian forces were then placed under the command of the Persian general Rustam for the counteroffensive against the Arabs in Mesopotamia.[86] Juansher was confirmed as commander (*sparapet*) of the Albanians on their arrival at Ctesiphon, fought at Qadisiyya, where he was wounded, was promoted (being granted some villages at the same time),

[86] Movses Daskhurants'i, 173.4–174.1, tr. Dowsett, *Moses Dasxuranc'i's History*, 109–10. Cf. J. Howard-Johnston, 'Armenian Historians of Heraclius: An Examination of the Aims, Sources and Working-Methods of Sebeos and Movses Daskhurantsi', in G. J. Reinink and B. H. Stolte, ed., *The Reign of Heraclius (610-641): Crisis and Confrontation*, Leuven 2002, 41–62, at 49–58, repr. in Howard-Johnston, *East Rome*, V.

and continued to serve the king loyally for another seven years.[87]

The Transcaucasian mobilisation was but a small part of a much larger operation, which put a great army into the field and which resulted in the ejection of the Arabs from lower Mesopotamia in 637. Similar processes should be envisaged as taking place whenever armies, great or small, were deployed in one or more theatres of war, in previous centuries. The Sasanian state, centralised, institutionally advanced, as was demonstrated by the scale of the infrastructure projects which it could organise as also by its stable and universal monetary system, had developed a command structure and an empire-wide military organisation of impressive efficiency. This was, of course, responsible for much more than mobilisation and direction of operations in wartime. Apart from recruiting, equipping, training and provisioning regular soldiers, it was responsible for distributing them across the empire's territory, allocating a majority to garrison duties on the frontier, others to the policing of potentially refractory areas, others still to strategically central positions, ready for deployment elsewhere.

There is, alas, all too little of the hard evidence – documentary, epigraphic, legal, literary – from which historians have been able to reconstruct the main features of the organisation of the contemporary Roman army and of its higher command. We have to scrabble around for odd, disconnected pieces of information. Three types of useful material can be picked up, from which to piece together some sort of a picture of Sasanian military organisation:

(1) a small number of official sealings testify to the existence of a set of four regional generals (*spāhbeds*) and a number (seven are currently known) of what were probably senior commanders of guards-regiments (*framādārs*);

(2) two well-informed Armenian historical texts, an account of the two fifth-century Armenian rebellions written by a contemporary, Łazar P'arpets'i, and the history attributed to Sebeos which dates from the middle of the seventh century, include detailed information about senior commanders operating in Armenia and the career of one Armenian general, Smbat Bagratuni, who rose to the very top of the army in the early seventh century – both these works seem to have had access to official Sasanian sources;

(3) perhaps the most valuable of all is a third Armenian text, the *Geography* of Ananias of Shirak, dating from the 660s – this includes a breakdown of the Sasanian Empire into four quarters, which correspond, almost certainly, to the four commands of the *spāhbeds*, and a breakdown of each of the four quarters into its constituent units.

In what follows I shall lay out the material culled from these sources about the structure of command, and shall then try to tease out some information about the functioning of the structures, in particular about the managerial capability of the high command as revealed in the crucial process of transforming the dispersed elements of the peacetime army into an effective instrument of war, available for use on any sector of the frontier. This vital task of combining units from different regional commands in an efficient and

[87] Movses Daskhurants'i, 174.1–177.2, tr. Dowsett, *Moses Dasxuranc'i's History,* 110–13.

timely manner into larger field armies was performed well on numerous occasions. Clues as to how it was achieved are to hand in the geographical distribution of guards-regiments and in the delineation of the boundaries of the regional commands.

Khusraw I Anūshīrvān (531–79) looms large in the versions of the official Sasanian history which have come down to us. This was not just because his reign stood at the limits of retentive memory at the time when that history became fixed, at the downfall of the empire in 651–2, but also because of the scale of the reform programme which he initiated, almost certainly right at the start of his reign, when he needed to secure his position by demonstrating his fitness to rule and by improving the functioning of the Sasanian state. It was Khusraw who promoted a literary and intellectual revival, and was probably responsible for commissioning the official dynastic history, the *Khwadāynāmag*, which, like its Christian analogues, reached back to the beginning of time. His prime concerns, though, seem to have been to increase the resources available to government, by shifting from a share-cropping system of taxation to one of fixed, annual liabilities, and to increase the striking power of the army – both rendered necessary by the proximity of a great and hostile empire in the west, itself being subject to a general institutional overhaul by Justinian.[88]

Apart from improvements to the inspection regime, to ensure that equipment was not mislaid nor allowed to deteriorate, the principal military reform involved the high command. Khusraw it is who is credited with dividing a unitary high command and instituting four regional commands, headed by *spāhbeds*.[89] Justinian's establishment of an independent Armenian field command under a *magister militum*, hived off from the unwieldy command of the *magister militum* of the East, cannot have escaped his attention.[90] A small number of holders of the *spāhbed* commands are known through their sealings, which have recently been subjected to systematic and thorough scrutiny by Rika Gyselen.[91] The iconography is uniform. The *spāhbed* is shown in full armour, riding an armoured horse and holding a lance, with a sheathed sword at his side. An emblem on the helmet (three crescents supine) indicates his rank, which is also stated in words. The inscription details the particular command held – *Khwarāsān* (East), *Nēmrōz* (South), *Khwararān* (West) or *Ādurbādagān* (North) – and the military post traditionally associated with each command – Parthian *aspbed* (Master of Horse – East), Persian *aspbed* (South),[92] *hazārbed* (Commander of a Thousand – West), and *aspbed* of the Empire (North). Eight *spāhbeds* are named on the eleven extant sealings, as are the kings under whom they served – Khusraw in five cases, Khusraw and Hormizd (Hormizd IV, 579–90) in two, Hormizd in one.

For the geographical definition of the commands, we turn to the short Persian section

---

[88] Christensen, *L'Iran sous les Sassanides*, 415–29; P. Huyse cited by J. Wiesehöfer, 'Iraniens, Grecs et Romains', *Studia Iranica* 32, Paris 2005, 139, n.240; Rubin, 'Reforms of Khusraw Anūshirwān'.

[89] Bosworth (tr.), *History of al-Ṭabarī*, v, 149–50.

[90] Malalas, xviii.10.

[91] R. Gyselen, *The Four Generals of the Sasanian Empire: Some Sigillographic Evidence*, Rome 2001.

[92] Omitted in the case of one of the three attested postholders (Pirag) – Gyselen, *Four Generals*, 40–41.

in Ananias of Shirak's *Geography*.[93] The largest command, in terms of the number of subordinated military districts, was the eastern, with 26. Most, if not all of these military districts were probably coterminous with civilian provinces. It stretched from Hamadan in Media to the southern flank of the Elburz at Komish, with an extension to Gurgan to the north, then over Abarshahr (including the important cities of Nev-Shabuhr [Nishapur] and Tus), Marv and Marv-rud, as far as the Oxus and Herat.[94] The second largest was the southern, with 19 subdivisions, which reached out from Khuzistan through the historic heartland of Persia proper to the wild lands of the far south-east as far as Zabulistan and the lower Indus plain (Sind and Debuhl). Key positions in the Gulf (in Bahrain and Oman) also belonged to the southern command.[95] The smallest command was the western, with a mere eight subdivisions.[96] Four were resource-rich – Kashkar (in the irrigated alluvium, below the metropolitan region),[97] Garmegan or Beth Garmai (north of the irrigated alluvium – the plain around modern Kirkuk, together with the nearby upland basin of Syarazur),[98] Nod-Ardashiragan or Adiabene (the upper Tigris plain together with the lower valleys of the Great and Little Zab, centering on Nineveh),[99] and Mayjinesteh (a corruption of Marjin/Mygdonia, on the right, west bank of the upper Tigris, extending to the frontier beyond Nisibis in the north and Singara in the south).[100] The other four covered the northern Zagros together with Media south of Hamadan, including Bisutun, strategic routes into the mountains *via* Kangavar and Nihavand and the important passes which emerge at modern Qasr-i Shirin and Pol-i Dokhtar.[101]

Finally, there is the northern command, about which we are better informed, thanks

---

[93] Ed. A. Soukry, *Géographie de Moïse de Corène*, Venice 1881, reproduced in facsimile as *Ashkharhatsoyts (AŠXARHAC'OYC'), the Seventh Century Geography Attributed to Ananias of Shirak*, ed. R. H. Hewsen, Delmar, NY 1994, 40. Translation and commentary in R. H. Hewsen, *The Geography of Ananias of Širak (AŠXARHAC'OYC'): The Long and Short Recensions*, Wiesbaden 1992, 72, 226–34.

[94] Localisation of districts: J. Marquart, *Eranšahr nach der Geographie des Ps. Moses Xorenac'i*, Abhandlungen der k. Gesellschaft der Wiss. zu Göttingen, Phil.–hist. Kl., ns.3.2, Berlin 1901, 47–93; R. Gyselen, *La géographie administrative de l'empire sassanide: Les témoignages sigillographiques*, Paris, 1989, 51–52, 84–85; R. Gyselen, *Nouveaux matériaux pour la géographie historique de l'empire sassanide: Sceaux administratifs de la collection Ahmad Saeedi*, Paris 2002, 148–51, 155, 162, 190–91, 193–94.

[95] Marquart, *Eranšahr*, 25–47; Gyselen, *Géographie administrative*, 70–73, 74–76, 85–88; Gyselen, *Nouveaux matériaux*, 165–68, 168–69, 169–70, 181, 183, 191–93, 194.

[96] Marquart, *Eranšahr*, 17–25. Ananias counts nine districts, having split Nod-Ardaširagan (Adiabene – see n.98 below) in two (Notartay and Širakan).

[97] M. G. Morony, 'Continuity and Change in the Administrative Geography of Late Sasanian and Early Islamic al-'Iraq', *Iran* 20, 1982, 1–49, at 30–4; Gyselen, *Géographie administrative*, 77–8.

[98] Morony, 'Continuity and Change', 14–18; Gyselen, *Géographie administrative*, 49; Gyselen, *Nouveaux matériaux*, 145–46.

[99] Morony, 'Continuity and Change', 5, 10–14; Gyselen, *Géographie administrative*, 56, 78–79; Gyselen, *Nouveaux matériaux*, 183–184.

[100] Hewsen, *Geography of Ananias*, 232; Gyselen, *Géographie administrative*, 79; Gyselen, *Nouveaux matériaux*, 134–136, 184.

[101] Morony, 'Continuity and Change', 5–6; Gyselen, *Géographie administrative*, 45–46, 53–54, 55, 82–84; Gyselen, *Nouveaux matériaux*, 157–58, 160, 161.

to the information which can be extracted from Armenian sources. Something can be learned about the upper echelons of the command structure below the *spāhbed*, as well as about the territorial extent of the *spāhbed*'s authority. The fourteen subdivisions were headed by Adurbadagan (what is now Iranian Azerbaijan, centering on Lake Urmia). The main constituent parts of Sasanian Transcaucasia formed five subdivisions - Armenia, Iberia, Albania, Balasagan (the Caspian Gates) and Siunia. Rayy (near modern Tehran) headed the larger eastern component of the command, which extended along the Elburz mountain range from Gilan to Dunbawand and included the Caspian lowlands (Amul and Tabaristan).[102]

The highest-ranking commanders serving under a *spāhbed* were *marzbāns*. Three are attested in the grand army operating on Roman territory between autumn 503 and autumn 504, one in command of the vanguard, another dispatched against Melitene, a third in command of the Amida garrison.[103] Over a century later it is as *marzbān* of Gurgan, within the eastern military quarter, that Smbat Bagratuni is credited with the final suppression in 601 of the rebellion of Khusraw II's maternal uncle Bistam, and with the revival of the war-damaged local economy.[104] He retired after eight years in post (600/1–607/8) but was recalled to active service, this time as commander-in-chief (so *spāhbed*), at a time of gathering crisis in the east (615–16), with authority to appoint his own *marzbāns*.[105] But we are best informed about the *marzbān* of Armenia. Several figure in Łazar of Pharb's detailed account of the Sasanian military responses to the Armenian rebellions of 450–1 and 482–4. This makes it plain that the post was in the gift of the crown and normally went to members of the Armenian nobility. *Marzbāns* could, of course, be dismissed, if they proved unsatisfactory, as was the case with the unpopular quisling Vasak in 451 (also sacked as Prince of Siunia), or if an absolutely reliable post-holder was needed, as happened early in 484 at end of the second rebellion when the *shāhānshāh* was planning his last, fatal expedition into the steppes (a Persian grandee, Shabuhr Mihran was appointed).[106]

Marzbāns were professional soldiers, since they could be entrusted with the direction of operations in the field, but they were also responsible for general administration in their area of competence. They were thus distinguished from regular provincial governors

[102] Ananias' total (13) does not correspond to the number of districts listed (14). Localisations: Marquart, *Eranšahr*, 94–136; Gyselen, *Géographie administrative*, 44, 45, 49–50, 57, 58–59, 63, 79–81; Gyselen, *Nouveaux matériaux*, 127–30, 131–34, 139–40, 146, 156–58, 164–65, 169, 176–77, 184–88.

[103] *Chronicle of Pseudo-Joshua*, cc.64, 66, 77.

[104] His command may have extended to the neighbouring provinces of Komish, Abarshahr and Tus – see R. Gyselen, 'Sources arméniennes et sources primaires sassanides: harmonie et dissonance', in M.-A. Amir Moezzi, J.-D. Dubois, C. Jullien and F. Jullien, ed., *Pensée grecque et sagesse d'orient: Hommage à Michel Tardieu*, Turnhout 2009, 293–306 at 301.

[105] Ps.Sebeos, 96.18–30, 98.8–17, 99.14–100.4, 100.27–103.21, with Thomson and Howard-Johnston, *Armenian History*, II *Historical Commentary* (cited henceforth as *Hist.Com.*), 181–89. A radically different, earlier chronology is proposed by Gyselen, 'Sources arméniennes', 299–305.

[106] Łazar, 47 and 83 (Vasak, *marzbān* of Armenia in 450-451, previously *marzbān* of Iberia), 118 (Atrushnasp Yozmandean, *marzbān* of Armenia in 482), 121 (Sahak Bagratuni, designated *marzbān* by Armenian rebels in 482), 121 (unnamed *marzbān* of Koprik'), 146 (Shapuh Mihran, *marzbān* of Armenia in 484).

(*shahrābs*, *ōstānādars*) whose authority was confined to civil affairs, and from senior military commanders who had no civil powers.[107] The title of the latter, Commander of a Thousand (*hazārbed* in Persian, *hazarapet* in Armenian, *chiliarchos* in Greek), should probably be taken to mean general, and could be applied to commanders operating at different levels – for example, the commander-in-chief in Transcaucasia when rebellion broke out in Armenia in 450 (*hazārbed* of the Aryans) or a field commander operating in Armenia alongside the *marzbān* in 482.[108] The post of *marzbān* could be combined with a military command in exceptional circumstances, as it was in Armenia a few years after the end of the 482–4 rebellion, when Vahan Mamikonean had proved his loyalty to the crown.[109]

Additional information about the roles of *spāhbed* and *marzbān* in Persarmenia can be culled from summaries of what look like official lists of generals and governors serving in Persarmenia in the late sixth and early seventh century, which are included in the history attributed to Sebeos, as well as from longer notices about operations on the Armenian front between 603 and 611.[110] The assassination of the *marzbān* Suren in Dvin in 572 was the signal for a general uprising and, once the Sasanians reacted militarily, for Roman intervention in force.[111] From spring 573, when the Persians found themselves under attack in north Mesopotamia and, probably, in the east (from the Turks) as well as in Transcaucasia, Gorgon Mihran (ps.Sebeos' Gołon Mihran), *spāhbed* of Adurbadagan, was sent in with 20,000 regular soldiers and additional auxiliaries from the Caucasus to direct military operations. He remained in post for seven years, in sole command during the first phase of containment, then taking part in the reimposition of Sasanian authority under the supreme command of Khusraw I himself in 576 and Tam Khusraw in 577–8.[112] With the accession of Hormizd IV in 579, he was replaced by a certain Varaz Vzur, who met with mixed fortunes, and, within a year, so from 580, by the *spāhbed* of the East ('the great Parthian and Pahlavi *aspbed*', i.e. the Parthian Master of Horse, of the Pahlav family), who remained in post for seven years, so into 586.[113] It was a period of Turkish introversion (rival leaders competing for supreme power) when it was relatively safe to combine the two commands of Adurbadagan and the East and to concentrate their forces on the northern, Transcaucasian sector of the western frontier.[114] By 586, with the fighting localised and attritional, the command in Armenia could be handed over to *marzbāns*, who were succeeded, in the years of peace between the great powers (13, if they are counted from the moment the Romans

[107] Gyselen, *Nouveaux matériaux*, 106–110.

[108] Mihrnerseh, *hazarapet* of Aryans in 450 (Łazar, 39); Vehvehnam, *hazarapet* of Armenia in 482 (Łazar, 118, 120–21).

[109] Vahan was *sparapet* of Armenia, a command apparently analogous to that of *hazārbed/hazarapet* but held by an Armenian (Łazar, 174–76). His appointment as *marzbān* was made on the recommendation of Andekan, Šapuh Mihran's successor as *marzbān* of Armenia (Łazar, 177–78).

[110] Lists: ps.Sebeos, 70.10–71.22, 105.21–25, 113.29–34, with *Hist.Com.*, 166–67, 189–90, 204–205. Longer notices: ps.Sebeos, 107.31–110.11, 111.11–112.19.

[111] Ps.Sebeos, 70.15–16, with *Hist.Com.*, 166.

[112] Ps.Sebeos, 70.17–71.4, with *Hist.Com.*, 166 (where Tam Khosrov is wrongly taken to be Gołon Mihran's successor rather than superior); Gyselen, *Four Generals*, 44.

[113] Ps.Sebeos, 71.5–8, with *Hist.Com.*, 166–7.

[114] Barfield, *Perilous Frontier*, 133–38.

formally backed the claim of the fugitive Khusraw II) by a series of civilian governors.[115]

The *marzbān*'s term of office seems to have been shorter on average than that of the *spāhbed*. The two *marzbāns* (Hrahat and Hratrin Datan) who succeeded the Parthian Master of the Horse in 586, were in post for four and two years respectively.[116] During the long tenure of Shahen who succeeded four short-lived holders of the command of *spāhbed* of Adurbadagan in 609 at the latest and was probably still in post in 626 when he was killed in battle in Asia Minor, there were five *marzbāns* based in Dvin, the capital of Persarmenia, the last of whom, Eroč Vehan (Rahzadh) had to cope as best he could with Heraclius' second invasion of Persarmenia in 627.[117] An incident, reported in ps.Sebeos and dating to the period of Smbat Bagratuni's temporary retirement, between 608 and 615, allows us to catch a glimpse of three tiers of Sasanian command: a *spāhbed*, either Shahen or his immediate predecessor, Ashtat Yeztayar, was in post, as we know from ps.Sebeos' list; a plan, supported by Smbat, took shape to rebuild the church of St. Gregory the Illuminator in Dvin; objections (vain – they were overruled by Khusraw) were lodged by the *marzbān* and the garrison commander on the grounds that the church would be too close to the citadel.[118] A similar three-tiered system of command features fleetingly in the biography of Juansher summarised by Movses Daskhurants'i. Juansher was, we are told, rewarded for his valour at the battle of Qadisiyya by being appointed general (so either *hazārbed* or *marzbān*, evidently a promotion from his previous post as *sparapet* of Albania) and, as such, confronted two antagonistic local military commanders (almost certainly commanders of urban garrisons) in the provinces of Mad and Hamadan and managed to bring their conflict to an end, thereby gaining esteem in the eyes of his superior, Khorazat, Rustam's successor as *spāhbed* of Adurbadagan.[119]

It may then be suggested, tentatively, that each of the four regional commands presided over a set of military districts-cum-provinces, that important fortified cities had their own garrison commanders, that professional military commanders might be appointed, from time to time, as circumstances demanded, to take charge of provinces as *marzbāns* and, *in extremis*, to operate alongside the provincial authorities, whether civil or military, as *hazārbeds*. It has also been seen that the system of four regional commands was not inflexible. If external pressure eased on one of the quadrants of the empire, the opportunity could be exploited to magnify the force brought to bear on another front, as happened in Transcaucasia in 580–6, when the Pahlav *spāhbed* of the East took over the northern command. Equally, if unusually large concentrations of troops were required for major operations, the mobile forces of two regional commands might be assigned to a single theatre of war, to carry out coordinated operations, as happened in 617 when two deep-penetrating attacks were launched into Asia Minor and again in 619 when Egypt was invaded in massive force. These two campaigns involved both *spāhbeds* whose commands abutted on Roman territory, Shahen *spāhbed* of Adurbadagan and Shahrvaraz *spāhbed* of

[115] Ps.Sebeos, 71.9–22.

[116] Ps.Sebeos, 71.9–13.

[117] Ps.Sebeos, 107.31–110.11, 111.11–112.19.

[118] Ps.Sebeos, 100.5–18, with *Hist.Com.*, 182–3.

[119] Movses Daskhurants'i, 175.4–176.1, tr. Dowsett, *Moses Dasxuranc'i's History*, 111–12.

the West.[120]

Scattered references to military officers bearing other titles (*k'rprm'an*, *tansardaran*, *kanārang*, *sālār*) are to be found in other sources – e.g. Pahlavi papyri from the ten-year occupation of Egypt (619–29) and a Roman report of intelligence received about the planned *putsch* against Khusraw II in early 628.[121] So there is much more to be said about the officer corps and its senior ranks. But one category of senior officer – the *framādār*, 'commander' – can be singled out for inspection forthwith, because of the relative abundance of precise documentation available on extant official sealings. Seven such commands are attested, each associated with a specific area. The most important was the *wāspuhragān-framādār* of Khusraw-shad-Kawad and Khusraw-shad-Ohrmazd, provinces which lay on the east bank of the Tigris and probably straddled the Nahrawan-Cut of Khusraw canal. Given this location and the meaning of *wāspuhr* ('special' or 'court'), this *framādār* may plausibly be identified as the commander of guards-regiments, strategically placed in the metropolitan area. From this position his troops could take charge of the capital's inner line of defense along the waterway, if ever it were threatened by internal or external enemies.[122]

It must be stressed, however, that the identification of a *framādār* as a guards commander is conjectural. Only in the cases of the *wāspuhragān-framādār* and *gund-i-kadag-khwadāyagān-framādār* ('commander of the army of the house-lords' – discussed below), can we be reasonably certain that the post was a military command. But it is surely not too hazardous to extrapolate and to identify the other five attested *framādārs* as commanders of guards-regiments stationed elsewhere in the empire.[123] Their bases were, it appears, so chosen, as to enable them to act both as strategic reserves and as independent counterweights to the regional forces under the command of *spāhbeds*. Three of these hypothetical guards-regiment commands were located in northern Khuzistan – those of the *framādārs* of Veh-Andiok-Shabuhr, Eran-khwarrah-Shabuhr and Mihragan-kadag – where they were well placed to maintain law and order in the rich, irrigated lands on either side of the lower Tigris, as well as to intervene, if necessary, in Persia proper to the south or in Media to the north.[124] A fifth command was based in Isfahan, in a key strategic position between Persia and Media, and a sixth in Adurbadagan, where it could support the *spāhbed* of the

---

[120] Asia Minor 617: ps.Sebeos, 113.23–8, with *Hist.Com.*, 203–4. Egypt 619: *Chronicle to 1234*, tr. A. Palmer, *The Seventh Century in the West-Syrian Chronicles*, TTH 15, Liverpool 1993, 128, with n.289 (parallel passage in the *Chronicle* of Michael the Syrian) for Shahrvaraz; *History of the Patriarchs of the Coptic Church of Alexandria*, ed. and tr. B. Evetts, *Patrologia Orientalis* 1, Paris 1907, 487 for Shahen.

[121] O. Hansen, *Die mittelpersischen Papyri der Papyrussammlung der Staatlichen Museen zu Berlin*, Berlin 1938, nos. 1 (23–27) and 58 (82–83); A. G. Perikhanjan, 'Pechlevijskie papyrusi sobranija GMII imeni A. S. Pushkina', *Vestnik Drevnej Istorii*, 77, 1961, 78–93, at 91–92; D. Weber, *Ostraca, Papyri und Pergamente*, Corpus Inscriptionum Iranicarum 3.4–5, London 1992, nos 19 (130–33) and 23 (136); Theophanes, *Chronographia*, ed. C. de Boor, Leipzig 1883–85, i, 325.10–326.20, tr. C. Mango and R. Scott, *The Chronicle of Theophanes Confessor: Byzantine and Near Eastern History AD 284-813*, Oxford 1997, 453–54.

[122] Gyselen, *Géographie administrative*, 35; Gyselen, *Nouveaux matériaux*, 119–20, 153–54.

[123] Gyselen, *Géographie administrative*, 37–38; Gyselen, *Nouveaux matériaux*, 115–16.

[124] Gyselen, *Géographie administrative*, 55; Gyselen, *Nouveaux matériaux*, 151–52, 161.

North's troops on the Caucasus or Armenian fronts as well as ensuring the security of the great fire-temple of Adurgushnasp at modern Takht-i Sulayman.[125]

The seventh and last attested *framādār* led 'the army of the house-lords', readily identifiable with the Armenian *tanuterakan gund* ('army of the heads of household'), the command of which was given to Smbat Bagratuni (apparently for the second time) when he was appointed *spāhbed* of the East in 615–16. It was an elite Armenian force, officered by Armenian princes and nobles and amounting to some 2000 cavalry. It had served with him in Gurgan during his tenure as *marzbān* (600/1–607/8), and continued to be stationed there afterwards. It came to join him at Komish for operations further east in 615.[126] The Sasanians, like the Romans, seem to have taken care to deploy ethnically distinct forces well away from their home regions. The best example beside the Armenian guards-regiments is that of the Daylamite units allocated to the northern command, under which they can be seen fighting Roman forces on several occasions in Lazica.[127]

To the main regular formations of the army, first those guarding the frontiers and serving in mobile field forces under *spāhbeds*, *hazārbeds*, and *marzbāns*, and second guards-regiments commanded by *framādārs*, should be added troops recruited from natural nurseries of fighting men within the empire – Kurds raised from the northern extremity of the Zagros who appear occasionally in sixth century sources, highlanders from Gilan as well as Daylam in the western Elburz, Caucasian Albanians (regarded as elite troops on a par with Huns in the fourth century), and Segestani (men from Sakastan in the far south-east, again picked out by Ammianus in the fourth century).[128] Little should be read into the non-appearance of units from Gilan, Albania and Sakastan in extant accounts of sixth- and early seventh-century campaigns in the west. It is far more likely that the Sasanians deployed these units in theatres of war not covered by the extant Roman and Armenian sources than that they ceased to exploit these rich sources of fighting manpower at the end of antiquity. No less important were foreign auxiliaries from the north, either recruited from outside the frontiers of the empire – Sabir Huns from the north Caucasus – or resettled on Sasanian territory – the Turks who were admitted and then divided up in 568–9 – and the many Arab tribes in the south who were incorporated into a nexus of alliances managed by the Sasanians' Nasrid client-kingdom from its capital at Hira.[129]

That is what can be seen of the late Sasanian army's organisation through such sources

---

[125] Gyselen, *Nouveaux matériaux*, 115–16, 127, 169–70.

[126] Gyselen, *Nouveaux matériaux*, 116; ps.Sebeos, 101.1–17. Cf. R. Gyselen, 'Le *kadag-xwaday* sassanide. Quelques réflexions à partir de nouvelles données sigillographiques', *Studia Iranica* 31, 2002, 61–69 and N. Garsoïan, 'Le "Guerrier des Seigneurs"', *Studia Iranica* 32, 2003, 177–84 who envisages a permanent base for this elite unit, in the heart of Persarmenia.

[127] Procopius, *Wars*, viii, 14.5, 12, 42; Agathias, *Histories*, iii, 17.6, 18.1–11, 22.5–8, 26.1–8, 28.6–7.

[128] References in n.23 above.

[129] Sabir Huns: Procopius, *Wars*, viii, 13.6–7, 14.3–5 and 11, 16.8, 17.10; Agathias, iv, 13.7; Blockley, *History of Menander*, fr.23.1. Turks: Ibn Miskawayh, *Tajārib al-umam*, tr. Rubin, 'Reforms of Khusraw', 280–82. Nasrid client-kingdom: M. J. Kister, 'Al-Ḥīra: Some Notes on its Relations with Arabia', *Arabica* 15, 1968, 143–69; F. M. Donner, *The Early Islamic Conquests*, Princeton 1981, 44–48; Hoyland, *Arabia and the Arabs*, 78–83, 236–43.

as survive. There were three distinct components:

(1) the regular army, divided into four regional commands,
(2) guards-regiments placed at strategic locations, and
(3) foreign auxiliaries.

Much, though, remains hidden from us. We know virtually nothing of the command structure within the regular army, below the highest level. Whereas individual units of the late Roman army can be identified with the help of inscriptions, papyri and the *Notitia Dignitatum*, we are entirely in the dark about individual units of the late Sasanian army, except for those identifiable by ethnic origin. The only regimental name to figure in a sixth century source, the *Immortals* who formed the main Persian reserve at the battle of Dara, may have been no more than an archaising usage of Procopius'.[130] Finally, a vital component of the Sasanians' armed forces, the troops responsible for the personal security of the *shāhānshāh* in court and on campaign, can only be glimpsed in passing.

VII. STRATEGIC AIMS

In conclusion, something should be said about the general strategic stance of the late Sasanian army, the rationale for its division into four commands, the functions of the individual regional commands, and the mechanisms for combining units from different commands into larger, unitary fighting forces for deployment in one or more theatres of war.

The general stance in Late Antiquity was one of aggressive defense. The army was poised to uphold the dignity of the king wherever it might be challenged, and, occasionally, especially when a foreign adventure might bind together fractious domestic interests, to make bold outward strikes. Both in terms of numbers, fighting quality and forward positioning, the army in the south-east and east was geared to projecting Sasanian power outwards and maintaining Iran's historic role as arbiter of Central Asian affairs. In the north and north-west, after the first phase of dynamic expansion, massive resources were allocated to the difficult tasks of defending the frontiers where they had stabilised in the second half of the fourth century, against the peoples of the north Caucasus and a much better-resourced rival empire. A military ethos, more pronounced than that of the Romans, ran through the population of highland Iran, from the grandest aristocrats and landed gentry down to the villagers who supplied most of the infantry. A *shāhānshāh*'s prestige or glory (*khwarrah*) rested ultimately on success in war or what could be construed as success in war.[131] Hence the surprisingly long duration of a unitary military command, which could, at any point, be assumed without bureaucratic difficulty by the reigning monarch. Hence the series of great kings whose deeds in war were commemorated in monumental inscriptions and reliefs and in the pages of the late Sasanian *Khwadāynāmag*.[132]

---

[130] Procopius, *Wars*, i.14.31, 45, 49.
[131] References in n.15 above.

Hence even as cultivated a ruler as Khusraw I, was remembered as much for his victories as for his thorough-going domestic reforms.[133]

Brute reality, the demands of assuring the security of so large and diverse a continental empire, which might be assailed from several quarters at the same time (as it was, we know, in the 350s, 421–2, 573, 615–16 and 626–9), should have led to the establishment of regional commands, each taking charge of a quadrant of the empire, long before the reign of Khusraw I. The long time-lag of some 250 years between the Roman division of command, instituted by Diocletian and Khusraw's reform is to be attributed to the overriding ideological imperative of maintaining the *shāhānshāh*'s direct control of warfare and personal command on major campaigns.[134] We do not know exactly when Khusraw took the decision[135] – I am inclined to place it in the difficult plague years, around the time (545) when the western war was confined, by mutual agreement, to Lazica – but from that point on, the adaptability of the Sasanian army and its speed of reaction were undoubtedly improved. Regional defense or mobilisation for local punitive or offensive action became easier and quicker, once the command was delegated to a *spāhbed* of high status and unquestioned authority within his quadrant. Equally, large-scale mobilisation for a major expedition, drawing on the resources of more than one quadrant, would be more manageable when the central authority had to deal with a few rather than many senior commanders. Another benefit of decentralisation is likely to have been better policing of refractory highland regions.

Each of the new commands had a clearly demarcated territory,[136] which included supply zones (rich, irrigated arable lands), recruiting-grounds (mainly in the mountains) and sectors of the frontier distinguished from each other by the nature of potential outside adversaries. The western command's principal task was to protect the richest component of the empire, Mesopotamia, by guarding the sector of the frontier facing the heavily militarised Roman forward zone in north Mesopotamia and Osrhoene. It also appears, from his control over the northern segment of the Zagros range, together with the flanking plains of Mesopotamia and the rolling hill country of south-west Media, that the *spāhbed* of the West was also expected to tap the mountains for recruits and to secure the strategic passes linking Mesopotamia and Media. The extension of his authority over the rich, grain-producing lowlands down as far as the metropolitan region and beyond it to the district around Kashkar was surely intended to guarantee provisions for his troops, whether garrisoning frontier fortifications or serving in units of the regional field army.

The southern command, which had its own allocated supply zone in Khuzistan and could recruit from the central and southern Zagros, including the old heartlands of Persia, probably had two prime tasks – the projection of Sasanian power inland from the Gulf coast of Arabia and the maintenance of control over the wild country of the far south-east,

---

[132] G. Herrmann, *The Iranian Revival*, London 1977, 87–94, 96, 100, 104–106.

[133] Bosworth (tr.), *History of al-Ṭabarī*, v, 150–62, 253–55, 264.

[134] M. Whitby, 'The Persian King at War', in E. Dąbrowa (ed.), *The Roman and Byzantine Army in the East*, Kraków 1994, 227–63.

[135] Bosworth (tr.), *History of al-Ṭabarī*, v, 149–50.

[136] *Contra* Gyselen, *Four Generals*, 15–16.

which could then act as a supplementary recruiting-ground. The eastern command, much the largest in terms of the number of its subdivisions, needed all the resources, human and material, provided by its territory (including provisions from the Gurgan plain and recruits from the Köpet Dagh), to man the hard-point defenses which affixed Sasanian authority on the ground and to field expeditionary forces large enough to operate against nomad adversaries. Finally, the northern command, responsible both for garrisoning the fortifications of the Caspian Gates and securing Persarmenia from the menacing Roman presence in west Armenia had as its allocation the Caspian lowlands and the Elburz range. It would not run short of supplies or fighting manpower.

Besides the all-important task of defense against external foes, the army had to uphold law and order throughout the empire and to guarantee the security of crown, palace and capital. Law and order probably fell within the remit of the *spāhbed* commands. Hence they reached deep into the interior of the empire. They were assuredly expected to keep the highlands quiescent and to assure free passage along the network of main routes. The only large area to be excluded from the four military quadrants was the metropolitan region. Behind its formidable water defenses – to the north the Nahrmalcha canal running from the Euphrates to the Tigris, the Euphrates itself to the west and the Nahrawan-Cut of Khusraw canal to the east – the irrigated alluvium which was the empire's single greatest arable asset, supporting a highly urbanised society, was relatively secure from attack. The palace guards-regiments, of which little is known but their existence, could police this interior zone, backed by the outer guards-regiments under the command of the *wāspuhragān-framādār* who were probably responsible for policing the Nahrawan-Cut of Khusraw canal. As for the desert approaches, where this heartland of the empire was in theory most exposed, the task of defense was delegated to the Nasrid client-kings of the Lakhm, ruling from Hira. Their army, consisting of directly recruited retainers, regular Sasanian troops and tribal levies, had little difficulty in discharging this duty, as well as helping to project Sasanian authority into the interior of Arabia and acting as a loyal force ready, if called upon, to intervene in Sasanian domestic politics.[137]

Ultimately, though, the army existed to defend Iran, in its late antique imperial manifestation, against whatever threats might materialise from the alien, outer world. If the danger were great or if a grand expedition were planned beyond the frontier, different component parts of the army would have to be brought together and combined to form an organic whole, capable of fighting the enemy on equal terms, divided perhaps for operational convenience into two or more corps but directed by a single supreme commander. There would be no difficulty in establishing the high command: either the *shāhānshāh* would take personal charge or he would appoint a general of his choice. But an assembly ground was needed, to which designated units from different commands could be directed and where they could be melded into a cohesive, responsive, adaptable fighting force – something analogous to the Gurgan plain south of the long wall but for the empire as a whole and safely withdrawn from its outer regions. It can be identified, on the basis

[137] See n.129 above. Bahrām V owed his throne to Lakhm backing (cf. Christensen, *L'Iran sous les Sassanides*, 274–76).

of oblique indications given in the *Geography* of Ananias of Shirak. The territorial commands of the four *spāhbeds* converged on the western angle of the Iranian plateau and Media, which is endowed, in its northern open swathe, with extensive and lush grazing-grounds. Each of the four commands had its own presence in this region, which may therefore be taken to be the military heartland of the state: the South had a subdivision centered on Isfahan; the West's consisted of the hill country, to the south of Hamadan (May or Mad); the north had the district of Rayy; the most surprising association, though, was that of the subdivision of Hamadan with the East.[138] This meant that North and East, as it were, leap-frogged over each other. Each had a bridgehead in the other's territory, and their two bridgeheads marched with the subdivisions of Mad and Isfahan to the south. Since all these military districts adjoined each other, together they could act as the venue for the mobilisation of a composite army, drawing on more than one regional command.

It is worth noting that the only discernible strategic reserve, the three guards units stationed in Khuzistan – in Veh-Andiyok-Shabuhr (the left bank of the Dez around Susa and Shustar), Eran-Khwarrah-Shabuhr (right bank of the Dez and Karkha rivers) and Mihragan-kadag (northern tip of Khuzistan), each under the command of a *framādār* – was within striking distance of this set of four adjacent military districts, on the far side of the central Zagros but close to the Pol-i Dokhtar Pass. From there they could be called upon to reinforce the regular field forces of the regional commands, particularly if the *shāhānshāh* was in command. Thus it can be argued that Media, together with the adjoining fertile margins of the plateau, constituted the military fulcrum of the Sasanian Empire, the designated zone for the assembly and mobilisation of grand armies. This helps to explain the choice of the large, mountain-girt basin of Bisutun, at the southern edge of Media, as the principal venue for the carving of monumental rock-reliefs commemorating the deeds in war and in the simulation of war (hunting) of Khusraw II, the greatest war-leader in the late Sasanian period.[139]

The military achievements of the late Sasanian army are partly to be explained by the ideological commitment of the troops and by the generalship of its commanders. But they would have been unattainable but for the development of a flexible, regionally structured and centrally controlled organisation, which facilitated both independent action by regional armies and their amalgamation into larger, grand armies for major offensives. As a result, the performance of the army at the end of antiquity was very impressive. We may single out the collective effort of 573, when the core territories of the empire were successfully defended against Armenian rebel forces backed by Roman troops in the west and against Turks in the east, while the elderly Khusraw I launched a brilliant counterattack from within the western quadrant.[140] Equally striking was the ability of the army to sustain the rolling offensive in the west, led by Shahen, *spāhbed* of Adurbadagan, and Shahrbaraz, *spāhbed* of the West, despite the serious defeat inflicted by the Turks on the regional army

---

[138] Cf. Marquart, *Eranšahr*, 70.

[139] Herrmann, *Iranian Revival*, 131–135; J. Howard-Johnston, 'Pride and Fall: Khusraw II and his Regime, 622–630', in G. Gnoli (ed.), *La Persia e Bisanzio*, Atti dei Convegni Lincei 201, Rome 2004, 93–113, repr. in Howard-Johnston, *East Rome*, IX, at 94–96.

[140] Whitby, *Emperor Maurice*, 254–58. See also n.62 above.

of the East commanded by Smbat Bagratuni in 615, their subsequent raiding expedition deep into the interior of Iran, and the effort put into Smbat's successful counteroffensive in 616.[141] Even more impressive was the strength of the offensive strokes which could be delivered and the army's resilience in times of crisis. Both relied on a well-established mobilisation system, which could reinforce one regional field army with detachments from the others and guards units.

Had Sasanian Iran been unable to achieve great concentration of force by combining units from different commands, we would be hard put to explain its survival through the sixth century, let alone the series of victories won by Khusraw I and Khusraw II or the army's ability to strike back with devastating effect after initial defeat and retreat, as in Armenia in 576 and Mesopotamia in 637.[142] As it was, in its late antique form, the Sasanian army more than matched the armies of earlier *shāhānshāhs*. For the Roman empire which was virtually conquered by 621 was not under serious pressure on other fronts and had only been weakened by internal division for two short periods. Equally the Turks who confronted Iran in the east and the north far exceeded their predecessors, Hephthalite, Kidarite and Hunnic, in territorial reach, wealth and military capability. No wonder Khusraw II could be portrayed in the *Shāhnāma* as master of the world.[143] No wonder the Arabs marveled at the wealth and grandeur of their Persian antagonists, and only succeeded in annihilating the empire when they suborned the *spāhbed* of Adurbadagan and thus left the last *shāhānshāh*, Yazdegird III, and the army of the East facing certain defeat.[144]

---

141 Ps.Sebeos, 101.26–103.13, with *Hist.Com.*, 183–89.

142 Whitby, *Emperor Maurice*, 262-265; Thomson and Howard-Johnston, *Armenian History*, 243–46.

143 J. Mohl, *Le livre des rois par Abou'lkasim Firdousi*, vii, Paris 1878, 221–23, 267–69.

144 Thomson and Howard-Johnston, *Armenian History*, 264–66.

8

Urban Militias in the Eastern Islamic World (Third–Fourth Centuries AH/Ninth–Tenth centuries CE)

Luke Treadwell

A paper on an amorphous and contested subject such as urban militias in the early Islamic world should begin with a definition of what a militia is and what it is not. A militia could not be a dynast's standing army or a *mamlūk* royal guard. Unlike these two institutions, it was usually composed of the citizens of a single city, who may have been part-time or professional soldiers. The militiamen were usually provided with equipment (in the case of infantry) and mounts (in the case of horsemen) and were sometimes remunerated for their service by the urban authorities, either by means of a cash payment, or a land grant. The existence of the militia as a formal military institution (if only part-time) distinguished it from ephemeral bands of vigilante fighters, a well-attested phenomenon in the early Islamic period, particularly in regions where caliphal or royal authority was too weak to maintain internal security and on the frontier where adjacent enemy territory offered rich rewards to raiders. These bands formed themselves *ad hoc* for the emergency defence of their territory or to pursue *ghazw*, either attaching themselves to a larger force of professional troops or forming raiding parties of their own. Being outside the control of the city authorities, they were often perceived as having a negative effect on social order and indeed, in some cases did act against the common good, by means of robbery and extortion.[1]

The institution of the militia is of interest to Islamic historians because as a self-sustaining civic organism it attests to the ability of the city which it serves to take charge of its own affairs without the assistance of the imperial or royal power.[2] The current consensus of opinion in the secondary sources, only lightly modified by recent voices

1 For volunteer fighters in the early Islamic period, see Bosworth, 'mutaṭawwiʿa', Mélikoff, 'ghāzī' and Taeschner, "ʿayyār', all in *EI²*. None of these articles makes any mention of the institution of the militia. See Cahen, 'aḥdāth, *EI²*, for a brief summary of Cahen's views on the 'urban militia', which are elaborated at length in C. Cahen, 'Mouvements populaires et autonomisme urbain dans l'aie musulmane du moyen age', *Arabica* 5:3, 1958, 225–50; ibid., 6:1, 1959, 25–56; ibid., 6:3, 1959, 233–65.

2 See B. Shoshan, 'The "politics of notables" in medieval Islam', *Asian and African Studies* 20, 1986, 181–87.

raised against the mainstream, is that the Islamic cities showed a marked reluctance to set up autonomous institutions by contrast with medieval Europe.[3] A review of the extent and function of the urban militias in the eastern Iranian world (the *Mashriq*) during the early Islamic period thus may have a contribution to make to the wider debate about these issues.

In the Islamic world, militias have traditionally been difficult to identify, because while there are several terms which can be used to designate a militia, none of them refers exclusively to the institution. Terminological profusion and imprecision has led modern historians to believe that the autonomous organisation of military forces by individual cities was rarely undertaken and constituted the exception to the rule.[4] The main problem is that the same terms (*aḥdāth, muṭṭawwiʿa, ʿayyārūn*) are used indiscriminately by our sources to refer to groups which the context allows us to identify as militias as well as to vigilante bands. The difficulty is compounded by the fact that even when the *aḥdāth* were acting as a formal militia (as in the case of fifth-century AH Damascus described by Cahen) which fought together over several years and was led by a cadre of captains, we have very little information on the remuneration and conditions of employment of the militiamen or their military training. As for the term *muṭṭawwiʿa,* most historians have long accepted that it usually designates volunteer warriors for the faith or vigilantes, because the word itself has been so defined by medieval Muslim authors, like the sixth-century author Samʿānī who wrote as follows:

> The *muṭṭawwiʿa* is a group that devotes itself to raiding and the *jihād* and populates the *ribāṭ*s on the frontiers...[5]

But as we shall see, in the Samanid world, the term was also used to refer to the urban

[3] One recent monograph which challenges the consensus regarding the formation of local military forces, albeit at the level of a dynasty (the Samanids) rather than a city, is J. Paul, *The state and the military: the Samanid case* (Papers on Inner Asia, no. 26), Bloomington 1994. In a later work, however, Paul argues that the urban militia was a rare and exceptional phenomenon in the pre-Seljuq *mashriq*, see J. Paul, *Herrscher, Gemeinwesen, Vermittler: Ostiran und Transoxanien in vormongolischer Zeit,* Beirut 1996, esp. 123–27.

[4] See e.g. C. Cahen, 'Mouvements populaires'; Paul, *The state and the military*, and idem, *Herrscher, Gemeinwesen*; *Vermittler*, and D. Tor, *Violent order: religious warfare, chivalry, and the* ʿAyyār *phenomenon in the medieval Islamic world,* Würzburg 2007. A much simplified characterisation of the views of these historians might be formulated on the following lines. Cahen saw the *aḥdāth* as a manifestation of the autonomous power of the Islamic Syrian city which was a direct inheritance from the classical Syrian city. Paul, who studies the Islamic East, does not consider the role of the urban militia to have been significant (see previous note). He argues instead that the dihqānate, or landowning gentry, were responsible for mobilising their peasants to fight on behalf of the Samanid ruler in the third century AH, somewhat on the model of medieval European baronial levies (see below, 'Conclusions', for my views of the role of the *dihqān* in the Samanid military establishment). Tor's emphasis upon the overriding significance of holy war as the motivating factor behind *ghazw* and *taṭawwuʿ* mirrors the views of many of the medieval Arabic and Persian sources which retroject a blanket notion of pious militancy onto the complex mosaic of regional military power in the pre-Seljuq period (see below 'Militiamen as *murābiṭūn*').

[5] *Wa hum jamāʿa farraghū anfusahum li al-ghazw wa al-jihād wa rābaṭū fī al-thughūr,* Samʿānī, *Kitāb al-Ansāb,* Hyderabad 1981, xii, 317.

militia, which was equipped, commanded, and probably paid, by the urban authorities. As for the *ʿayyārūn,* while this term is most commonly used to mean unregulated bands of local vigilantes, who are often perceived to be as much of a hindrance as a help to local security, there are examples in Samanid history which show the *ʿayyārūn* collaborating closely with city authorities in times of emergency and fighting alongside the *muṭṭawwiʿa.*

This paper focuses on a number of short passages in two texts, the *Book of Gifts and Rarities* of Rashīd Ibn al-Zubayr (fifth century AH) and the chronicle of Ibn Ẓāfir al-Azdī (sixth century AH), which give accounts of the militia in Samanid times. But we begin with a brief review of the evidence for city militias in the early Abbasid period, including the Sīstānī evidence from the early career of Yaʿqūb b. Layth, the Saffarid.

MILITIAS IN THE ABBASID PERIOD

Although evidence is scanty, urban militias seem to have played a key role in regional politics during the early Abbasid period, at the very time that the caliph's power was at its peak. As Kennedy points out, this would suggest that the Abbasids conceded a fair degree of autonomy to local provincial elites. Both Mosul and Fustat, the capitals of the Jazira and Egypt, remained largely under the sway of local elites up to the Civil War which followed the death of Hārūn al-Rashīd in 193/808–9. Local notables controlled the judiciary and the military in both cities, because caliphal governors rarely had the time or the contacts, during their short tenure of office, to make much impact on the local scene. In Mosul, policing duties within the city were undertaken by the caliphal governor, but the *rawābiṭ,* a mounted corps of up to 4000 local tribesmen, defended the city against the depredations of the Kharijites who inhabited the nearby steppelands and occasionally demanded taxes from recalcitrant tribesmen.[6] In Fustat, by contrast, the local militia known as the *jund,* could field up to 5000 troops who acted both as an urban police force and a (sometimes ineffective) mobile force that could be deployed against external threat: they received stipends and were commanded by local notables.[7] This model would no doubt be replicated for many other Abbasid cities of the late second century AH, especially those beyond the central Islamic lands of Iraq and Syria, if the historical evidence were available.

The Civil War between Amīn and Maʾmūn (193/808–196/811) brought wholesale change to the political map of the Dār al-Islām. Some provinces, like Egypt, were taken over by powerful military governors appointed by the caliph who destroyed the local elites and took direct control of the military and administrative apparatus, while others, like the Jazira fell out of the caliphal orbit altogether and into the hands of local elites who ruled independently of Baghdad. After a brief resurgence of caliphal authority which began with

---

[6] H. Kennedy, 'Central government and provincial élites in the early ʿAbbasid caliphate', *Bulletin of the School of Oriental and African Studies* 44, 1981, 30–31; C. F. Robinson, *Empire and elites after the Muslim conquest: the transformation of northern Mesopotamia,* Cambridge 2000, 159ff.

[7] Kennedy, 'Central government', 34–36.

the foundation of Samarra in the early third century and lasted until the middle of that century, the caliphate entered a period of decline which culminated in the Buyid conquest of Baghdad in 334/945–6. As the caliphal centre became weaker, urban militias began to reassert their presence, particularly in the *Mashriq*, where the constant presence of the Turkish threat had always ensured a high degree of militarisation among the population, but also in the central Islamic lands, where the reach of the Abbasid army became increasingly confined to the capital. Few details are available, but Kennedy has noted that Mosul and Kufa both had effective urban militias (*junds*) which defended the city against the Kurds and Qarāmiṭa respectively, while the citizens of Hīt and Raqqa also managed to repel attacks.[8] Responsibility for local defence was also taken up by tax-farmers like ʿAlī al-Rāsibī at Junday Shapur, Sūs and Mādharāya.[9]

In Khurasan and adjacent regions the ubiquitous Kharijites destabilised large pockets of territory. The ineffectiveness of Tahirid rule from the 240s/850s onwards meant that urban populations could expect no protection against the Kharijites or any other marauders and were forced to set up their own defence networks. While modern historians have acknowledged that the residents of *mashriqī* cities were capable of taking up arms, the evidence has often been lacking to distinguish between armed rabbles or groups of 'young men' (*fityān*) which could be mobilised in emergencies and quickly disbanded, from urban militias which operated on a regular basis.[10] The consensus of the secondary sources is that local resistance movements commonly consisted of informal and loosely organised groups of volunteers, vigilantes and pious Muslims anxious to restore order and eradicate heretics. The degree of organisation among these movements is generally assumed to have been fairly low insofar as the sources give us any information about this topic.

THE SAFFARID 'MILITIA'

Yet the history of the first years of the Saffarid warlord, Yaʿqūb b. Layth (253/867–265/878) implies a higher degree of organisation among local armed bands. The earliest anti-Khārijī movements in Sistan originated from the armed citizenry of the cities of Bust (N. Afghanistan) and Zaranj (the capital of Sistan province). Yaʿqūb first appears as a follower of one Ṣāliḥ b. al-Naḍr, the leader of the *ʿayyārs* of Bust, who led his troops from Bust to Zaranj in 239/853–4 to plead before the Tahirid governor that his only motive in raising a band of armed followers was to seek revenge from the Kharijites who had killed his

[8] Urban populations were left to their own devices particularly in the reign of Muqtadir, when Abbasid authority reached a nadir. The *jund* of Kufa fought off the Qarāmiṭa in 293/905–6 (ʿArīb al-Qurṭubī, *Ṣilat ta'rīkh al-Ṭabarī*, ed. M. J. de Goeje, Leiden 1897, 12–13); while the *jund* of Mosul protected their city against the Kurds in 301/913–14 (idem, 42). The populations of Hīt and Raqqa successfully defended themselves against marauders (Miskawayh, Aḥmad b. Muḥammad, *Tajārib al-umam*, in *The Eclipse of the ʿAbbasid caliphate*, ed. and tr. H. F. Amedroz and D. S. Margoliouth, Oxford, 1920, I, 183; ʿArīb, *Ṣilat ta'rīkh al-Ṭabarī*, 134). All references in this and the following note are taken from H. Kennedy, *The armies of the caliphs: military and society in the early Islamic state*, London 2001, 163.

[9] ʿArīb, *Ṣilat ta'rīkh al-Ṭabarī*, 44.

[10] See Paul, *Herrscher, Gemeinwesen*; *Vermittler*, and *idem*, 'The Seljuq conquest(s) of Nishapur: A reappraisal', *Iranian Studies* 38, 2005, 575–85.

brother.[11] Yaʿqūb later turned against his patron, accusing him of favouring his fellow Bustīs over the Sīstānīs, which confirms the point that Ṣāliḥ's closest followers were from that city.[12] Ṣāliḥ's record of success against the Kharijites and his bold confrontation with the Tahirid governor suggest that by the time he left Bust, his troops were competent soldiers, not an urban rabble. All the more so for Yaʿqūb himself who rose to the post of *amīr* of Sistan in 247/861–2. He was a highly effective commander who administered a rigorous process of recruitment for new soldiers, imposed rigid discipline, and had a very efficient military administration. His troops were Sīstānīs, many of them former Kharijites whom he had persuaded to join his army. Before he began his forays into Khurasan, it seems that he was a successful militia leader, who managed to combine the various armed groups fighting in Sistan, among them Ṣāliḥ's Bustī militia, the ex-Khārijīs, and his own 'Sīstānī' *ʿayyārs*, into an interregional militia, whose role was to bring security to the province.[13] Yaʿqūbī, a contemporary source, tells us that Yaʿqūb received permission from the Tahirid governor of Khurasan to 'gather together / muster (*jamʿ*)' the *muṭṭawwiʿa* of Sistan.'[14] Ibn al-Athīr describes him as *mutawallī amr al-mutaṭawwiʿa* and states that his troops were given the task of maintaining order and 'regulating the roads and guarding them.'[15] As we shall see in the following section, the term *muṭṭawwiʿa* was used in Transoxania to designate a city militia.

It was surely no coincidence that militias were prevalent in Sistan, since Sistan was an anarchic border region far from the metropolitan centre. Transoxanian militias were part of a more complex military scenario and their relation to their (Samanid) rulers was different to that of their Sīstānī counterparts. The primary function of the militia in Transoxania was not to suppress local dissidents like the Kharijites, since the latter were not active in the region. The militia had two tasks: the first was to man the frontier posts (*ribāṭs*) which the Tahirids, the Samanids and their client princes, like the Afshīnid rulers of Ushrūsana, built along the fringes of the deserts and mountains that enclosed the sedentary zone; and second, to protect their native cities from attack. Both tasks were undertaken in collaboration with the Samanid *amīrs*, with whom the militia commanders had good relations. The Samanids relied on the militias rather than their standing army for these tasks because the defence of the extensive frontier required large numbers of men who could operate on a rotating basis. The closest sources of manpower available to the Samanids were the Transoxanian cities and their hinterlands. We find ample evidence in textual sources to prove that this was where the majority of *murābiṭūn* were recruited.

---

[11] C. E. Bosworth, 'The armies of the Ṣaffārids', *Bulletin of the School of African and Oriental Studies* 31, 1968, 541, citing *Tārīkh-i Sīstān*.

[12] C. E. Bosworth, *Sistan under the Arabs, from the Islamic conquest to the rise of the Saffārids (30–250/651–864)*, Rome 1968, 116.

[13] See Bosworth, 'The armies of the Ṣaffārids', for Yaʿqūb's military administration.

[14] Yaʿqūbī, *Taʾrīkh al-Yaʿqūbī*, Dar al-Sadir, Beirut 1960, ii, 495.

[15] Ibn al-Athīr, *al-Kāmil fī al-taʾrīkh*, ed. C. J. Tornberg, Dār Ṣādir reprint, Beirut 1965, vii, 185.

MILITIAS IN THE SAMANID PERIOD

The accounts of the Samanid militias describe events which occurred in the late third and early fourth centuries AH and derive from two main sources, Ibn Ẓāfir al-Azdī's *Akhbār al-duwal al-munqaṭi'a* (The History of the discontinued dynasties)[16] and Rashīd Ibn al-Zubayr's *Kitāb al-hadāyā wa al-tuḥaf* (*Book of Gifts and Rarities*).[17] Both works were composed long after the events they describe and neither author directly cites his sources for the Samanid material on the militias.[18] Some of Ibn Ẓāfir's most detailed information appears in a long account of the death of the Samanid *amīr* Aḥmad b. Ismā'īl in 301/913–14 which may have been written by an eyewitness to the events, while other passages in his work probably originate in one or other contemporary chronicle.[19] Both sources contain legendary elements and material relating the heroic deeds of pious urban citizens. These passages may have been based on oral accounts with which storytellers entertained their audiences.[20] The obscurity of the source material aside, there is a striking unanimity between these two authors' remarks on the militia which lends some credence to the picture that they paint. We begin with the detailed account relating to the Bukharan militia's defence of the city against the Samanid *ghilmān,* who in 301/913–14 attempted to occupy Bukhara and put their own candidate on the throne in place of the recently assassinated *amīr* Aḥmad b. Ismā'īl.

When news of the slave troops' intentions reached the governor of the city, Muḥammad b. Aḥmad, he:

> ... hastily mounted his horse, rode to the gate of the citadel and secured it. Then he gave the order for the *muṭṭawwi'a* to mount their horses (or alternatively: he supplied

---

[16] As Madelung points out, the original title given to the full version of this work by Ibn Ẓāfir was *akhbār al-duwal al-islāmiyya*, see W. Madelung, 'The identity of two Yemenite historical manuscripts', *Journal of Near Eastern Studies* 32, 1973, 176.

[17] For an edition and translation of Ibn Ẓāfir's chapter on the Samanids see W. L. Treadwell, 'Ibn Ẓāfir al-Azdī's account of the murder of Aḥmad b. Ismā'īl and the succession of his son Naṣr', *Studies in honour of Clifford Edmund Bosworth,* ii, ed. C. Hillenbrand, Leiden 2000, 397–419, and idem, 'The account of the Samanid dynasty in Ibn Ẓāfir al-Azdī's *Akhbār al-duwal al-munqaṭi'a,*' *Iran* 43, 2005, 135–71. Hamidallah produced an Arabic edition of the *Book of Gifts and Rarities* entitled *Kitāb al-dhakhā'ir wa al-tuḥaf,* Kuwait 1959, and reminded his readers that the manuscript he edited was in fact a eighth-century abridgement of the original fifth-century text. For the first English translation of the passage examined in this paper, see C. E. Bosworth, 'An alleged embassy from the emperor of China to the *amīr* Naṣr b. Aḥmad – a contribution to Samanid military history', *Yādnāme-ye Īrānī-ye Minorsky,* ed. M. Minovi and I. Afshar, Tehran 1969, 17–29. For a recent English translation of the whole book, which casts doubt on Ibn al-Zubayr's authorship and suggests the alternative title (*Kitāb al-hadāya wa al-tuḥaf*) see G. al-Qaddūmī, tr. *Book of gifts and rarities,* Cambridge, Mass. 1996.

[18] Ibn Ẓāfir cites two authors, Thābit b. Sinān and Farghānī, in his chapter on the Samanids, both of whom are also referred to in the Book of Gifts (Qaddūmī, *Book of gifts*, 19). But in the latter text, no reference to either source appears in the passage relating to the Samanid militia.

[19] For more on the historiography of Ibn Ẓāfir's account, see Treadwell, 'Ibn Ẓāfir al-Azdī's account'.

[20] See Bosworth, 'An alleged embassy', for comments on the historicity of Rashīd Ibn al-Zubayr's account.

> mounts for the *muṭṭawwiʿa*) and despatched a thousand of them to guard the governor's palace and the treasury.[21]

The governor's first action was to deploy the *muṭṭawwiʿa,* all of them mounted on horses, to guard key buildings. The word *istarkaba* which is used to describe the governor's action could either mean that he gave the order for them to mount their horses, or that he supplied the militiamen with horses to ride. As we will see below, the Samanid *amīr* Aḥmad had provided large numbers of horses for the militiamen who fought against the Turkish invaders of Transoxania in 297/909–10, four years before his death. The passage continues:

> He then ordered the *ʿayyārs* to take up their weapons. He brought out the banners and marched them out to a place known as al-Sahla.[22]

Although Ibn Ẓāfir gives us little information about these *ʿayyārs*, it is likely that they were divided into sections according to their domicile in the city (hence the importance of the banners, which may have been the banners of the individual city quarters although this cannot be verified) and that they were infantrymen. Their deployment to the area known as al-Sahla, an empty piece of ground near the city walls, suggests that they formed the front line against the advancing enemy, while the more mobile cavalry remained behind them, ready to move quickly to wherever they were needed when the *ghilmān* arrived.

> The *ghilmān* made their way towards them and found the cavalry drawn up in ranks, and the banners (of the *ʿayyārs*) unfurled. The city notables were mounted on their horses, each one with his retainers. They approached one of them, Abū Yaʿqūb Isḥāq b. Ibrāhīm, the *shaykh al-balad* and master armourer, who had more than a thousand followers in the city.[23]

The *ghilmān* found themselves confronted by the massed ranks of militiamen, consisting of both cavalry and footsoldiers, led by the urban notables. One of these notables, Abū Yaʿqūb, is referred to as *shaykh al-balad wa ustādhuhā fī ʿamal al-silāḥ,* signifying that he was the chief notable of Bukhara and the city's master armourer. The position of *shaykh al-balad* was probably an official urban post while the word *ustādh* could either be a title or an honorific term denoting his eminence as a craftsman skilled in the manufacture of weaponry. He was obviously a prominent citizen with many followers: Ibn Ẓāfir tells us that he employed more than a thousand apprentices, presumably craftsmen who worked in his workshops. The *ghulām* commanders addressed themselves to Abū Yaʿqūb first, which suggests that the master armourer was acting as the field commander of the militia. As we shall see below, the city authorities issued equipment and weapons to the militia on

[21] *Bādara bi al-rukūb wa jāʾa ilā bāb al-quhandiz wa istawthaqa minhu wa istarkaba al-muṭṭawwiʿa wa wakkala minhum alf rajul bi-dār al-imāra wa bayt al-māl* (Ibn Ẓāfir in Treadwell, 'Ibn Ẓāfir al-Azdī's account', 399 and 406).

[22] *Wa amara al-ʿayyārīn bi-labs al-silāḥ wa akhraja al-bunūd wa kharaja bihim wa waqafa bihim fī makān yuqālu lahu al-sahla* (Ibn Ẓāfir in Treadwell 'Ibn Ẓāfir al-Azdī's account', 399 and 406).

[23] *Fa taqaddamū ilayhim fa-idhā al-khayl maṣfūfa wa al-bunūd manshūra wa al-mashāyikh ʿalā khuyūlihim kull wāḥid maʿa aṣḥābihi fa-balaghū ilā aḥadihim wa huwa abū yaʿqūb isḥāq b. ibrāhīm shaykh al-balad wa ustādhuhā fī ʿamal al-silāḥ wa lahu fī al-balad akthar min alf tilmīdh* (Ibn Ẓāfir in Treadwell, 'Ibn Ẓāfir al-Azdī's account', 399 and 407).

another occasion. It may be that this was also the case in 301/913–14 and that Abū Yaʿqub had a pivotal role in leading the militia, both as the quartermaster who supplied their weaponry and as their field commander.

The Bukharan *muṭṭawwiʿa* succeeded in disarming the 6000-strong regiment of *ghilmān* and forcing them to pledge allegiance to Aḥmad's young son, Naṣr, as his successor. They then went on to play a leading role in the subsequent conflict with Naṣr's great-uncle, Isḥāq b. Aḥmad, who marched on Bukhara to seize the throne for himself, with a huge army of 37,000 troops, including large numbers of Turks from the eastern province of Farghana. Naṣr's army was less than half the size at 17,000 troops: it consisted of 10,000 troops of the *ʿāmma jaysh bukhārā* (the commoners of the Bukharan army), a contingent of *mamlūks*, a group of freemen and 3000 cavalrymen sent to Naṣr's assistance by the ruler of Khwārazm. The *ʿāmma jaysh bukhārā* were probably members of the same *muṭṭawwiʿa* which had defended the city against the regicidal *ghilmān*. Naṣr's forces suffered heavy casualties but turned the unequal contest in Naṣr's favour and secured victory against the Samarqandīs.[24]

The militia's victory against the *ghilmān* and the Turkish tribesmen who fought for Isḥāq was clearly a momentous triumph. While we lack any further detailed evidence for this militia, we do have three short references to the commanders of a similar body of troops in Samarqand which date from the third century AH. All three references name the officers as *ṣāḥib jaysh al-ghuzāt bi-samarqand*.[25] While the title has the meaning 'Commander of the army of *ghāzīs* of Samarqand', it is likely that this army resembled a city militia, rather than group of volunteer *ghāzīs* who fought independently of the city authorities, since the word *jaysh* implies a permanent military presence rather than an ephemeral band of 'holy warriors'. The Samarqandī militia survived after the Samanid conquest of the eastern provinces had been completed, at least until the middle of fourth century AH (if not longer). The post of *ṣāḥib al-jaysh al-samarqandī* (note by this time the absence of a reference to the *ghuzāt*) was held by one Abū Isḥāq Ibrāhīm b. Aḥmad al-Bakrī (d. 348/959–60).[26]

---

24 See Treadwell, 'The account of the Samanid dynasty', 163–64, for the description of these two armies.

25 The following references were first collected by J. Paul, 'The histories of Samarqand', *Studia Iranica* 22, 1993, 83. For the title of *ṣāḥib jaysh al-ghuzāt bi-samarqand* see Zīrak al-Aʿraj (the Lame) (d. 248) (Najm al-Dīn ʿUmar al-Nasafī, *Kitāb al-qand fī ta'rīkh ʿulamā' samarqand*, ed. Y. al-Hadi, Tehran 1999, no. 284 where he is known as Zibrak; for correction see Paul, 'The histories of Samarqand', 83; and Saʿīd b. Saʿd al-Shāshī (d. 296) (Nasafī, *Kitāb al-qand*, no. 320); and Aḥmad b. Qāsim b. al-Hayyāj (date unknown) (Nasafī, *Kitāb al-qand*, no. 1178). For the designation *min ru'ūs al-ghuzāt bi-samarqand* held by one ʿĀmir b. Isḥāq b. Rāwakhsh (Paul demonstrates that he was active in the early third century AH), see Nasafī, *Kitāb al-qand*, no. 1068.

26 Nasafī, *Kitāb al-qand*, 47, no. 5. For his genealogy, see W. L. Treadwell, and V. Kalinin, "A unique *fals* of Binkath (Shāsh) dated 186 AH", *Oriental Numismatic Society Newsletter*, 2003.

MILITIAMEN AS MURĀBIṬŪN

The Samarqandī army must have been deployed on the eastern Transoxanian frontier in the early third century when the Samanids were still in the process of expanding and consolidating their border with the Turks. The most vital task performed by the militias of Samarqand, Bukhara and other great cities of Sogd was to man the *ribāṭ*s or fortified enclosures, which were constructed in the newly conquered eastern regions and along the borders that separated the steppe lands from the settled regions of Transoxania and eastern Khurasan after the main thrust of the Samanid conquests was completed in 227/841–2.[27] *Ribāṭ* is a term which has generated much discussion among Islamicists and covers buildings with many different functions; military forts, caravanserais for traders, hostels for travellers, and refuges for pious retreat. It is probable that the earliest Samanid *ribāṭ*s were built to serve as military strongholds, and that the ancillary functions of the building type grew out of the military fort. As we will see from the examples of Farāwa and Dīzāk, the *ribāṭ* was a fortified complex that comprised buildings which served several different functions, including accommodation, storage, and places of worship.[28]

Fortified *ribāṭ*s were constructed at strong points along the northern border of the Samanid state, from Isfiyāb in the east, to the Dihistān steppe, north of Jurjān, in the west. Several *ribāṭ*s were built around Isfiyāb after its conquest, with the aim of consolidating the control of the urban hinterland. *Ribāṭ*s were also constructed along the southern rim of the two great steppe regions to the north of Transoxania and Khurasan, the Qarā Qum and the Qizil Qum. In Ushrūsana to the east of Samarqand, *ribāṭ* construction began in the early third century. Iṣṭakhrī tells us that on the road leading from Samarqand to Khojand, which passed through Ushrūsana, there were numerous *ribāṭ*s that were built facing the Ghuzz steppe to the north, all of them manned by Samarqandīs. He singles out the region of Dīza (Dīzak) in Ushrūsana as a place where *ribāṭ* construction was particularly dense and tells us that it included the most famous *ribāṭ* in Transoxania, in a place known as Khudaysir.[29] This building had been put up by the Afshīn Ḥaydār himself and had a spring within its walls. Another group of *ribāṭ*s which lay within the region of Nūr, to the north of Samarqand, may have been constructed at the same time as the Ushrūsanī forts.

Further to the west, a line of *ribāṭ*s ran along the border between the Ghuzz steppe and the mountainous northern fringes of Jurjān. Tahirid patronage was important in this case. The huge *ribāṭ* of Farāwa, built by ʿAbdallāh b. Ṭāhir (213/828–230/844) during Ma'mūn's caliphate, comprised three interlinked forts, one surrounded by a moat, which were capable

---

[27] These are the regions where our sources identify concentrations of *ribāṭ* building: others may have escaped the notice of our meagre source base. Naymark summarises the archaeological evidence, see A. I. Naymark, 'The Size of Samanid Bukhara: A Note on Settlement Patterns in Early Islamic Mawarannahr,' in *Bukhara: the Myth and the Architecture,* ed. Attilio Petruccioli, Cambridge, Mass. 1999, 39–60.

[28] See also Chabbi, 'ribāṭ', *EI*².

[29] Iṣṭakhrī, *Kitāb al-masālik wa al-mamālik,* ed. M.J. de Goeje, Leiden 1870, 327 (Khudaysir); Narshakhī, *Tārīkh-i Bukhārā,* ed. Rizawi, Tehran 1351, 17 (Nūr). Iṣṭakhrī's description of Dīzak suggests that the construction of military outposts created a secure zone which attracted hostels for travellers and unfortified habitations.

of housing men, horses and a weapons store.[30] That of Dihistān, described by Ibn Ḥawqal, was capacious enough to comprise a mosque within its walls.[31]

The evidence suggests that a line of forts was constructed along the southern edge of the buffer zone between the fertile settled lands and the steppe, which was designed to monitor and regulate the flow of nomads into the *Mashriq*. A line of *ribāṭ*s extending from Marv to Amul and from Amul up the course of the River Oxus towards Khwarazm, and from Khwarazm to Bukhara, may also have been instigated by the Tahirids.[32] *Ribāṭ*s were also constructed on the eastern and southern flanks of the Samanid state for the same purposes as the northern forts, but about these we are very poorly informed. *Ribāṭ*s were built according to need and fell out of use when no longer required or when they became uninhabitable. The numerous *ribāṭ*s of Paykand are a case in point. Narshakhī tells us that they were manned by the inhabitants of the villages of the Bukharan oasis and that they were in active use until 240/854–5.[33] Their defensive function declined thereafter, perhaps as a result of the improvement in regional security which resulted from the construction of Tahirid *ribāṭ*s in Khwarazm to the north.[34]

The proliferation of *ribāṭ*s was an innovation of real significance, for the Sogdians had attempted nothing of the kind before the arrival of the Muslims, probably because Sogdiana had lacked the political cohesion necessary for such grand projects. The Abbasid governor of Shāsh had built a great wall to the north of Shāsh in the late second century, but this structure is not mentioned in the extant Samanid sources. It seems that the Samanids and their Tahirid overlords adopted a new defensive strategy, which was founded on the construction of multiple centres where military force could be concentrated in order to respond to imminent threat. Defence was the priority against the Turkish threat, for there was no incentive to mount regular expeditions deep into enemy territory. Here the contrast with the Byzantine border is clear. In the Near East, the *ghuzāt* sought prizes, both ideological and material, by striving to take territory from their Roman enemies, to capture prisoners

---

[30] Muqaddasī, *Aḥsan al-taqāsīm fī maʿrifat al-aqālīm*, ed. de Goeje, Leiden 1906, 320, and Samʿānī , *Kitāb al-Ansāb*, Hyderabad 1979, x, 166.

[31] Ibn Ḥawqal, *Kitāb ṣūrat al-arḍ*, 2nd ed. J. H. Kramers, Leiden 1939, 383.

[32] See Naymark, 'The Size of Samanid Bukhara', 50 and notes 88 and 89, for references to the archaeological research that has identified these lines of *ribāṭ*s. See for the *ribāṭ*s connecting Khwārazm and Bukhara, Y. P. Manylov, 'Trassy torgovykh putei iz Bukhary v Khorezm v. X vv.', *Formirovannie i ravvitie trass Velikogo Shelkovogo Puti v Tsentral'noi Azii v drevnosti i srednevekov'e. Tezisy dokladov mezhdunarodnogo seminara IUNESKO*, Tashkent 1990, 62–64. See also Muqaddasī , *Aḥsan al-taqāsīm*, 292 (and note g thereto) and 243, for references to the *qarya* (settlement) of the Khwarazmians and the Bukharans on the river bank, which were most likely crossing points of the river manned by Khwarazmians and Bukharans. For the *ribāṭ* of Farabr, slightly inland from the river, which was built by the Samanid Naṣr II (301/913–331/942) in memory of his father Aḥmad who was murdered there, and which provided accommodation for travellers, see Muqaddasī, *Aḥsan al-taqāsīm*, 291.

[33] Narshakhī, *Tārīkh-i Bukhārā*, 25 = idem, *The history of Bukhara*, tr. R. N. Frye, Cambridge, Mass. 1954, 18.

[34] See Naymark, 'The Size of Samanid Bukhara', note 91, for the *ribāṭ*s of Paykand, which he interprets as hostels rather than forts. In the fourth century AH, Ibn Ḥawqal, *Kitāb ṣūrat al-arḍ* , 383 and 388, notes that the *ribāṭ* of Dihistān (to the north of Jurjān) fell into disrepair. In this case it seems that the site was abandoned due to problems in the supply of water.

and plunder, but above all, to occupy settlements which could be declared as having been won back from the enemy in an endless tug-of-war between the two sides which neither ever won outright.[35] The Turkish frontier offered different opportunities. Here there were few great towns to capture and little value to be had from the laborious and highly dangerous enterprise of conquest. In fact the border, once established by Samanid and Tahirid arms, benefited both parties. It was fringed by market towns where the tribesmen sold the slaves they had captured in battle against their tribal enemies, as well as commercial products from the northern lands. Depending on its location and the course of events in its vicinity, a *ribāṭ* or group of *ribāṭ*s could serve one or more of three purposes, economic, administrative and political. It could regulate access to the settled lands for tribesmen seeking markets for their animal products (dairy, meat and leather); keep order in the regions which tribesmen frequented to graze their flocks, some of which were just north of the frontier (e.g. Nur, to the north of Bukhara); and provide information about tribal movements and early warning of potential incursions from the deep steppe. *Ribāṭ* construction also provided a conduit for private investment and pious endowment by locals who were not part of the ruler's administration, but wished to make a contribution. A Samarqandī named Abū Aḥmad *al-muṭṭawwiʿī*, for instance, built one such structure in the village of Qatwān, just to the north of Dīzak, the same region against which Naṣr (I) b. Aḥmad is known to have led a military action in 235/849–50.[36]

The construction of frontier *ribāṭ*s demonstrates that after the main wave of conquest was complete, both the Samanids and Tahirids took a grip on the internal security of the region by securing major routes and providing defences against Turkish raids. The question is who manned the *ribāṭ*s? Our sources, which mostly postdate the Samanid period by a couple of centuries or more, have been taken to imply that the job was done by *ghāzī*s, in the sense of 'holy warriors' who were intent on taking the fight to the Turkish heathens, and *muṭṭawwiʿa,* in the sense of pious Muslims who wished to prove their devotion to Islam by performing superogatory duties which exceeded the normal responsibilities expected of good Muslims. Among these *murābiṭūn,* so it has been claimed, were men from all over the Muslim world who flocked to the eastern frontier to demonstrate their devotion to the cause.[37]

In fact there is reason to believe that this later retrojection of individualised pious intent as the driving force behind the operation of the *ribāṭ*s is quite misleading. If we look at the evidence, we see that in most cases where the collective origin of the *murābiṭūn* is mentioned, they are men from the great Sogdian cities and their hinterlands, in other words, the same reservoir of men on whom the militias themselves drew. In the case of the numerous *ribāṭ*s of Paykand, Narshakhī tells us that they were staffed by men from

[35] See C. E. Bosworth, 'The city of Tarsus and Arab-Byzantine frontiers in early and middle Abbasid times', *Oriens* 33, 1992, 268–86, on the frontier city of Tarsus, two thirds of whose inhabitants are said to have been 'batchelors' (*ʿuzzāb*), that is freelancing young men who wished to pursue the *jihād* against Rūm.

[36] Samʿānī, *Kitāb al-Ansāb*, Hyderabad 1992, vii, 261, gives his name as Abū Aḥmad *al-zāhid al-muṭṭawwiʿī* and identifies him as the uncle of the qāḍī Muḥammad b. Janāḥ al-Sanjadīzakī (d. 305 AH: the *nisba* refers to a city quarter in Samarqand).

[37] This is the view of Tor, *Violent order.*

the villages of the Bukhara region; in the case of Dīzak, we hear that they were occupied by Samarqandīs; in the case of Isfiyāb, a dangerous, if profitable location, far away on the eastern border, the burden was shared by the men of Samarqand, Bukhara and Nakhshab.[38] Given the function of the military *ribāṭ*s as listening posts and barrack houses, they needed to be occupied and maintained throughout the year, though some may have been most active during the season when the tribesmen approached the settled lands. They were not platforms for launching seasonal raids into enemy territory, like the Anatolian *ṣā'ifa* (summer expedition): they were permanent military establishments. Such establishments could only be run by a rotating garrison which would have to be relieved at regular intervals. The *murābiṭūn* had to have local knowledge, otherwise they would have been unable to do their job of monitoring the movement of tribesmen. It is true that such *ribāṭ*s would have had room for foreigners, for pious men wishing to test their taste for *zuhd* to the limit, for ne'er-do-wells, and even old men who were not fit for active service in the army.[39] But their core personnel were drawn from the *muṭṭawwiʿa* militia whose military role we are examining.

MILITIAMEN RESISTING INCURSIONS FROM THE STEPPE

In addition to their role as *murābiṭūn*, the *muṭṭawwiʿa* were called into the field when Turkish steppe tribes attacked Transoxania. In these cases, only a handful of which are documented, the *muṭṭawwiʿa* saw action outside the confines of the city and the *ribāṭ*s and acted as fast-moving mobile units which harassed, and if we are to believe our sources, often got the better of, the huge armies of the enemy. The first case occurred in 291/903–4, when an enormous Turkish force, probably seeking revenge for Ismāʿīl b. Aḥmad's conquest of Talas a decade earlier, was repelled by the Samanid army and the *muṭṭawwiʿa*. Ṭabarī, a rather distant and laconic observer of the Samanid scene, states that a general call to arms was declared (*wa nūdi'a fī al-nās bi al-nafīr*) and that many of the *muṭṭawwiʿa* went out to fight (*fa kharaja min al-muṭṭawwiʿa nās kathīr*).[40] The phrase could be read to mean that the call to arms was answered by civilians who volunteered to join the resistance, but a more plausible reading is that the *muṭṭawwiʿa* constituted a fixed body of troops, many of whose members responded to the mobilisation. The passage is too short to support further analysis on these lines, but when Transoxania was threatened by attack from the steppe in 297/909–10, Ibn Ẓāfir tells us that the Samanid *amīr* Aḥmad assembled the commanders of the standing army and the militia in his court:

---

[38] For Paykand, see Narshakhī, *Tārīkh-i Bukhārā*, 25; for Dīzāk, see Iṣṭakhrī (note 29 above); and for Isfiyāb, see Muqaddasī, *Aḥsan al-taqāsīm*, 273. Note also the settlements of the Khwarazmians and the Bukharans on the Oxus River (see above, note 32).

[39] Cf. the tale of Muḥammad al-Ṣandalī, an old soldier who was dismissed from the Samanid army and told to spend the rest of his life in a *ribāṭ*, but ended his life leading a rebellion against the Samanid governor of Sistan (Ibn Ẓāfir in Treadwell, 'The account of the Samanid dynasty', 155).

[40] Ṭabarī, *Ta'rīkh al-rusul wa al-mulūk*, ed. M. J. de Goeje, Leiden 1879–1901, iii, 2249.

> (Aḥmad) looked at the commander of the *muṭṭawwiʿa*, ʿAbdallāh b. ʿUbayd al-Ḍabbī, and said: 'I imagine you are going to say that this will require many men and the people / militiamen are without means and have no equipment. (I will provide) you with money, horses and equipment.' He (the commander) went out and assembled the people/ militiamen.[41]

This passage explains the relationship between the Samanid *amīr* and the militia leader. Once the *amīr* had guaranteed to provide funding, mounts and equipment for the militia, the commander mustered his men. One might wonder why a properly constituted militia would need provisioning on such a scale by the *amīr*. The answer is nowhere to be found in the sources, but one or two suggestions can be made. First, it should be remembered that this was a truly massive attack by the Turks, who are said to have numbered 400,000 men, and that the normal resources of the militia would have been insufficient to meet the challenge without extra assistance. It may also have been the case that the Samanids deliberately chose to limit the militia's resources in order to limit their military potential. As we saw in the story of the defence of Bukhara in 301/913–14, the militiamen were capable of overcoming a very large force of the royal Turkish guards, and of winning pitched battles against overwhelming numbers of Turkish tribesmen. However well disposed its leaders were to the Samanids, the *amīr*s must have been wary of the militia's strength and may have chosen to control its regular access to horses and hardware in the city for this reason. On this occasion in 297/909–10, the militiamen resorted to 'guerrilla tactics' in the face of overwhelming numbers. According to Ibn Ẓāfir, one small Bukharan contingent of five hundred men managed to set fire to a Turkish camp in a heavily wooded area, causing huge loss of life, while another rescued a group of Khwarazmian soldiers who had been taken prisoner by the enemy.[42]

Another very large Turkish army attacked Transoxania in 301/913–14, just before Aḥmad's death, but details of the successful defence of the region are lacking.[43] Towards the end of the reign of Aḥmad's son, Naṣr, in 327/938–9, the threat of steppe power reappeared in a more benign, though still potent, form. An embassy from a Turkish ruler, probably a Uighur *khān*, arrived in the region, making unspecified demands that may have been linked to a claim for a large amount of tribute which the Turkish king believed was owed to him by the Samanids. In response to their presence, and with the aim of demonstrating his military might, Naṣr mobilised his standing army and the militias across Transoxania. According to the *Book of Gifts and Rarities*, he began by ordering the governor of Farghana to muster the standing army and militia (*yajmaʿ juyūsh farghāna wa al-muṭṭawwiʿa*) and commanded all the governors of adjacent provinces to do likewise. In Bukhara:

---

41 *Thumma naẓara ilā ṣāḥib jaysh al-muṭṭawwiʿa wa huwa ʿabd allāh b. ʿubayd al-ḍabbī wa qāla lahu ka-annī bika taqūlu inna hādhā yaḥtāj ilā khalq wa al-nās mastūrūn wa laysa lahum ʿudda fa-aḥḍir al-rijāl wa laka al-amwāl wa al-khuyūl ...wa al-ʿudad fa kharaja wa jamaʿa al-nās* (Ibn Ẓāfir in Treadwell 'The account of the Samanid dynasty', 139 and 154). For an alternative translation of *mastūrūn* (meaning 'concealed') see ibid., 154.

42 Treadwell, 'The account of the Samanid dynasty', 154.

43 ʿArīb, *Ṣilat taʾrīkh al-Ṭabarī*, 43.

> he told the commander of the *muṭṭawwiʿa* to take as many weapons as he needed from the armoury and as many mounts too ... he ordered that horses be brought (to Bukhara) from every place ...[44]

Once again, as in 297/909–10, it is the Samanid *amīr* who releases weapons from his armoury and horses from the royal stables for the use of the militia. In the event, 40,000 *muṭṭawwiʿa*, every one with a cuirass (*jawshan*), are said to have been on parade when the foreign ambassadors arrived at Dabusiya, just outside Bukhara. The ambassadors, bedazzled by the display of power they encountered before even entering Bukhara, asked their minders how the Samanids, whom they had believed to be weak and incapable, could possibly field such a large number of troops. They are told about the *muṭṭawwiʿa* that:

> they are the holders of land-grants (*iqṭāʿāt*), who have been assigned estates for supporting themselves, their families and their dependents, and for financing the upkeep of their mounts and weapons. From the income of these estates there is also a surplus which they can use for trading purposes and for almsgiving to the poor.[45]

The mention of *iqṭāʿ*s is interesting, since the Samanids are generally thought to have made little use of land grants in lieu of military pay, unlike their Buyid neighbours or Seljuq successors. Perhaps the *iqṭāʿ* was a mechanism used by the Samanids in the fourth century AH to attract fighting men to the frontier regions in an era when the huge wealth that was pouring into the region from trade with the steppe had begun to make the life of the *murābiṭ* less attractive than it had been in the third century. These *muṭṭawwiʿa* seem to have been organised in communal estates, and, unlike their urban comrades, appear to have been self-sufficient as regards horses and equipment. One should not forget, of course, that this information was conveyed to the ambassadors by the commander of the militia. It may be that Ibn al-Zubayr relied on a source that deliberately exaggerated the role of the *muṭṭawwiʿa* in order to persuade them that they were permanent residents of the frontier, while in fact they were nothing more than the *murābiṭūn* who manned the *ribāṭs*. On the other hand, we know that some *ribāṭs* were endowed as *waqfs* (charitable trusts) which would have meant that their occupants, like the *muqtaʿ*s of Ibn al-Zubayr's account, would have been able to live in them free of charge and cultivate the surrounding area and graze their stock there.[46]

When the ambassadors finally reached Bukhara, already quite overwhelmed by the number and strength of the Samanid forces they had already encountered:

> The banners of (the various quarters of) Bukhara were all displayed, amounting to one thousand seven hundred in all. Each banner was accompanied by a group of *ʿayyārs*,

[44] *Amara naṣr li- ṣāḥib jaysh al-muṭṭawwiʿa an ya'khudha min khizānat al-silāḥ mā iḥtāja wa min al-dawwāb ḥājatahu...wa amara bi-iḥḍār al-dawwāb min kull makān* (Ibn al-Zubayr, *Kitāb al-dhakhā'ir*, 142).

[45] *Hā'ulā'i aṣḥāb al-iqṭāʿāt alladhīna uqṭiʿū ḍīyā'an takūnu ma'ūnatahum wa ma'ūnata dawwābihim wa silāḥihim wa ʿayālihim wa man nazila ʿalayhim minhā wa yafḍilu li kulli wāḥid minhum min tilka al-ḍayʿa mā yakūnu li-tijāratihim wa...ṣadaqātihim ilā al-fuqarā'* (Ibn al-Zubayr, *Kitāb al-dhakhā'ir*, 143).

[46] See Ibn al-Jawzī, *al-Muntaẓam fī ta'rīkh al-mulūk wa al-umam*, Hyderabad 1357, vi, 77, for the *waqfs* which the Samanid Ismāʿīl b. Aḥmad assigned to frontier *ribāṭs*.

> each of which numbered between two hundred and one thousand ʿ*ayyārs* alone (i.e. exclusively ʿ*ayyārs*). All these banners were in addition to the flags of the *ghāzīs*.[47]

The ʿ*ayyārs* were deployed in bands of several hundred men, each one of them accompanied by the banner of their particular city quarter or village settlement.[48] The reference to the flags of the *ghāzīs* may be significant. The term *ghāzī* may here be used as a synonym for the *muṭṭawwiʿa* or it may alternatively refer to 'holy warriors' who were not members of the urban militia who had congregated in the city prior to setting out for the frontier. In any event, these *ghāzīs* were more likely to have been locals than foreigners. The wars of conquest of the early third century which would have provided foreigners with opportunities for war booty were long over: profits were made from the steppe through trade in the great markets of the metropolitan cities rather than on the border of the *Dār al-kufr.*

CONCLUSIONS

This paper has noted that militias, in the sense of autonomous urban self-defence forces with an institutional structure, were not uncommon in the early Islamic period, even at the time when the centralised Abbasid state was at its most powerful. In general, militias flourished on the periphery of the state, when control was weak. The difficulty in identifying militia activity arises from the multiplicity of terms which are used in the sources to describe them and the overall lack of the type of source which might provide useful information. The so-called local or city histories (of Nishapur, Bukhara and Qumm, to name three) which become common from the fourth century AH onwards focus their attention on the urban scholarly class and are largely uninterested in urban institutions of any kind. This paper has not entirely succeeded in overcoming these terminological and historiographical obstacles. For example, the references to the resistance mounted against the marauders of Hīt and Raqqa in the third century, may have been the work of the urban citizenry who rushed to save their city in a last-ditch defence, rather than the work of a trained militia. But I would contend that wherever the terms *jaysh* and *jund* are found, these refer to militias rather than untrained bands of citizens. The same obviously goes for the Samanid *muṭṭawwiʿa,* although in this case, it is the context (slight though it is) which proves the point, not the term (*muṭṭawwiʿa*) alone.

The militia was competent for the tasks for which it was trained, including city defence, frontier defence and 'guerrilla' warfare against invaders (the latter two apply in the Samanid case, at least). But it was clearly not intended to function as part of a royal army, to travel long distances, mount sieges, or provide any of the specialist services which were required

[47] *Wa qad ukhrijat bunūd bukhārā wa li-bukhārā alf wa sabʿ miʾa band yakhruju maʿa kulli band min al-ʿayyārīn mā bayna miʾatay rajul ilā alf rajul ʿayyārīn khāṣṣatan siwā aʿlām al-ghuzāt* (Ibn al-Zubayr, *Kitāb al-dhakhāʾir,* 143).

[48] The number of banners, even if greatly exaggerated, cannot easily be accounted for by the city quarters of Bukhara, however large the city had grown by the 320s/930s (cf. the dozen or so banners which are displayed in today's parades in the Sienna palio!). It is likely that the ʿ*ayyārs* were also drawn from the villages of the extensive agricultural hinterland which surrounded the city. Note the association of banners (*bunūd*) with the ʿ*ayyārs* in 301/913–14 (see above).

of a standing army. The only exception to this was the Saffarid case, where the absence of a caliphal military presence in the province allowed Yaʿqūb to build his city militia into a sophisticated supra-urban militia which formed the core of the professional army that he later used to pursue his ambitious strategic goals throughout Iran.

The Bukharan militia was a potent military force, but it was not suited to operate outside Transoxania. Its leaders were on good terms with the Samanids and their representatives. In the accounts cited above, we see them in the best possible light, probably because the narratives originated in the urban context in which they flourished. Militias were inevitably a double-edged sword for the ruler, however useful they were in some circumstances. They could not be relied upon with the same degree of confidence as royal troops because they were not part of the royal court and their priority was to defend the city, rather than the ruler (though these two goals coincided in Bukhara in 301/913–14). The military history of the Florentine Republic reveals that the city militia was often militarily ineffective, unreliable and occasionally prone to pursuing agendas that differed from that of the city's ruling council.[49] The Florentine example, well attested from a variety of different sources, including city chronicles as well as a huge archive, reminds us that we know little about the conditions under which militiamen served in Transoxania. Did they serve, as in Florence, in payment of dues which they owed to the city, either to be remitted in cash if they could afford it, or in military service if they could not?[50] Were the mounted *muṭṭawwiʿa* of Bukhara the equivalent of the commoner knights of the Iberian Reconquista (*caballeros villanos*), while the *ʿayyārūn* played the role of the *peonías* infantrymen?[51] Our sources are too slim to support further enquiry of this kind. What is clear, however, is that the *ʿayyārūn* could be just as dangerous and destabilising a force in Samanid Transoxania as elsewhere, when the conditions were apt. In the latter part of the fourth century AH, as the Samanid state began to crumble, an *ʿayyār* force led by a man with the *nisba* Panāfghānī is said to have been responsible for the destruction of Nasaf, one of the great cities of the region.[52]

The Transoxanian militia was recruited not from the rural areas, but from the cities and their hinterlands. A distinction should be maintained between the mobilisation of the militia in the various accounts given above, and the much rarer cases in which a general mass levy of all subjects, including peasants as well as citizens, was called. These general levies were called only in the last resort. One example occurred in 287/900, when the Samanid *amīr* Ismāʿīl had to repel an attack from an unaccustomed quarter, that is from the Saffarid state which lay to the south of the Oxus River. Ṭabarī and Narshakhī tell us that the *dahāqīn* and *tunnā'* (landowners) reponded to Ismāʿīl's call along with large numbers

[49] See C. C. Bayley, *War and society in Renaissance Florence: the* De Militia *of Leonardo Bruni*, Toronto 1961, ch. 1 for the military background.

[50] *Taṭawwuʿ* can convey the meaning of enrolment in an armed force (R. Dozy, *Supplément aux dictionnaires arabes*, Leiden, 1881, vol. 2, 68, s. v. '*ṭawaʿa*'). The term *muṭṭawwiʿa* could have designated a militia whose members were not conscripted into military service, but voluntarily chose to do military service as a way of fulfilling a civic obligation. For a modern example of a 'volunteer' force which formed part of a professional army, see the Volunteer force of the British army (formed in 1859), which became the Territorial Army in 1908.

[51] See E. Laurie, 'A society organised for war: medieval Spain', *Past and Present* 35, 1966, 54–76.

[52] Nasafī, *Kitāb al-qand*, 48, no. 8; 87, no. 103; 533, no. 930.

of peasants. Much to the consternation of his courtiers, Ismāʿīl distributed rations to all those peasants who, terrified by his claim that the Saffarids were intent on annihilating the population of Transoxania, answered his call. They included men who were able (i.e. trained) to bear arms and those who were not. The peasant levies were said to have ridden horses with wooden stirrups, a sign to observers that they were unaccustomed to waging war and militarily incapable.[53] In this case, the term applied to their leaders, the *dahāqīn,* does refer to rural landlords and is probably a synonym for *tunnā'*. But the rural landlords did not mobilise their peasants on a regular basis.[54] The term *dihqān,* when it is found in reference to Samanid army commanders (i.e. in the famous description of the Samanid army by Ibn Ḥawqal,[55] among others), undoubtedly refers to the client princes who fought for the Samanids and the other noblemen of high status, both Persians and Arabs, who led the free soldiers (as opposed to slaves) in the Samanid ranks.

Finally one might ask what the evidence presented here for the early Islamic militia can contribute to the debate about the capacity of Islamic cities to function and act autonomously. The consensus appears to be that unlike the medieval European city, the Islamic city did not display much evidence of a capacity to organise itself, judicially, militarily or administratively. The evidence for militia activity in the third and fourth/ninth and tenth-century *Mashriq* suggests that urban communities were indeed capable of organising their own defence independently, and sometimes in opposition to the royal powers with which they usually collaborated. Was the case of Samanid Transoxania an exception to the rule, which should be explained by Transoxania's proximity to the Turkish steppe? Or was it rather symptomatic of a wider trend in early Islamic urban history, which the Abbasid and Saffarid examples cited above seem to support? The question remains open.

---

[53] Narshakhī, *Tārīkh-i Bukhārā,* 122; *idem, The History of Bukhara,* 89–90; Ṭabarī, *Ta'rīkh*, iii, 2194; *Tārīkh-i Sīstān* (anon.), ed. Bahar, Tehran 1935, 256; Muḥammad b. Khāwand Shāh Mīrkhwānd, *Tārīkh-i rawḍat al-ṣafā'*, ed. N. Sabuhi, Tehran 1339, iv, 17.

[54] For the contrary view, see Paul, *The state and the military.*

[55] Ibn Ḥawqal, *Kitāb Ṣūrat al-arḍ*, 471.

9

The Long Shadow of Pre-Islamic Iranian Rulership: Antagonism or Assimilation

D. G. Tor

It has been observed that "each age's vision of the past is formed by its present concerns. It is from the standpoint of the present that we look back on the past to tell us who we are, where we came from, how we became as we are today, where we may be going ....".[1] Amongst all the variegated human pasts which have cast their shadow over subsequent historical epochs, the pre-Islamic Iranian past surely cast one of the most enduring and deepest. Scholars have long acknowledged that the pre-Islamic Iranian past heavily influenced not only its Iranian heirs, who continued to treasure the memory of ancient glory, nor just the Arabs who conquered the Sasanian Empire and the lands within its cultural and mercantile orbit, but the entire Islamic empire and civilization that were built in the centuries following the conquest.

Other civilizations of Antiquity influenced the Muslims as well; yet the Muslims did not absorb all elements indiscriminately and equally from all, but absorbed only certain very specific and limited aspects from each. Thus, the Hellenistic influence in Islam was expressed largely in philosophy and science; the Greeks (apart from the Islamicized Qur'ānic figure of Alexander) are represented in Islamic literature and high culture by Galen, Plato, and Aristotle, not Pericles or Demosthenes.[2] The absorption of Iranian elements into Islamic culture was similarly selective; pre-Islamic Iran cast a very long shadow over the Islamic world, but not equally in all areas. Nowhere is the shadow cast by the Iranian Late Antique past more apparent than in everything connected to rulership.

Various aspects of the Islamic-era fascination with pre-Islamic Iranian kings and kingship have long been noted and analysed. Scholars have differed, however, regarding the

---

[1] J. S. Meisami, 'The Past in Service of the Present: Two Views of History in Medieval Persia', *Poetics Today* 14, 1993, 247.

[2] P. Crone, 'Post-Colonialism in Tenth-Century Islam', *Der Islam* 83, 2006, 19, notes: "Culturally, too, the pre-conquest Near East was resurfacing in a recognizable way ... Iranian rulers plus Persian culture and the Persian language on the one hand and that of Greek science and philosophy (without the rulers) on the other".

significance of this Iranian strand in Islamic political and cultural life: Was the use of pre-Islamic Iranian political and cultural paradigms antagonistic to, and in competition with, Islamic culture and ideals? Certain scholars have viewed the recrudescence of various aspects of the ancient Iranian political heritage as in some ways a reaction, to at least a degree anti-Islamic in and of itself, against the new Islamic civilisation. Such scholars view the adoption and assimilation of the Iranian political tradition as an "outlet" for "Persian resentment",[3] a "conflict ... between two conceptions of monarchy: the traditional Iranian ... and the Islamic."[4] Such scholars view the two political traditions, Islamic and Iranian, as inimical to one another- a pre-modern "clash of civilizations", as it were.[5]

This paper will suggest, first, that all of the seemingly separate and disparate manifestations of the Islamic fascination with Iranian rulership of Antiquity – ranging from the widespread revival of Sasanian titulature, symbols of rulership, and even genealogies, to the adoption of Sasanian rulership as an Islamic political model in Muslim literature and political theory – were actually constituent components of one larger, coherent phenomenon: namely, the incorporation of the ancient Persian ideal of rulership into Islamic civilization after the ideological failure of the caliphate; and, furthermore, that this phenomenon was not anti-Islamic, as has sometimes been posited, but that, on the contrary, this tradition was suitably modified and adapted in order to assimilate it harmoniously into Islamic culture and political life. The question, it should be emphasized, is not whether or not a national or cultural identity or patriotism existed – obviously, cultural identity has existed for all of recorded human history; rather, the undecided issue is whether or not the embracing of the ancient Iranian heritage of kingship stood in opposition to Islamic identity or as a natural complement to it; whether it was combined with Islam or directed against it.

Methodologically, this paper will accomplish its goal in two ways: First, it adopts a holistic approach by looking at a larger historical picture, both synchronously and across a far broader stretch of time than has previously been examined in this context, yet with due attention given to the relative chronology of various related phenomena. For one of the best proofs that the resurfacing of the Sasanian model of rulership was the result of an Islamic embracing and assimilation of that model, rather than of an antagonistic, anti-Islamic, neo-Sasanian revival, is the chronological and geographical breadth of the phenomenon. Obviously, if those who adopt the Sasanian model include not only tenth-century imperfectly-Islamicized Iranians, but a broad swathe of impeccably Muslim Arabs ranging from a tenth-century Andalusian litterateur to a fifteenth-century Arab *qāḍī* in Yemen, one arrives at very different conclusions than one would have, had the phenomenon

---

[3] W. Madelung, 'The Assumption of the Title Shāhānshāh by the Būyids and 'The Reign of the Daylam (*Dawlat al-Daylam*)", *Journal of Near Eastern Studies* 28, 1969, 85.

[4] Meisami, 'The Past in Service of the Present', 257.

[5] Thus Gibb, for instance, asserts that "... the Sasanian strands which had been woven into the fabric of Muslim thought [in the ninth century] were, and remained, foreign to its native constitution... in open or latent opposition to the Islamic ethic, and the Sasanian tradition introduced into Islamic society a kernel of derangement, never wholly assimilated yet never wholly rejected". Cf. H. A. R. Gibb, 'The Social Significance of the Shuubiya, *Studies on the Civilization of Islam*, Princeton 1982, 72.

been manifested across a far more limited time span and ethnic, social, political, and geographical range. The second methodological approach is the examination of the specific historical context in which the Sasanian ideal was first resurrected and in which it flourished, in order to cast light on the reasons behind the widespread adoption of the ancient Iranian governing tradition.

Previous studies which have examined the Islamic-era fascination with the political legitimacy and charisma of the Late Antique Persian kings[6] all have focused on one particular aspect of the phenomenon in isolation, be it the revenant pre-Islamic Persian themes in literature; the era of Daylamite political dominance; the usage of Late Antique Persian ruling titulature and genealogies; or the reverence displayed toward ancient Persian traditions of kingship and the embracing of the Sasanian model as the paragon of rulership. Yet, this atomistic approach leads to the same results as those obtained in the well-known story of the men told to go into a dark room and describe what they find there, each of whom touches a different body part of an elephant and then attempts to describe the entire animal on the basis of the isolated portion of anatomy he felt, resulting in such varying identifications as a snake; a tree-trunk; and a thin, leathery sail. In like manner, when scholars focus on only one isolated aspect of a broader phenomenon, divorced from both its phenomenological and historical contexts, they risk misapprehending not only the contours of the overall elephant, but also the significance of each of the constituent parts on which they had been focusing.

All of the various discrete manifestations of the revival of the Late Antique Persian ideal of rulership, then, really constitute one phenomenon, consisting of two complementary categories or sub-manifestations, one political and the other cultural: Namely, the practical use of the Sasanian tradition as a political means of legitimising rulership, and the adoption of Sasanian rulership as an Islamic political model in Muslim literary texts and treatises. The overall phenomenon itself was an attempt to fill a gaping hole in Islamic political life with the already available and successful model of the Iranian past.

The late eighth and early ninth centuries were critical in the formation of both the Islamic religion and, concomitantly, Islamic political theory and reality. This formative time witnessed the transfer of the religious authority of the caliphate to the nascent Sunni clerics – the *ʿulamāʾ*.[7] As noted by Crone, the Abbasids were, consequently, left bereft of a legitimising political rationale for governmental power; their only viable option, given their situation, was "thus to fuse the Sasanian tradition with Islam".[8]

That is, since the Abbasids failed doctrinally as a Shiite revolution, and since nascent Sunnism had no place for them – neither as a 'blessed dynasty' nor as an imperial government – a vacuum in legitimising political ideology was created; in Lapidus's words, "insofar as the Abbasid empire had in part been built up on the efforts to identify Islam

---

[6] On the charisma or divine glory of the Iranian kings, see Gherardo Gnoli, *sv* "Farr," *Encyclopaedia Iranica*; E. Yarshater, 'Iranian Common Beliefs and World-View', *Cambridge History of Iran*, iii, *The Seleucid, Parthian, and Sasanian Periods*, ed. E. Yarshater, Cambridge 1983, 345.

[7] On this process see e.g. I. Lapidus, 'The Separation of State and Religion in the Development of Early Islamic Society', *IJMES* 6, 1975, 363–85; D. G. Tor, 'Privatized Jihad and Public Order in the Pre-Saljuq Period', *Iranian Studies* 38, 2005, 555–73.

[8] P. Crone, *Slaves on Horses: The Evolution of the Islamic Polity*, Cambridge 1980, 62.

and the caliphate, this loss ... was politically catastrophic".[9] This was the reason for the political collapse of the Abbasid caliphate in the ninth century; but it was also the reason for the revival of Late Antique Iranian traditions of rulership, which, as one would expect, find their clearest expression following the Abbasid collapse;[10] since there was no viable Sunni Islamic political alternative, Muslim intellectuals simply adopted what must have seemed to them the best available working model – Islamicizing it, however, in the process.

The resurrection of the Sasanian model was, therefore, an attempt by Muslims to provide a solution to a perceived need or lack within Islamic civilisation, not to revert to an outside, rival or inimical civilisation. This will become much clearer when we review each of the relevant sub-manifestations in historical context, and see the ways in which the Iranian tradition of rulership was made to harmonise with an Islamic framework.

Perhaps the earliest instance of this cultural survival of the Sasanian model, and its paradigmatic use, occurs in the 860s, during the reign of Muntaṣir. The timing is significant; it is no accident that the recrudescence of Iranian ideals of rulership occurred in the wake of the Abbasid political failure. According to Ṭabarī, writing in the early tenth century, the political paradigm to which people looked after Muntaṣir's involvement in the murder of his own father, Mutawakkil, was a Sasanian one:

> I often heard people say, when the caliphate passed to al-Muntaṣir, that from the time he acceded to rule until his death he would live for six months, as did Shīrawayh b. Kisrā after he killed his father. This [account] was spread among the populace and notables alike.[11]

This co-optation of the Sasanian kings into the Islamic historical canon is even clearer in Masʿūdī's recounting of this popular linkage in the public mind between the old Iranian kings of kings and the Islamic caliphs: in his version, which is attributed to an Abbasid official of Muntaṣir's time, there are two rulers who provide the historical model (in this case, literally: their portraits appear together on a carpet): Shīrawayh, who killed his father Khusraw Aparvīz (Khusraw II), and the Umayyad caliph Yazīd III, who murdered his cousin al-Walīd II. In this story, both the Umayyad and the Sasanian ruler are employed as prescriptive or normative models; since each of them ruled for only six months, it is clear to the courtier that Muntaṣir, too, will rule for only six months.[12]

What is important about these stories is, first, the indication they give that the absorption of the ancient Iranian heritage into the Islamic mythology of rulership appears to have occurred already in connection with the Abbasids, in the ninth century – well before the

---

[9] I. Lapidus, *A History of Islamic Societies*, Cambridge 1988, 125.

[10] It is significant that the first (and most famous) complaints about the Sasanian inspiration of Abbasid administrative practices were written by Jāḥiẓ (d. 869), during precisely this time; see E. Yashater, 'The Persian presence in the Islamic world', *The Persian presence in the Islamic world*, ed. Richard Hovannisian and Georges Sabagh, Cambridge 1998, 70–73.

[11] Joel L. Kraemer (tr.), The *History of al-Ṭabarī, XXXIV, Incipient Decline*, Albany 1989, 219; Ṭabarī, *Taʾrīkh al-Ṭabarī*, ed. M. A. Ibrāhīm, Beirut n.d., ix, 252 (ed. M. J. de Goeje *et al.*, Leiden 1879–1901, iii, 1496).

[12] Mas'ūdī, *Murūj al-dhahab wa-ma'ādin al-jawhar*, ed. M. M. Qamīḥa, Beirut n.d., iv, 148–49.

period of the heterodox Daylamites. The use of the pre-Islamic Iranian kings and heroes as an historical model or paradigm, according to this evidence, was alive in the minds of the most Islamized class of the empire, the Abbasid courtiers, and in this context at least was in no way part of some neo-Sasanian revival.

Regarding the actual political manifestations of the phenomenon, perhaps the most frequently noted revivification of the Late Antique Iranian political tradition is the eventual embracing, beginning in the tenth century, of Sasanian-era titles, particularly '*shāhānshāh*', frequently accompanied not only by the title, but by all the trappings of ancient Iranian kingship, real and imagined. Some scholars have attempted to ascertain the significance of this embracing of Sasanian political traditions by studying solely the example of the most extreme outliers, politically and religiously, of the phenomenon: Heterodox or imperfectly Islamized figures such as Asfār b. Shīrūya and Mardāvīj b. Ziyār, who built golden thrones, desired crowns modeled after those of the Sasanian kings, ordered the rebuilding of the audience hall of the Sasanian kings at ancient Ctesiphon, planned to conquer Iraq, and called or intended to call themselves by the Sasanian title of *shāhānshāh*.[13]

It is not methodologically sound to take the extreme fringe of a political movement as one's representative sample; yet this is what some otherwise excellent scholars have done. Because they were examining the phenomenon of the revival of Iranian political models in an atomistic context, solely or largely as one of a number of manifestations of neo-Persianism on the part of undeniable religious deviants such as Asfār b. Shīrūya and Mardāvīj (the latter in particular was clearly well outside the religious mainstream – even the Shiite religious mainstream – if there is any truth to Ibn al-Athīr's contention that Mardāvīj proclaimed that the spirit of King Solomon had taken up residence in himself),[14] the scholars who followed this path have tended to conclude that the adoption of ancient Iranian elements of kingship was necessarily *eo ipso* the sign of a neo-Persian revolt directed against Islam, due either to a desire for "a restoration of the Persian empire and kingship", including the Zoroastrian religion;[15] or, in Minorsky's view, an anachronistic ninth century appearance of Persian nationalism.[16] Yet, while Asfār b. Shīrūya and Mardāvīj b. Ziyār may have utilized the memory and the heritage of ancient Iranian kingship as part of an un-Islamic program, this does not in itself mean that any and all use of that heritage was perceived by mainstream Muslims in the classical period as anti-Islamic. That is, just because the pre-Islamic Iranian tradition of rulership *could* be utilized as part of an anti-Islamic program, this does not mean that it was normally – let alone necessarily – perceived by the Muslims of that time as antagonistic to Islamic rule and traditions.

Indeed, we have just seen in the foregoing examples from Ṭabarī and Masʿūdī that the

---

13 Ibn al-Athīr, *al-Kāmil fī'l-tā'rīkh*, ed. C. J. Tornberg, Dār Ṣādir reprint, Beirut 1399/1979, viii: 192, 302; Abū Bakr Muḥammad b. Yaḥyā al-Ṣūlī, *Akhbār al-Rāḍī wa'l-Muttaqī*, ed. J. Heyworth Dunne, E. J. W. Gibb Memorial Trust, Beirut 1401/1982, ii, 62; Miskawayh, *Tajārib al-umam*, ed. Amedroz. Baghdad, n.d. (reprint of the 1915 Egyptian edition), i, 317–18; C. E. Bosworth, 'The Heritage of Rulership in Early Islamic Iran and the Search for Dynastic Connections with the Past', *Iran* 11, 1973, 57.

14 Ibn al-Athīr, *al-Kāmil*, viii, 298.

15 Madelung, 'The Assumption of the Title Shāhānshāh', 86–87.

16 V. Minorsky, 'La Domination des Dalamites', *Iranica: Twenty Articles*, Tehran 1964, 25–26.

caliphs' own Muslim officials, in the heart of Islamic Baghdad, considered Sasanian kingship to be as much a part of their political heritage and paradigm as they considered the Muslim caliphs to be – and even if Ṭabarī was inventing the incident, the fact that a pious Muslim of his stature was not only conversant with, but saw nothing wrong with utilizing the ancient Iranian example – at a chronological point well before Mardāvīj's career – shows us that the adoption of the Iranian kingly model was indeed, as Ṭabarī depicts, ubiquitous throughout Muslim society in the late ninth century, at least in the eastern lands, and not just limited to an imperfectly Islamicized or anti-Muslim fringe.

More importantly for our evaluation of these early adoptions of Sasanian titulature, we see that similar symbols and titles were adopted, both at that time and subsequently, by other dynasties that could not by any stretch of the imagination be accused of atheist, anti-Islamic, or Zoroastrian sentiments. Most famously, there were the ninth- and tenth-century Buyid rulers of western Iran and Iraq,[17] who went much further than the aforementioned rulers in their imitations of Sasanian glory, including the claim of descent from Bahrām V[18] – yet who also, as Madelung himself notes, took great pains to emphasize their status as 'defenders and restorers' of Islam.[19] In fact, ʿAḍud al-Dawla, the greatest of the Buyid rulers, is even curiously entitled in one of his official documents 'King of Islam *shāhānshāh*'.[20]

This analysis is confirmed by the fact that it was not only Shiites or those of dubious Islamic commitment who assumed or utilized the title of *shāhānshāh*; other dynasties also did so, most outstandingly the highly orthodox Samanids, Ghaznavids, and Seljuqs. Thus, as noted by Treadwell, the Samanids, like the Buyids, called themselves by this title on at least one medallion.[21] Similarly, Bosworth has pointed out that official Ghaznavid panegyrists such as Farrukhī, Manūchihrī, and 'Unṣurī, all applied this epithet to the Ghaznavid sultans in their court productions,[22] as well as other old Iranian titles such as 'Khudāvand'; 'Khusraw'; and 'Khusraw-yi Mashriq'.[23] The vehemently and avowedly Sunni Seljuqs officially proclaimed themselves as *shāhānshah* on the vast majority of their coins;[24] and even, in a strange echo of the Buyid titulature, 'Shāhānshāh King of Islam'.[25]

Finally, the political significance of such titulature must be understood in the broader context of a widespread utilization of other pre-Islamic Iranian titles of rule. There is

---

[17] Bosworth, 'The Heritage of Rulership', 57.

[18] Qazvīnī, *Tārīkh-i Guzīda*, ed. 'A. Navā'ī, Tehran 1362, 409. See also Bīrūnī's disparagement of this claim; *The Chronology of Ancient Nations*, tr. Sachau, London 1878, 45.

[19] Madelung, 'Assumption', 98.

[20] Madelung, 'Assumption', 108.

[21] Luke Treadwell, '*Shāhānshāh* and *al-Malik al-Mu'ayyad*: The Legitimation of Power in Sāmānid and Būyid Iran', in F. Daftary and J. Meri, *Culture and Memory in Medieval Islam: Essays in Honour of Wilferd Madelung*, London 2003, 318–37.

[22] C. E. Bosworth, 'The Titulature of the Early Ghaznavids', *Oriens* 15, 1962, 219.

[23] C. E. Bosworth, 'The Titulature of the Early Ghaznavids', 223; idem, 'Heritage of Rulership', 61.

[24] e.g. Toghril Beg: Tübingen Münzkabinett FB4 B1; Alp Arslan, Tübingen FB5 C3; Malikshāh, Tübingen FB5 D5; Berkyāruq, Tübingen 2002-16-149; Sanjar, Tübingen 96-32-41, and so forth.

[25] Tübingen FB5 C4, 94-22-46, and so forth.

abundant testimony to the prevalence at this time of the usage of other, lesser eastern Late Antique ruling titles. One of the most important and prevalent of these lesser titles was 'Ispahbadh', an ancient Iranian military title.[26] This was employed in particular around the Caspian Sea region, by local dynasties such as the Bāvandids, who ruled in Ṭabaristān for more than 700 years. According to the anonymous tenth-century work *Ḥudūd al-ʿālam*, the Bāvandid kings, named after their eponymous ancestor Bāv, were called by the title 'Ispahbad-i Shahriyār' or 'Sipahbad-i Shahriyār-kūh' from Late Antiquity onwards.[27]

Another local Caspian-sea area dynasty employing the title Ispahbad was that of the Bādūspānid Ispahbads. This dynasty could truly be called a Late Antique relic, since it ruled in the mountainous areas of Māzandarān from pre-Islamic times throughout our entire period and beyond it.[28] They were also said to have used the title of Ustāndār, which was a Sasanian administrative term meaning literally 'the holder of an *ustān* or province'.[29] Similarly, the minor dynasty of the Kākūyids also used the title 'Ispahbad', which they were actually granted by their Buyid overlords.[30]

Pre-Islamic Iranian regional titles, in fact, were common not only all over the Persian-speaking world – for instance, the local rulers of the eastern provinces of Jūzjān and Khuttal in the late ninth century are respectively known as the 'Gūzgān khudāh' and the 'Khuttalānshāh' or 'Shīr Khuttalān',[31] along with many similar examples noted by Frye –[32] but even farther afield, and even outside of Iran. Thus, not only is the ancient term 'Ikhshīd' used for the ruler of Farghana in the late ninth century;[33] we see this title actually being bestowed by the caliph Rāḍī in the early tenth century as an honorific upon the caliphal general and then governor in Egypt, Muḥammad b. Tughj.[34] This latter instance of the employment of pre-Islamic Iranian titulature, one should note, is almost exactly contemporaneous with Mardāvīj's identical practice; we are therefore not dealing with an originally anti-Islamic practice that somehow became acceptable over time, but with the simultaneous and widespread adoption of this practice by figures who are beyond reproach on this score; it is difficult to view the revival of ancient Iranian titles as an anti-Islamic or Persian nationalist gesture if the Abbasid caliph himself is employing them as well.

Another, related aspect of the embracing of Late Antique Iranian political traditions of rulership was the use of genealogical connections, both real and imagined, with the pre-Islamic past as a legitimising means.[35] Again, this practice has been interpreted by various

---

26 See C. E. Bosworth, 'Ispahbadh', *EI2*.

27 Ibn Isfandiyār, *Tārīkh-i Ṭabaristān*, ed. 'A. Iqbāl, Tehran 1366/1947, 322–23; Anon., *Ḥudūd al-'ālam min al-mashriq ilā al-maghrib*, ed. M. Sutūda, Tehran 1340/1962, 147.

28 Ibn Isfandiyār, *Tārīkh-i Ṭabaristān*, 319–321.

29 As C. E. Bosworth, 'Ustāndār', *EI2*, notes; see also Ibn Isfandiyar, *Tārīkh-iṬabaristān*, 51, where he equates term specifically with "wālī."

30 C. E. Bosworth, 'Dailamīs in Central Iran: The Kākūyids of Jibāl and Yazd', *Iran* 8, 1970, 73; H. Rabino di Borgomale, 'Les dynasties locales du Gīlān et du Daylam', *Journal Asiatique* 237, 1949, 313.

31 Ibn Khurradādhbih, *al-Masālik wa'l-mamālik*, ed. M. de Goeje, Leiden 1889, 40.

32 R. Frye, 'Some Early Iranian Titles', *Oriens* 15, 1962, 352–59.

33 Ibn Khurradādhbih, *al-Masālik wa'l-mamālik*, 40.

34 Ṣūlī, *Kitāb al-awrāq*, ed. J. Heyworth Dunne, Beirut 1982, ii, 44.

35 In Meisami's words: "One aspect of this enterprise was the manufacture of legitimising

scholars, in relation to dynasties with bad press, as indicating anti-Islamic tendencies. Thus, the attempts by the anonymous local history of Sistan to invent a Sasanian genealogical *isnād* for the ninth-century Saffarid dynasty,[36] together with a poem about the Saffarids sporting a similar claim,[37] led Stern to conclude that this reverence for the Sasanian past indicated "a political manifest with a quite particular objective[:] ... Persian national restoration".[38] Similarly, Madelung interpreted the invention of a Buyid genealogy back to Bahrām II as "a restoration of the Sassanid empire".[39]

The difficulty with these interpretations – wholly apart from the question of the nature of Saffarid ideology[40] – is that it was not just the unpopular dynasties which were indulging in this practice, but virtually everybody else as well. Thus, the Tahirids – again, a ninth-century dynasty, thoroughly Muslim, and earlier than the heterodox Daylamites – claimed descent from the ancient Iranian hero Rustam;[41] while the aforementioned Bāvandid dynasty of the Caspian region claimed that its eponymous founder, Bāv, was, according to one story, supposedly named to his position by the emperor Khusraw II; there was also a different claim, that the lineage itself went back to the Sasanian emperor Qubād.[42]

Bīrūnī, when discussing the bloodline of his Ziyārid patron, brags of his patron's connection to the Bāvandid family, and asserts as fact the Qubādian genealogy. He also makes a point of noting that Qubād was 'the father of Anūshīrvān', thus demonstrating that the name of Anūshīrvān (Khusraw I) still conferred glory.[43] This supposed bloodline, in fact, was still making an impression on people in the twelfth century; thus, Niẓāmī ʿArūḍī Samarqandī, the Ghūrid court author, notes that Firdawsī "came to Ṭabaristān to the Sipahbad Shīrzād of the House of Bāvand, who was king in Ṭabaristān; they are a great noble family; their genealogy is connected to Yazdegird the son of Shahriyār".[44] Niẓāmī ʿArūḍī then quotes from Firdawsī's *Shāhnāma* dedication to the Bāvandid ruler: "I will

---

genealogies". Meisami, 'The Past in Service of the Present', 249–50.

[36] *Tārīkh-i Sīstān*, ed. Bahār, Tehran 1935, 200–202. This assertion of Sasanian blood is reasserted in the section introducing Ya'qūb's kinsman Azhār b. Yaḥyā, 204.

[37] Yāqūt, *Mu'jam al-udabā'*, Beirut 1420/1999, 262–63. On the very problematic provenance of this poem see Tor, *Violent Order*, 169–72.

[38] S. M. Stern, 'Ya'qūb the Coppersmith and Persian National Sentiment', *Iran and Islam: A Volume in Memory of Vladimir Minorsky*, ed. C. E. Bosworth, Edinburgh 1971, 545. Bosworth concurs, stating that "ideas seem to have appeared among their entourage which might be described as having a proto-Persian nationalist tinge ...". See C. E. Bosworth, *The History of the Saffarids of Sistan and the Maliks of Nimruz*, Costa Mesa 1994, 13.

[39] Madelung, 'Assumption', 106. Despite Bīrūnī's scepticism (*Chronology*, 45-46), Ibn al-Athīr, at least, presents the genealogy as authentic; *al-Kāmil*, viii, 264–65.

[40] On which see D. G. Tor, 'Historical Representations of Ya'qūb b. al-Layth al-Ṣaffar: A Reappraisal', *Journal of the Royal Asiatic Society* 12, 2002, 247–75.

[41] Mas'ūdī, *Kitāb al-tanbīh wa'l-ishrāf*, 347.

[42] C. E. Bosworth, 'Bāvandids', *EI2*; also idem, *The New Islamic Dynasties*, New York 1996, 165.

[43] Bīrūnī, *The Chronology of Ancient Nations*, tr. Sachau, London 1879, 47. As Touraj Daryaee notes (*Sasanian Persia: The Rise and Fall of an Empire*, London 2010, 29): "Khusro I (531–79) represents the epitome of the philosopher-king in Sasanian and Near Eastern History... Khusro I's reforms and changes to the empire were to become a blue-print for Kings and Caliphs and Sultans alike."

[44] Samarqandī, *Chahār maqāla*, ed. M. Qazvīnī, Tehran 1375, 80.

dedicate this book to you instead of to Sultan Maḥmūd, for this book is entirely about the stories and deeds of your ancestors".[45]

Barthold comments regarding the names of both the Bādūspānid and the Bāvandid dynasties: "The names of most members of both these dynasties (Shahriyār, Rustam, Yazdegird, Ardashīr, and so on), like those of the Ziyārids and Buwayhids, show how long were retained, despite Islam, the traditions of the Sasanian epoch in these regions".[46] It is also worth pointing out, however, that this coexisted alongside a very Islamic tradition, as indicated by the fact that, for instance, the same Bādūspānids with the very Iranian names also boast of a king who received the *laqab "shāh ghāzī"*.[47] In other words, in this case the Iranian model being adopted is, again, one of rulership (the names are of great kings and heroes of the past, not just random pre-Islamic Iranian names); and it clearly complements rather than flouts Islamic identity.

Perhaps the most interesting cases of this genealogical practice are those in which ethnic Arabs tout such connections to ancient Iranian royalty. Most spectacularly, according to the tenth-century author Tha'ālibī the Umayyad caliph Yazīd b. al-Walīd b. ʿAbd al-Malik, whose mother was a Persian slave, used to boast of his descent from the Persian King of Kings.[48] Then there is the case of the Sharwān Shāhs, an ethnically Arab dynasty that assumed a Persian identity and lineage, as indicated both in its changing prosopography and its forged pedigree back to Bahrām V or, alternatively, Khusraw I.[49] So widespread does this legitimising practice seem to have been, that we find not only political rulers, but even Abbasid court poets claiming Sasanian descent.[50]

The most decisive refutation of the view that the embracing of a genealogy derived from the pre-Islamic Iranian rulers stood in some way in contradiction to Islam, though, is the empirical fact that we also find the dynasties with the most highly reputable, orthodox Sunni reputations adopting this practice. Thus, as noted previously, the Tahirid dynasty claimed descent from the legendary pre-Islamic Iranian hero Rustam b. Dāstān.[51] Then there is the Samanid claim to Sasanian descent, well-documented in our sources. For instance, the Samanid-era geographical work *Ḥudūd al-ā'lam* states: "The Amir of Khurasan sits in Bukhara. He is from the House of Sāmān and among the descendants of Bahrām Chūbīn. They are called 'The King of the East' [*malik-i mashriq*]. He has officials [*'ummāl*] throughout all Khurasan".[52]

---

[45] Samarqandī, *Chahār maqāla*, 80.

[46] W. Barthold, *An Historical Geography of Iran*, tr. Svat Soucek and ed. C. E. Bosworth, Princeton 1984, 240.

[47] Ibn Isfandiyār, *Tārīkh-i Ṭabaristān*, 321.

[48] Tha'ālibī, *The Book of Curious and Entertaining Information: The Laṭā'if al-ma'ārif of Tha'ālibī*, tr. C. E. Bosworth, Edinburgh 1968, 73.

[49] Bosworth, 'Heritage of Rulership', 60; idem, *The New Islamic Dynasties*, 140–42.

[50] Abū'l Faraj al-Iṣbahānī, *Kitāb al-aghānī*, Beirut 1412/1992, xii, 61: "He is Muḥammad b. al-Ḥārith b. Buskhunnar, called by the *kunya* Abū Jaʿfar; according to what they claim, they were *mawālī* of al-Manṣūr. The clientage of service is attributed to him, not the clientage of manumission... and Muḥammad used to claim that he was among the descendants of Bahrām Chūbīn".

[51] Mas'ūdī, *Kitab al-tanbih wa'l-ishraf*, 347.

[52] Anon., *Ḥudūd al-ā'lam*, 89.

Another Samanid-era contemporary, the tenth-century Arab geographer Ibn Ḥawqal, writes of Transoxiana: "The kings of these lands and of the rest of Khurasan are the House of Sāmān, and they are among the descendants of Bahrām Chūbīn, whose reputation among the Persians for strength and courage has endured".[53] Note that Ibn Ḥawqal, himself an Arab, sees nothing extraordinary or inimical to Islam in the persistence of this historical memory. The polymath Bīrūnī, for his part, writes that "nobody denies" the fact of Samanid descent from Bahrām Chūbīn, and claims the same distinction for the Khwarazm-shāhs and the Shīrvānids, whose most peculiar genealogical claims we have already seen.

To many of our medieval authors, moreover, the Samanids' claim to Sasanian lineage indeed constituted a legitimising factor. Bīrūnī, who was no Shuʿūbī, comments on these claims, to which he personally gives credence: "The fact that claims to some noble lineage...are just and well-founded, always becomes known somehow or other, even if people try to conceal it, being like musk, which spreads its odour, although it be hidden".[54] Likewise, the Ghaznavid-era historian Gardīzī adduces this Samanid genealogy, stretching through Bahrām Chūbīn and ancient Iranian royalty back to the legendary first king of Iran, Kayūmarth,[55] as does the thirteenth-century *Tārīkh-i Guzīda*, which introduces this genealogy with the assertion that "Sāmān was of the seed of Bahrām Chūbīn".[56]

Furthermore, the Samanids were not the only impeccably Islamic and orthodox dynasty to adopt the Sasanian royal heritage as part of its legitimising project. Their successors in Iran, the ethnically Turkish Ghaznavid dynasty, for example, were also given a royal Sasanian genealogy. As Bosworth has noted, "The fictitious genealogy elaborated for the Ghaznavids ... links them with the Persian Sasanian past, and not with some ancient, princely family of the Turks, an affiliation which would have been just as easy to make and more plausible".[57] Thus, Jūzjānī's *Tabaqāt-i Nāṣirī* states that the Ghaznavid founder, Sebuktegin, "was among the descendants of Yazdegird Shahriyār", and that after the killing of Yazdegird "his followers and dependents escaped to Turkistan and made alliances with [the locals]. After two or three generations had passed, they became Turks ...".[58]

The Ghaznavid example is an important case in point, because it demonstrates that what was of the essence was not whether a bloodline actually went back to Sasanian times, nor whether a family managed to cling to power and political importance throughout the centuries – but that Sasanian practices, titles, and genealogies, real or imagined, were embraced and adopted by Muslims as a legitimising political enterprise that was in no way perceived as conflicting with Islam.

Further confirmation that this legitimising political use of the Sasanian heritage was evidence of the Islamic capacity for assimilation, rather than of Iranian anti-Arab or anti-Islamic antagonism, can be found in the fact that the use of this heritage is not some passing Shuʿūbī phenomenon limited to the ninth through eleventh centuries, but, rather,

[53] Ibn Ḥawqal, *Kitāb ṣūrat al-arḍ*, ed de Goeje, Leiden 1939, 468.

[54] Bīrūnī, *Chronology*, 48.

[55] Gardīzī, *Tārīkh-i Gardīzī*, 325.

[56] Qazvīnī, *Tārīkh-i Guzīda*, 376.

[57] C. E. Bosworth, 'The Titulature of the Early Ghaznavids', *Oriens* 15, 1962, 220.

[58] Minhāj-i Sirāj Juzjanī, *Ṭabaqāt-i Nāṣirī*, ed. 'Abd al-Ḥayy Ḥabībī, Tehran 1363, i, 226.

is of much longer duration. Thus, for instance, a fourteenth-century Indian dynasty of the Central Deccan both claimed descent from Bahrām V and widely employed Sasanian symbols.[59] In short, the embracing of Late Antique Iranian traditions of rulership was not some bizarre Late Antique recrudescence indicating anti-Islamic values; but, rather, merely one aspect of the quite widespread phenomenon of the incorporation of the pre-Islamic Iranian heritage into Muslim civilization and culture.

But perhaps the best proof that the assimilation of the ancient Iranian traditions of rulership was done not in opposition to the Islamic ideal, but in complement to that ideal, is to be found in the second sub-category of the Islamic adoption of the Late Antique Iranian past. This is what we defined as the cultural and literary adoption of ancient Iranian kingship as an Islamic ideal by the vast Muslim literary corpus. Here, too, we see once again that this embracing of the pre-Islamic past lasted long beyond the existence of anything that could be called a Shuʿūbī movement.

The fact that this incorporation of the past becomes, if anything, more pronounced as time goes on indicates that we are not talking about a mere preservation or reversion to the pre-Islamic past, but a transformation and adaptation of it. Thus, from the tenth century onwards there is the significant appearance of entire books whose setting is a fictionalized royal court, either of pre-Islamic times or else containing outstanding pre-Islamic elements – from Firdawsī's *Shāhnāma* in the tenth century to Niẓāmī Ganjavī's *Haft Paykar* and Ibn Khudādād's *Samak-i ʿayyār* in the twelfth.[60] One of the best representatives of this Islamization and Iranization of the past, its remolding into one harmonious whole with medieval Islamic civilization, is Niẓāmī's *Iskandar-nāma*, written around the year 1200,[61] in which the ancient Greek pagan king was transmuted into "the model of the Muslim hero, the Iranian knight, through his own merits worthy of acceding to the rank of prophet of the One God".[62] Even more interesting than books written about or set in the Late Antique Iranian past, though, is the use of and reference to the pre-Islamic Iranian past as a living cultural heritage and model for emulation in the author's own time. This is found throughout various literary genres, but is especially evident in advice literature, political writings, and above all the "Mirrors for Princes".[63] There were two active periods of the composition of such works: the first occurring in the early Abbasid era, when Manṣūr was casting about for a legitimising ideology after the original Abbasid Kaysānī Shiism had proven unworkable; and the second during the early Seljuq period of the mid-eleventh century.[64]

[59] Mehrdad Shokoohy, 'Sasanian Royal Emblems and their Reemergence in the Fourteenth-Century Deccan', *al-Muqarnas* 11, 1994, 65–78.

[60] Niẓāmī Ganjavī, *Haft Paykar*, Tehran 1340/1961; Ibn Khudādād, *Samak-i ʿayyār*, ed. Parvīz Khānlarī, Tehran 1342.

[61] On the dating of this work see F. de Blois, *Persian Literature: A Bio-Bibliographical Survey. Volume 5: Poetry of the Pre-Mongol Period*, second ed., London 2004, 366–70.

[62] A. Abel, 'Iskandar Nāma', in *EI2*, Leiden 1978, iv, 127–29.

[63] See A. K. S. Lambton, 'Islamic Mirrors for Princes', *Atti del Convegno internazionale sul tema: la Persia nel Medioevo*, Rome 1971, 419–42.

[64] "The genre of mirrors for princes had flourished under the early Abbasids, as Persian imperial ideals and administrative practices were introduced into Arabic-Islamic culture. But from the end of the third/ninth century until the late sixth/twelfth century there was no major development in

The first wave can be viewed as marking the introduction of "the Sassanian kings of Persia...as model rulers", initially by Ibn al-Muqaffa', then by his emulators such as Ibn Qutayba and pseudo-Jāḥiẓ.[65] These works were all written in Arabic. The second wave of this genre begins appearing in the eleventh century – and, again, if we restore this cultural development to its historical context, we can trace it to the political and religious history of the time. It is surely not coincidental that this second flowering of the political advice and theory genres appeared after the Seljuqs had conquered Baghdad yet failed to restore political power to the Abbasid caliphs. Since it was now very clear who wielded the reins of power henceforth among Sunnis – to wit, military commanders who had no juridical authority under Muslim law – Muslims needed a new ideological model of political authority; and, since Persian was now the dominant language of culture throughout the eastern Islamic lands, and Persian dynasties were the political force which had arisen on the ruins of the eastern caliphate, most of the works of this second wave were composed in Persian.[66]

One of the earliest such works was the *Qābūs nāma*, written around the year 1082,[67] in which the princely author begins by proudly reminding his son that:

> "Your grandmother, my mother, was the daughter of Prince Marzubān b. Rustam b. Sharvīn ... whose thirteenth-generation ancestor was Kābūs b. Qubād, the brother of King Anūshīrvān the Just [Khusraw I]; and your mother was the daughter of the King Ghāzī Mahmūd b. Nāṣir al-Dīn".[68]

It is fitting that Kay Kā'ūs should thus harmoniously blend at the outset the Islamic and the Iranian elements of his son's genealogical pedigree, just as the work itself blends the same elements in its philosophical pedigree.

Thus, Khusraw Parvīz's famous minister Buzurgmihr appears in various anecdotes throughout the work, always as a paragon of wisdom, ranging from his wise and repeated acknowledgment of his own human limitations to his pontificating on the reason for the fall of the Sasanians (Answer: "in their great affairs they relied upon petty officials").[69] Similarly, the author tells his son to heed the collective distilled wisdom of the wise, particularly of Khusraw I, who is always referred to in this literature by the title "Anūshīrvān the Just". Kay Kā'ūs joins Anūshīrvān with the Islamic past by informing the reader that

---

the genre until its resurgence in the early Saljuq period". See J. Meisami, *Persian Historiography until the End of the Twelfth Century*, Edinburgh 1999, 145.

[65] F. Rosenthal, *Political Thought in Medieval Islam*, Cambridge 1962, 67–68; C. E. Bosworth, 'Administrative Literature', *The Cambridge History of Arabic Literature: Religion, Learning, and Science in the 'Abbasid Period*, ed. M. J. L. Young *et al.*, Cambridge 1990, 165–66.

[66] On this second wave see P. Crone, *God's Rule*, New York 2004, 152–64. On the challenge posed by the Seljuqs to Sunni political theorists and jurists, see A. K. S. Lambton, 'Aspects of Saljūq-Ghuzz Settlement in Persia', *Islamic Civilisation 950–1150*, ed. D. S. Richards, Oxford 1973, 106, and D. G. Tor, 'Sultan', *Encyclopedia of Islamic Political Thought*, ed. Gerhard Böwering, Patricia Crone, *et al.*, Princeton, forthcoming.

[67] Kay Kā'ūs, *Qābūs nāma*, ed. Gh. Yūsufī, Tehran 1378, 263.

[68] Kay Kā'ūs, *Qābūs nāma*, 5.

[69] Kay Kā'ūs, *Qābūs nāma*, 38–39, 46, 220.

the caliph Ma'mūn made a pilgrimage to Anūshīrvān's tomb and had the inscription on it translated into Arabic.[70]

The most famous of the eleventh-century 'Mirrors for Princes', Niẓām al-Mulk's *Siyāsat nāma*, likewise depicts the ancient Iranian kings as a model for emulation, together with the practices of various, selected Islamic rulers. In fact, the pre-Islamic rulers of Iran have been made over entirely in an Islamic image. A few examples of different types should suffice to illustrate this point. First, Niẓām al-Mulk co-mingles pre-Islamic and Islamic figures freely, using them both as paradigms. In his chapter warning against the mischief of women, the author's examples include pre-Islamic figures such as Kay Kā'ūs and Siyāvush, Darius, Khusraw and Shīrīn, and Buzurgmihr, interspersed with ʿA'isha and the Prophet, Joseph, and the caliph Ma'mūn.[71] Likewise, in his chapter on judges, Niẓām al-Mulk's two models are the Ṣaḥāba and the Persian Kings of Antiquity, whom he praises for their accessibility and impartial justice.[72]

Second, Niẓām al-Mulk holds up the Sasanian kings in particular, and their viziers, as the embodiment and epitome of kingly virtue. Sometimes this consists in his quoting approvingly the statements of Sasanian kings on a particular subject;[73] on other occasions it lies in his citing their historical example and actions as illustrations of righteous or just government.[74] In the chapter on viziers, perhaps the one that lay closest to the author's own heart, *all* of the anecdotes are taken from the ancient Iranian past.[75]

Niẓām al-Mulk also praises his Islamic heroes, such as Maḥmūd of Ghazna, for following certain excellent pre-Islamic Iranian customs, for instance in paying his army in cash instead of land grants.[76] Thus, Niẓām al-Mulk, an orthodox Shāfiʿī Muslim, approves of the Islamic adoption of Sasanian models; obviously, he perceives no opposition between the two models. In fact, he states outright that "The Sasanian kings [*mulūk-i Akāsira*] in justice, magnanimity, and manliness [*muruvva*] surpassed all other kings; especially Anūshīrvān the Just."[77]

Nowhere is the thorough Islamization of the Sasanian kings better seen than in Niẓām al-Mulk's use of them, particularly Anūshīrvān, as a model for proper *religious* attitudes. Thus, in his chapter on land grants and administration (chapter 5), Niẓām al-Mulk's only model is Anūshīrvān the Just, who is not only held up as the paragon of the righteous ruler – but to whom is also attributed great piety and respect for God.[78] Nor is this a lone aberration: In his chapter on the ruler's duty to maintain proper religion, Niẓām al-Mulk

[70] Kay Kā'ūs, *Qābūs nāma*, 50, 55. On the special role played by Ardashīr and Anūshīrvān in Islamic political thought, see L. Marlow, *Hierarchy and Egalitarianism in Islamic Thought*, Cambridge 1997, 83–90.

[71] Niẓām al-Mulk, *Siyar al-mulūk*, ed. H. Darke, Tehran 1378, 243–46.

[72] Niẓām al-Mulk, *Siyar al-mulūk*, 56–59.

[73] Niẓām al-Mulk, *Siyar al-mulūk*, 251.

[74] Niẓām al-Mulk, *Siyar al-mulūk*, 30, 98.

[75] Niẓām al-Mulk, *Siyar al-mulūk*, 31–42.

[76] Niẓām al-Mulk, *Siyar al-mulūk*, 134–35.

[77] Niẓām al-Mulk, *Siyar al-mulūk*, 174–75; the laudatory statement appears on the latter page.

[78] Niẓām al-Mulk, *Siyar al-mulūk*, 43–55.

at one point somewhat bizarrely cites Ardashīr and the Qur'ān as joint authorities.[79]

In the same chapter, his examples of ideal rulers include a promiscuous blending of figures from Iranian Antiquity and the Muslim past: Afrīdūn, Alexander, Ardashīr and Anūshīrvān the Just; 'Umar I and II; Hārūn al-Rashīd, Ma'mūn, and Muʿtaṣim; Ismāʿīl b. Aḥmad Sāmānī; and Maḥmūd of Ghazna, concluding "[People still] recite blessings and praise for them".[80] Even the Sasanian viziers – or at least Buzurgmihr – are made over into paragons of religious virtue; in a section treating the *sententiae* of 'the great religious figures', Niẓām al-Mulk's virtuous examples include equally Buzurgmihr and ʿAlī b. Abī Ṭālib.[81] He even views the religious disorders of his own time through the prism of pre-Islamic history and the Mazdakite disorders of Sasanian time, using Late Antiquity to teach a moral lesson about Islam itself. [82]

More importantly for our thesis, contrary to what previously has been thought, it is not the case that Muslims dropped the Sasanian paradigm in the eleventh century.[83] The legitimising use and incorporation of the pre-Islamic heritage of rulership continued throughout the pre-Mongol period; again, well after the end of any movement or phenomenon that could be labelled as Shuʿūbī or anti-Islamic – and it extended far beyond Iran.

Thus, we find the twelfth-century Amirs of Khuttal insisting upon their descent from Bahrām V.[84] In the same vein, Niẓāmī ʿArūḍī's twelfth-century advice manual tells us that for a scribe to be accomplished, he needs to master the Qur'ān, the Sunna, "the memoirs of the Companions, the proverbs of the Arabs, and the wise words of the Persians".[85] Similarly, the work portrays the ancient Iranian kings as paradigms of rulership, noting approvingly that good Muslim rulers such as Maḥmūd of Ghazna based themselves on the customs of kings "such as the Pīshdādī, Kayānī, and Sasanian kings and the caliphs, whose custom it was to contend for glory and compete in justice and virtue ...".[86]

Rāvandī's didactic history of the Seljuqs, *Rāḥat al-Ṣudūr*, written around the turn of the thirteenth century, employs the Sasanian model in a similar paradigmatic fashion. Thus, throughout his work, Rāvandī quotes approvingly, in various contexts, the alleged *ḥadīth* (for lack of a better term) of figures such as Ardashīr and Anūshīrvān regarding the conduct of kings. Thus, when explaining approvingly that Toghril modeled himself on "the laudable actions of the kings of yore", Rāvandī cites Ardashīr on proper royal administrative

---

79 Niẓām al-Mulk, *Siyar al-mulūk*, 80.

80 Niẓām al-Mulk, *Siyar al-mulūk*, 81–82.

81 Niẓām al-Mulk, *Siyar al-mulūk*, 179–80.

82 Niẓām al-Mulk, *Siyar al-mulūk*, 306, 257–78.

83 Bosworth, 'Heritage of Rulership', 62: "The era in which powers established in Iran on the ruins of the 'Abbāsid caliphate automatically tried to forge a connection with the glorious traditions of ancient Iran, draws to an end in the eleventh century".

84 The *amīr* bears the very Persian name of Farrukh-Shāh; M. Fedorov, 'New Data on the Appanage Rulers of Khuttalān and Wakhsh', *Iran* 44, 2006, 201.

85 Niẓāmī 'Arūḍī, *Chahār maqāla*, 22.

86 Niẓāmī 'Arūḍī, *Chahār maqāla*, 39–40. On the question of the historicity of the Kayanids, see A. Christensen, *Les Kayanides*, Copenhagen 1931, 27–35; other scholars, however, are more skeptical.

practices;[87] when discussing the reign of Sultan Sanjar b. Malikshāh, Rāvandī again quotes Ardashīr to the effect that prosperity depends on justice and good administrative policy;[88] when expounding upon justice, he cites Anūshīrvān,[89] and so forth. What is striking is that all of these these *sententiae* are adduced *in Arabic*, which Rāvandī then has to translate for his readership into Persian; that is, they came from an Arabic-language tradition, not a Persian one.

The influential thirteenth century work *Dastūr al-vizāra* also looks to the Late Antique Persian kings for inspiration. When searching for the ultimate example of Ozymandias-like fallen greatness in the ministerial sphere, it quotes a poem stating that "the memory of Buzurgmihr is obliterated in this era".[90] In his chapter "In remembrance of the praises of kings and stories and songs about them which have remained eternal and perpetual in books of the time", Iṣfahānī names "Ardashīr Bābak and his son Shāpūr" as the greatest and most virtuous of kings.[91]

Iṣfahānī, like Niẓām al-Mulk, also connects the pre-Islamic Persian historical tradition with the Islamic one. In his chapter on the discretion and vigilance of the vizier in service of the king, Iṣfahānī adduces an anecdote in which the first Abbasid caliph, Abū al-'Abbās, was sitting and holding an evening conversation whose subject was the glory of the Iranian kings of yore.[92] In other words, much of the Islamic literary corpus is characterized by an unself-conscious blending of the Pre-Islamic Persian tradition with the Islamic religious one.

The widespread adoption of the Sasanian model was characterized not only by chronological diffusion but also by ethnic and geographical diffusion. Thus, the final refutation of the idea that the incorporation of the Sasanian kings and their traditions into Islamic civilization was somehow inimical to Islam or a resentful Persian nationalist response to the Arabs is the fact that Arabs and Arabic literature, across the centuries, embraced the Sasanian model as well. Moreover, this phenomenon begins in the tenth century, precisely at a time when one would expect Arabs to have rejected the practice, had the revival of the Sasanian model been a mere expression of Shuʿūbism or anti-Arab feeling.

Thus, the tenth-century Arabic geographer Muqaddasī states that "ʿUmar b. al-Khattāb ... said: Lo, I learned justice from Kisrā".[93] Muqaddasī also considered the old Iranian lineage as bestowing legitimacy: he writes of the Samanids that:

---

[87] Rāvandī, *Rāḥat al-Ṣudūr va-Āyat al-shurūr dar Āl Saljūq*, ed. M. Iqbāl, Tehran 1364/1985f., 97.

[88] Rāvandī, *Rāḥat al-Ṣudūr*, 186. On the stock use of the tradition cited by Rāvandī, see A. K. S. Lambton, 'Justice in the Medieval Persian Theory of Kingship', *Studia Islamica* 17, 1962, 100.

[89] Rāvandī, *Rāḥat al-Sudūr*, 74. Rāvandī also combines sacred and ancient Persian history in his chapter on 'The great ones and kings of yore', 352-353. The Sasanian past, interestingly, also features in his discussion of the game of chess, and the improvements made to it by Buzurgmihr; 407–408; explained further on, 410.

[90] Maḥmūd b. Muḥammad b. al- Ḥusayn al-Iṣfahānī, *Dastūr al-Vizāra*, ed. Riḍā Anzābī Nizhād, Tehran 1364/1985f., 37.

[91] Iṣfahānī, *Dastūr al-vizāra*, 93.

[92] Iṣfahānī, *Dastūr al-vizāra*, 108.

[93] Muqaddasī, *Aḥsan al-taqāsīm fī ma'rifat al-aqālīm*, ed. De Goeje, Leiden 1906, 18.

> their origin goes back to Bahrām Gūr; therefore God has given them victory and power. They are among the best of kings in conduct and administration; the most sublime in the knowledge of God and the people of that knowledge. Among the sayings of the people: 'If a tree were to revolt against the house of Sāmān, it would wither'.[94]

If anything, there is a tendency, as we have seen in Niẓām al-Mulk's work, to Islamicize Iranian kings. This can be seen in a statement Muqaddasī makes when discussing Khuzistan:

> Regarding al-Ahwāz, Shāpūr when he built it in two parts, called one of them by the name of Allāh, may He be magnified and exalted, and the other by his [own] name; then he united the two under one name, and its name was Hormuzdārāwshīr [sic] ...[95]

That is, even the ancient Iranian royal worship of Ahura Mazda/Ohrmazd has been Islamicised to the point where the Zoroastrian deity is explicitly equated with Allāh- and Muqaddasī was no Unitarian. Note that this is an Arab author writing in Arabic.[96]

Other Arabic sources, too, draw on the memory of Late Antique Iranian rulership: when describing the downfall of the Afshīn, for instance, Maqdīsī's tenth-century *Kitāb al-bad' wa'l-ta'rīkh*, declaims an elegy in which the acme of glory and nobility is "*Banī Kā'ūs, awlād al-'ajam*".[97] Similarly, belletristic texts in both Persian and Arabic preserve and glorify the memory of Sasanian rulership. Thus, the *Kitāb al-aghānī* features the Persian kings in a poem about the transience of glory, in which both Khusraw I (Anūshīrvān) and Shāpūr are mentioned by name.[98] Likewise, "Bahrām Gūr son of Yazdegird son of Shāpūr" puts in an appearance as well.[99]

In like fashion, the anonymous eleventh-century Arabic work *Kitāb al-dhakhā'ir wa'l-tuḥaf*, a catalogue of marvelous gifts, opens with the Sasanian kings – the only pre-Islamic gift-givers and recipients to be mentioned – starting with an account of various magnificent gifts exchanged by Khusraw I with neighboring rulers.[100] Other sections of the work begin similarly, with an account of Sasanian times and practices clearly setting a standard to which Islamic rulers are then compared – for example the chapter on receiving envoys;[101] again, this is an Arabic, not a Persian text.

More importantly, this work, too, depicts, as a natural matter of course, the caliphs as the continuators of Sasanian traditions and practices. For instance, it states:

[94] Muqaddasī, *Aḥsan al-taqāsīm*, 338.

[95] Muqaddasī, *Aḥsan al-taqāsīm*, 406.

[96] This is not to say that he was not influenced by the Iranian tradition – in fact, that is precisely the point. On this subject see J.H. Kramers, "L'Influence de la tradition Iranienne dans la geographie Arabe," *Analecta Orientalia*, Leiden 1954, i, 147–56.

[97] Maqdīsī, *Kitāb al-bad' wa'l-ta'rīkh*, ed. Cl. Huart, Paris 1899–1919, ii, 300.

[98] Abū'l-Faraj al-Iṣbahānī, *al-Aghānī*, ii, 131.

[99] Abū'l-Faraj al-Iṣbahānī, *al-Aghānī*, ii, 137

[100] Anon., *Kitāb al-dhakhā"ir wa'l-tuḥaf*, ed. M. Ḥamīd Allāh and Ṣ. Munajjid, Kuwait 1959, 3–5.

[101] Anon., *Kitāb al-dhakhā"ir wa'l-tuḥaf*, 127.

> The Nawrūz gifts that were brought to the Kings of Persia every year by the *dahāqīn* of Iraq numbered ten million, and the Mihragān gifts one hundred million. Afterwards, in Islamic times, they were brought to the caliphs.[102]

The caliphate is here portrayed as a harmonious continuation of ancient Persian kingship.

This tendency is even more apparent in the chapter on plunder taken in conquests and shares of booty in raids. While the first example is of the Prophet, and the second pertains to the booty obtained by the Muslims in the battle of Qadisiyya, the text then passes quite casually to the amount of booty accumulated in the treasury by Khusraw II, his son Shirawayh, and grandson Ardashīr, before passing back to the *jihād* of the early Muslim conquests.[103] That is, an eleventh-century Arabic text incorporates Late Antique Iran into one seamless whole with Islamic civilization – not in opposition to Islam, but by co-opting the Sasanian past in much the same fashion that the Qur'ān co-opts and refashions the Biblical past.

This characteristic, moreover, is found throughout Arabic literature. Thus, one of the great Arabic litterateurs of the tenth century, Abū Ḥayyān al-Tawḥīdī, sets forth the Sasanian kings and viziers and their sayings as paragons of wisdom, justice, and statesmanship; Khusraw Anūshīrvān (Khusraw I), Khusraw Aparvīz (Khusraw II), Bahrām Gūr (Bahrām V), and the vizier Buzurgmihr appear repeatedly in this role.[104] At least some of the Iranian kings also assumed larger than life proportions. For example, Tawḥīdī writes "it is said of the things in which Khusraw excelled that his height was sixteen spans; his heart was seven spans; and he would eat every day a grilled foal from among the horses, as well as [several] she-kids ...".[105] Moreover, the writer assumes a basic familiarity with the legendary royal Sasanian biographies and their protagonists on the part of his reader, launching into anecdotes without feeling it necessary to explain his references: "When Khusraw killed Buzurgmihr"; "Khusraw said to Maria, the daughter of the Byzantine Emperor"; and so forth.[106] In other words, this was part of a living tradition, the assumed cultural background of all readers of polite Arabic literature.

The incredibly far-flung geographical extent to which Iranian Late Antiquity became absorbed into Islamic culture is best illustrated, perhaps, by the adoption of the Sasanian model at the far Western end of the Islamic world, by the Andalusian Ibn ʿAbd Rabbih (d. Cordoba, 940), in his work *al-ʿIqd al-farīd*. Here, as in the other writings we have examined, the Iranian kings and viziers of Late Antiquity, from Khusraw Aparvīz to Ardashīr,

---

[102] Anon., *Kitāb al-dhakhā"ir wa'l-tuḥaf*, 5.

[103] Anon., *Kitāb al-dhakhā"ir wa'l-tuḥaf*, 245.

[104] Tawḥīdī, *al-Baṣā'ir wa'l-dhakhā'ir*, ed. Wadād al-Qāḍī, Beirut 1999; Anūshīrvān : iv, 17–18; vi, 63; 9:103, ix, 159, 177; Aparvīz: iv, 120; 8:79; Khusraw: ii, 184–85; iv, 42, 96, iv, 169, 174; v, 132; vi, 130, 221; vii, 176; vii, 194–95; ix, 14; xiii, 184–85; Bahrām Gūr: vii, 183; Buzurgmihr: i, 22, 136; ii, 141; iii, 157; iv, 15, 80, 96, 113, 120, 153, 170, 171, 216–17; v, 12, vii, 157, and so forth.

[105] Tawḥīdī, *al-Baṣā'ir wa'l-dhakhā'ir*, ii, 80–81.

[106] Tawḥīdī, *al-Baṣā'ir wa'l-dhakhā'ir*, vii, 43 and vi, 129; similarly, one encounters references such as "Khusraw said to Shīrīn"; "Khusraw wrote to Hormuzd"; "When Khusraw Aparvīz was forced to flee from before Bahrām Chūbīn"; "Anūshīrvān wrote to the Ispahbad of Khurasan"; respectively vii, 155; vii, 181; viii, 79; ix, 182.

Anūshīrvān, and Buzurgmihr, are held up as the embodiment of justice, statecraft, and kingly virtue.[107]

The same Islamicizing tendency toward the Sasanian past is also present in this work, in very pronounced form. First we find, in similar anecdotes, both Anūshīrvān the Just and a generic Sasanian emperor instructing their satraps regarding religious priorities: "Make use of people of valour and generosity; for they are the people of Allāh's favourable judgment".[108] Even more specifically Islamicizing is the depiction of Ardashīr's instructions to his son: "O my son, bestow your speech upon people of high rank; your gifts upon the men of *jihād*; your joy in men of religion ...".[109] Similarly, we have 'Alī b. Abī Ṭālib asking "one of the Persian nobles" which of the Persian kings was most praiseworthy (the noble names Ardashīr and Anūshīrvān/Khusraw I).[110] Short of the Prophet's endorsement, there is no higher Islamic certificate of approval.

Yet another salient fact that refutes the Shuʿūbī partisan interpretation of the meaning and scope of Late Anique Iranian calques in Islamic culture is, once again, the chronological extent of the Sasanian incorporation into Arabic literature. As was the case with Persian literature, these calques continue to be used well past the eleventh century, and long after any possible Shuʿūbī movement or controversy had disappeared. Thus, for example, the twelfth-century Baghdadi Ḥanbalite cleric Ibn al-Jawzī, in his work *al-Adhkiyā'*, adduces anecdotes which feature Khusraw b. Hormuzd, Khusraw II, and Shīrūya.[111]

One even finds one of the leading fifteenth-century clerics of Yemen, Ḥamza b. ʿAbdallāh al-Nāshirī, in his work on hunting and falconry, featuring the Sasanian kings, their doings, sayings, and pronouncements. Thus various *sententiae* of "Khusraw" are quoted,[112] and anecdotes involving these kings and their prowess – among them Khusraw I, Bahrām b. Hormuzd, Bahrām V, Shāpūr, and Khusraw II[113] – are recounted. Even in a work of this sort, the Persian kings are held up and admired as exemplars. Thus, Bahrām V figures as the first person said to have hunted the merlin; and, in a different passage, the best of all Persian marksmen.[114]

To conclude: Islamic culture was not some weak and self-contained flower, wilting under the stressful threat of an assertive and revenant ancient Iranian tradition. First of all, Islamic culture was an assimilative one; and, second, it was not an indiscriminately assimilative one. It took what it needed – and only what it needed, and as needed – from

[107] Abū 'Umar Aḥmad b. Muḥammad Ibn 'Abd Rabbih, *Kitāb al-'iqd al-farīd*, ed. I. al-Ibyārī, Beirut, n.d., Khusraw Aparvīz: i, 26, i, 41, 42, 43; ii, 244–45, 413; iv, 146; Ardashīr: i, 40; Anūshīrvān: ii, 413; vi, 395–98; Buzurgmihr: i, 245; ii, 226, 300, 360, 412; iii, 78-82; vi, 331.

[108] Ibn 'Abd Rabbih, *Kitāb al-'iqd al-farīd*, i, 120, 245–46.

[109] Ibn 'Abd Rabbih, *Kitāb al-'iqd al-farīd*, i, 38.

[110] Ibn 'Abd Rabbih, *Kitāb al-'iqd al-farīd*, ii, 267.

[111] Ibn al-Jawzī, *al-Adhkiyā'*, Beirut, 1418/1998, 208-209, 217-219.

[112] Nāshirī, *Intihāz al-furaṣ fī'l-ṣayd wa'l-qanas*, ed. 'A. M. Al-Ḥabashī, Abu Dhabi 2002: "Khusraw said: A windy day is good for sleeping; a cloudy day for hunting; a rainy day for drinking; a sunny day for necessities;"p. 36; "A falcon is a better friend than patience; it never misses an opportunity", 143.

[113] Nāshirī, *Intihāz al-furaṣ fī'l-ṣayd*, 97–98, 296–311, 312–13.

[114] Nāshirī, *Intihāz al-furaṣ fī'l-ṣayd*, 148, 281.

other cultures. Thus, precisely which element was adopted from the Late Antique Iranian past is significant, not random. Just as Greek culture was prized for its philosophy, Late Antique Iran was raided for its tradition of rulership.

To say that the 'Islamic ideal of rulership' was in conflict with the Iranian ideal that was actively embraced and absorbed into Islamic culture from the Abbasid era onwards is simply not accurate. The original Islamic ideal of the caliphate proved impossible to put into practice; this is why, according to classical Sunni theory, there have been no real caliphs at all since the first four; the Islamic ideal, after the death of the Prophet, existed for less than thirty years.[115] In short, the Iranian ideal saved the Islamic polity at a crucial moment, when the caliphate had failed and was in the process of collapse; it was one of the two legitimising factors – the other being the *jihād*- that was able to turn mere *amīr*s, or military commanders, into sultans – legitimate political authorities.[116] The essential reason why the Iranian ideal was revived, reshaped, and given a new lease on life was precisely the lack of a viable mainstream Islamic ideal after the ideological implosion that followed on the heels of the Abbasid failure.

Nor did Islamic civilization adopt the ancient Iranian ideal unmodified; it re-shaped and Islamicized it. The neo-Sasanian attributes of independent Iranian dynasties are not a return to Late Antiquity. In light of the foregoing, it is possible to say of certain elements of Iranian Late Antiquity, particularly of its tradition of rulership, not that they survived, but that they were revivified in a transfigured, Islamicised form. In the end, the Late Antique Iranian heritage of rulership did not fade, but, rather, "suffer[ed] a sea-change/ into something rich and strange".

Acknowledgements

The author is deeply grateful to Patricia Crone and Edmund Bosworth for reading and commenting upon this article; and to Luke Treadwell, Chase Robinson, Teresa Bernheimer, and the other participants who commented upon the oral presentation of this research at the Oxford Centre for Late Antiquity seminar in January 2008.

[115] This is what Crone has referred to as "The de-politicization of the community of believers"; see P. Crone, *God's Rule: Government and Islam: Six Centuries of Islamic Political Thought*, New York 2004, 30–32.

[116] On the legitimising function of *jihād* for the autonomous dynasties see D. G. Tor, 'Privatized Jihad', *passim*, and idem, *Violent Order*, Chapters 3, 4, 5, and 6. This is not to preclude other, more minor means of legitimation – among them caliphal recognition; but that sort of buttressing tended to constitute the icing on the cake rather than the main ingredient: caliphal endorsement never clinched or doomed any dynasty's bid for political rule, as can be seen from the time of the Saffarids to the hapless volte-faces caused by the caliphal execution of the warring sides' bidding in the Seljuq succession struggles after the death of Malikshāh.

INDEX